# Electricity and Electronics

## LABORATORY MANUAL

by

**Dale R. Patrick**
Professor of Industrial Education and Technology
Eastern Kentucky University
Richmond, Kentucky

**William E. Dugger, Jr.**
Professor and Program Area Leader
Industrial Arts Education
Virginia Polytechnic Institute and State University
Blacksburg, Virginia

South Holland, Illinois
THE GOODHEART-WILLCOX COMPANY, INC.
Publishers

# INTRODUCTION

This Laboratory Manual is intended for use with the text, ELECTRICITY AND ELECTRONICS. The experiments presented are designed to help you better understand the theoretical concepts of electricity and electronics.

When using this lab manual and textbook, be sure to follow the recommended procedures. If you are unsure about safe practices, ask your instructor.

Before proceeding with the experiment, study the textbook and read the laboratory manual. Listen to the instructor's lecture on the theoretical material to be covered and try to relate this to the experiment you will perform.

Note that each experiment has certain common parts:

The INTRODUCTION will give you a quick review of the material covered in the textbook. The EXPERIMENT OBJECTIVES briefly state the performance objectives of the experiment. The REFERENCE material specifically gives the chapter and pages of the text, ELECTRICITY AND ELECTRONICS, that should be studied.

The MATERIALS AND EQUIPMENT list tells you what test equipment and components are needed to perform the experiment. The PROCEDURE gives the correct step-by-step activity called for by the experiment. Record the answers in the space provided. The QUESTIONS at the end of each experiment will help you review the results.

We hope you enjoy working on these experiments. At the same time, we hope this lab manual will increase your interest and understanding of this exciting field of electricity and electronics.

Dale R. Patrick
William E. Dugger, Jr.

# CONTENTS

1 SCIENCE OF ELECTRONICS

Experiment 1-1 STATIC ELECTRICITY . . . . . . . . . . . . 9

Experiment 1-2 STATIC CHARGE BY INDUCTION . . . . . . . 11

Experiment 1-3 THE LAW OF CHARGES . . . . . . . . . . . 13

Experiment 1-4 ATTRACTION AND REPULSION OF
CHARGED OBJECTS . . . . . . . . . . . . . 15

Experiment 1-5 CURRENT ELECTRICITY . . . . . . . . . . 17

2 SOURCES OF ELECTRICITY

Experiment 2-1 VOLTMETER ORIENTATION . . . . . . . . . 19

Experiment 2-2 MEASURING CELL VOLTAGE . . . . . . . . 23

Experiment 2-3 PRIMARY CELLS . . . . . . . . . . . . . . 25

Experiment 2-4 SECONDARY CELLS . . . . . . . . . . . . 27

Experiment 2-5 BATTERIES . . . . . . . . . . . . . . . . 29

Experiment 2-6 SOLAR CELLS . . . . . . . . . . . . . . . 31

Experiment 2-7 AMMETER FAMILIARIZATION . . . . . . . . 33

Experiment 2-8 ELECTRICITY FROM HEAT . . . . . . . . . 37

Experiment 2-9 MEASURING AC WITH A VOM . . . . . . . . 39

Experiment 2-10 PRESSURE SOURCES OF ELECTRICITY . . . 41

3 CIRCUITS AND POWER

Experiment 3-1 DETERMINING WIRE SIZES . . . . . . . . . 43

Experiment 3-2 OHMMETER FAMILIARIZATION . . . . . . . 45

Experiment 3-3 COLOR-CODED RESISTORS . . . . . . . . . 49

Experiment 3-4 OHM'S LAW VERIFICATION . . . . . . . . . 51

Experiment 3-5 SERIES DC CIRCUITS . . . . . . . . . . . 53

Experiment 3-6 PARALLEL DC CIRCUIT
CHARACTERISTICS . . . . . . . . . . . . . 57

Experiment 3-7 SERIES-PARALLEL DC CIRCUITS . . . . . . . 61

4 MAGNETISM

Experiment 4-1 PERMANENT MAGNETS . . . . . . . . . . . 63

Experiment 4-2 PERMANENT MAGNET FIELDS . . . . . . . . 65

Experiment 4-3 ELECTROMAGNETS . . . . . . . . . . . . . 67

Experiment 4-4 ELECTROMAGNETIC FIELDS . . . . . . . . 69

Experiment 4-5 ELECTROMAGNETIC RELAYS . . . . . . . . 71

## 5 GENERATORS

Experiment 5-1 GENERATOR PRINCIPLES . . . . . . . . . . 73

Experiment 5-2 ROTATING ELECTRIC GENERATORS . . . . 75

Experiment 5-3 ROTATING DC GENERATOR . . . . . . . . 77

Experiment 5-4 FIELD COIL GENERATORS . . . . . . . . . 79

Experiment 5-5 AC AND DC GENERATOR OUTPUT . . . . . . 81

Experiment 5-6 OSCILLOSCOPE FAMILIARIZATION . . . . . 83

## 6 INDUCTANCE AND RL CIRCUITS

Experiment 6-1 DC RL CIRCUITS . . . . . . . . . . . . . . 85

Experiment 6-2 AC RL CIRCUITS . . . . . . . . . . . . . . 87

Experiment 6-3 MUTUAL INDUCTANCE . . . . . . . . . . . 89

Experiment 6-4 TRANSFORMER FIELDS . . . . . . . . . . . 91

Experiment 6-5 TRANSFORMERS . . . . . . . . . . . . . . . 93

Experiment 6-6 TRANSFORMER WINDINGS . . . . . . . . . 95

Experiment 6-7 INDUCTIVE REACTANCE . . . . . . . . . . 97

## 7 CAPACITANCE IN ELECTRICAL CIRCUITS

Experiment 7-1 CAPACITOR TESTING . . . . . . . . . . . . 99

Experiment 7-2 CAPACITOR CHARGING AND
DISCHARGING ACTION . . . . . . . . . . . 101

Experiment 7-3 RC TIME CONSTANT . . . . . . . . . . . . 103

Experiment 7-4 CAPACITOR CIRCUITS . . . . . . . . . . . 107

Experiment 7-5 CAPACITIVE REACTANCE . . . . . . . . . . 109

## 8 TUNED CIRCUITS: RCL NETWORKS

Experiment 8-1 SERIES RESONANT PRINCIPLES . . . . . . . 111

Experiment 8-2 SERIES RESONANT CIRCUITS . . . . . . . . 115

Experiment 8-3 PARALLEL RESONANT PRINCIPLES . . . . . 117

Experiment 8-4 PARALLEL RESONANT CIRCUITS . . . . . . 119

Experiment 8-5 FILTER CIRCUITS . . . . . . . . . . . . . 121

Experiment 8-6 HIGH-PASS, LOW-PASS FILTERS . . . . . . 123

## 9 ELECTRIC MOTORS

Experiment 9-1 PERMANENT MAGNET MOTORS . . . . . . . 125

Experiment 9-2 SERIES DC MOTORS . . . . . . . . . . . 127

Experiment 9-3 SHUNT DC MOTORS . . . . . . . . . . . 129

Experiment 9-4 UNIVERSAL MOTORS . . . . . . . . . . . 131

Experiment 9-5 INDUCTION MOTORS . . . . . . . . . . . 133

## 10 INSTRUMENTS AND MEASUREMENTS

Experiment 10-1 METER RESISTANCE . . . . . . . . . . . . 135

Experiment 10-2 AMMETER SHUNTS . . . . . . . . . . . . 137

Experiment 10-3 VOLTMETERS . . . . . . . . . . . . . . . 139

Experiment 10-4 OHMMETERS . . . . . . . . . . . . . . . 141

Experiment 10-5 AC VOLTMETERS . . . . . . . . . . . . . 143

## 11 VACUUM TUBES AND SEMICONDUCTORS

Experiment 11-1 SEMICONDUCTOR DIODE TESTING . . . . . 147

Experiment 11-2 SEMICONDUCTOR DIODE
CHARACTERISTICS . . . . . . . . . . . . . 149

## 12 POWER SUPPLIES

Experiment 12-1 SEMICONDUCTOR HALF-WAVE
RECTIFIERS . . . . . . . . . . . . . . . . . 153

Experiment 12-2 FULL-WAVE RECTIFICATION . . . . . . . . 157

Experiment 12-3 BRIDGE RECTIFIERS . . . . . . . . . . . 159

Experiment 12-4 FILTER CIRCUITS . . . . . . . . . . . . . 161

Experiment 12-5 VOLTAGE REGULATION . . . . . . . . . . 165

Experiment 12-6 VOLTAGE DOUBLER POWER SUPPLIES . . . 167

**13 ELECTRON AMPLIFIERS**

Experiment 13-1 TRANSISTOR FAMILIARIZATION . . . . . . 169

Experiment 13-2 TRANSISTOR TESTING . . . . . . . . . . 173

Experiment 13-3 TRANSISTOR ALPHA . . . . . . . . . . . 175

Experiment 13-4 COMMON EMITTER AMPLIFIERS . . . . . . . 177

Experiment 13-5 AC SIGNAL AMPLIFICATION . . . . . . . . 179

Experiment 13-6 TRANSFORMER COUPLED AMPLIFIERS . . . 183

Experiment 13-7 PUSH-PULL AMPLIFIERS . . . . . . . . . 187

**14 ELECTRONIC OSCILLATORS**

Experiment 14-1 OSCILLATOR PRINCIPLES . . . . . . . . . . 191

Experiment 14-2 HARTLEY OSCILLATORS . . . . . . . . . . 193

Experiment 14-3 COLPITTS OSCILLATORS . . . . . . . . . 197

Experiment 14-4 CRYSTAL OSCILLATORS . . . . . . . . . . 199

**15 RADIO TRANSMITTERS**

Experiment 15-1 CW TRANSMITTERS . . . . . . . . . . . . 201

Experiment 15-2 AMPLITUDE MODULATION . . . . . . . . . 203

Experiment 15-3 AM TRANSMITTERS . . . . . . . . . . . . 207

Experiment 15-4 FREQUENCY MODULATION . . . . . . . . 211

Experiment 15-5 FM TRANSMITTERS . . . . . . . . . . . . 213

**16 RADIO RECEIVERS**

Experiment 16-1 AM COMMUNICATION SYSTEM . . . . . . . . 215

Experiment 16-2 RF TUNING CIRCUITS . . . . . . . . . . . 217

Experiment 16-3 AM SIGNAL DEMODULATION . . . . . . . . 219

Experiment 16-4 A HETERODYNING CIRCUIT . . . . . . . . 221

Experiment 16-5 IF AMPLIFIERS . . . . . . . . . . . . . . 223

Experiment 16-6 SOUND TRANSDUCERS . . . . . . . . . . . 225

Experiment 16-7 FM RECEIVERS . . . . . . . . . . . . . . 227

## 17 TELEVISION

Experiment 17-1  MONOCHROME TELEVISION RECEIVERS . . 229

Experiment 17-2  MONOCHROME TELEVISION RECEIVER
CONTROLS . . . . . . . . . . . . . . . 233

## 18 ELECTRONICS IN INDUSTRY

Experiment 18-1  LIGHT DETECTORS . . . . . . . . . . . . 235

Experiment 18-2  LDR CONTROL CIRCUITS . . . . . . . . . 237

Experiment 18-3  RC TIMERS . . . . . . . . . . . . . . . 239

Experiment 18-4  RADIO CONTROL . . . . . . . . . . . . 241

## 19 TEST INSTRUMENTS

Experiment 19-1  BRIDGE MEASURING CIRCUITS . . . . . . 243

Experiment 19-2  TRANSISTOR TESTER . . . . . . . . . . . 245

## 20 INTEGRATED CIRCUITS

Experiment 20-1  AND GATES . . . . . . . . . . . . . . . 249

Experiment 20-2  OR GATES . . . . . . . . . . . . . . . . 253

Experiment 20-3  NOT GATES . . . . . . . . . . . . . . . 255

Experiment 20-4  NAND GATES . . . . . . . . . . . . . . 259

Experiment 20-5  NOR GATES . . . . . . . . . . . . . . . 263

Experiment 20-6  BINARY COUNTERS . . . . . . . . . . . 267

MATERIALS AND EQUIPMENT LIST . . . . . . . . . . . . . . . 271

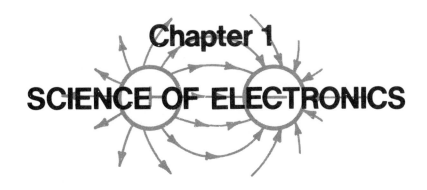

# Chapter 1
# SCIENCE OF ELECTRONICS

## Experiment 1-1  STATIC ELECTRICITY

### INTRODUCTION

Nearly everyone has had an experience with static electricity. Simply walking across a carpeted room while dragging your heels generates a static charge on your body. Then, touching another person or a metal object usually releases the charge with a spark. Sliding across the seat of an automobile will also generate a static charge. Touching a metal object will release the static charge through a spark.

Static electricity is commonly produced by friction between two or more objects. One object will lose some of its electrons to the second object because of friction. This loss of electrons causes the first object to show a net positive charge. The object gaining electrons likewise changes by becoming overbalanced in the negative direction. Static electricity is best produced when conditions are very dry.

### EXPERIMENT OBJECTIVES

As a result of this laboratory experience, you should be able to accomplish the following:
1. Generate static electricity by friction.
2. Observe static charges on the electroscope.
3. Prove the Law of Charges that like charges repel.

### REFERENCE

Gerrish and Dugger, ELECTRICITY AND ELECTRONICS, Chapter 1, pages 7 to 9.

### MATERIALS AND EQUIPMENT

1 — Electroscope
1 — Vulcanite rod
1 — Glass or lucite rod
1 — Piece of wool cloth
1 — Piece of silk cloth

### PROCEDURE

1. Pick up vulcanite rod and briskly rub it with a piece of wool cloth. Through this action, you have caused many electrons from wool to be transferred to rod. Therefore, rod has taken on a _____ charge while wool is _____ charged because of friction.
2. Discharge rod by touching it to a metal object. Repeat process several times. Try discharging rod to bench, cloth, or any other large surface object in laboratory.
3. Place vulcanite rod and wool cloth on bench and pick up glass rod. Rub it briskly with silk cloth. Glass or lucite rod, in this case, loses many of its electrons to silk cloth. Therefore, rod becomes _____ charged while cloth is _____ charged due to friction.
4. Discharge rod by touching it to some other object. Repeat charge and discharge operation several times on different objects. Were you able to observe a spark during discharge action? _____

   _____

5. Carefully remove electroscope from storage cabinet and place it on workbench.
6. Study structure of electroscope. Particularly note location of two metal leaves. Describe original position of two leaves.

   _____

   _____

7. Touch metal ball of electroscope with one hand and alternately touch bench, a metal object or floor if possible. Does any of this alter position of two leaves? _____

   _____

8. Pick up vulcanite rod and rub it briskly with wool cloth. Place cloth on bench top and touch end of rod to metal ball of electroscope. What happens to metal leaves of electroscope? _____

   _____

9. Remove rod from electroscope. How do metal leaves respond to this action? Repeat process two or three times while observing action. To discharge electroscope, place cloth and rod both on bench and touch metal ball with your hand. If they do not return to their original position, try touching a water pipe, metal machine or floor with one hand and electroscope with other hand.

10. Repeat charge and discharge process with glass or lucite rod and silk cloth. Since rod, in this case, takes on a different charge, how do leaves respond when electroscope is touched with rod? _____

    _____

11. Repeat charge and discharge action several times while observing electroscope.

12. Return all parts to storage cabinet.

### QUESTIONS

1. Is there any difference in the electroscope action between steps 8 and 10 with a different charge on each rod? Explain why.

2. What are some examples of static electricity other than those mentioned in this experiment?

3. Which law of static charges applies to this experiment?

# Experiment 1-2  STATIC CHARGE BY INDUCTION

## INTRODUCTION

A static charge developed on an object by friction establishes an invisible field. This field tends to influence other objects even when they are in direct contact. Bringing a neutral object into the static field of a charged object tends to rearrange the electrons in such a way that the neutral object becomes charged. Many neutral objects, therefore, become charged by simply being in the presence of a static field. This method of charging an object is called "charging by induction."

In this experiment you will develop a static charge on a rod by friction. The charged rod will then be used to influence the charge on an electroscope by the induction process. The nearness of the charged rod directly influences the strength of the developed charge.

A prime example of charging by induction occurs during a thunderstorm. A strong negative static charge on a cloud repels electrons away from the objects immediately below it. Then, if the difference in potential charge becomes great enough, a discharge will occur, causing a huge spark or bolt of lightning.

When the static charge developed on an object touches an uncharged object, it is transferred by the "conduction process." Charging by conduction must be achieved by direct contact; charging by induction is accomplished by transfer of static fields.

## EXPERIMENT OBJECTIVES

As a result of this laboratory experience, you should be able to accomplish the following:

1. Place a static charge on different rods by friction.
2. Charge an electroscope by conduction.
3. Charge an electroscope by induction.

## REFERENCE

Gerrish and Dugger, ELECTRICITY AND ELECTRONICS, Chapter 1, pages 7 to 11.

## MATERIALS AND EQUIPMENT

1 — Electroscope
1 — Vulcanite rod
1 — Glass or lucite rod
1 — Piece of wool cloth
1 — Piece of silk cloth

## PROCEDURE

1. Charge vulcanite rod by rubbing it vigorously with wool cloth.
2. Charge electroscope by conduction process. Then, remove rod from contact. Describe reaction of electroscope leaves. _____

_____

_____

_____

3. Place your hand on contact ball of electroscope to discharge it.
4. Charge vulcanite rod again by rubbing it with wool cloth.
5. Bring charged rod near contact ball of electroscope without making contact. Describe reaction of electroscope leaves.

_____

_____

_____

_____

6. Move rod close, then move away from contact ball while observing electroscope leaves. Describe your observations. _____

_____

_____

_____

_____

7. Repeat this procedure with silk and glass rod. Developed charge on glass rod will be positive when compared with vulcanite rod.
8. Describe observations made in step 7.

_____

_____

_____

_____

9. Return all equipment to storage cabinet.

**QUESTIONS**

1. In this experiment, you charged the electroscope. What is meant by the term charging by conduction?

2. Explain what is meant by the term charging by induction.

3. What causes a static field to be developed on an object.

# Experiment 1-3 THE LAW OF CHARGES

## INTRODUCTION

One of the fundamental principles of static electricity deals with the Law of Charges. This law simply states that like charged objects produce a repelling action while unlike charged objects cause attraction. This law is extremely important because it has many applications in the study of electricity.

In the physical structure of an atom, the Law of Charges applies to electrons and protons. The negative charge of an electron causes it to be attracted to the positive charge of the nucleus. Individual electrons likewise tend to repel each other as they revolve around the nucleus.

The Law of Charges also applies to static electricity. A negatively charged body, for example, will attract a positively charged body. A repelling action will occur when two negative or two positive charged bodies are brought together. The static charge developed by an object is commonly produced by friction.

In this experiment, you will investigate the charging and discharging of an object by friction. The developed charge will then be transferred to another object by the conduction process. Like charged objects will show a repelling action; unlike charged objects will demonstrate the attraction principle.

## EXPERIMENT OBJECTIVES

As a result of this laboratory experience, you should be able to accomplish the following:
1. Charge pith balls with static electricity.
2. Confirm the Law of Charges.

## REFERENCE

Gerrish and Dugger, ELECTRICITY AND ELECTRONICS, Chapter 1, pages 10 to 12.

## MATERIALS AND EQUIPMENT

1 — Wooden base, wire stands
1 — Length of thread with a pith ball attached to each end
1 — Vulcanite rod
1 — Piece of wool cloth
1 — Glass or lucite rod
1 — Piece of silk cloth

## PROCEDURE

1. Assemble wire stand by placing wire into drilled hole in wooden base unit. Place assembled unit upright on bench. See Fig. 1-3-1.

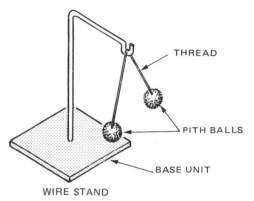

THREAD

PITH BALLS

BASE UNIT

WIRE STAND

Fig. 1-3-1

2. Position two pith balls so that one is suspended 3 or 4 in. lower than other.
3. Charge vulcanite rod by rubbing it with wool cloth. This action causes rod to develop a negative static charge.
4. Touch charged rod to bottom pith ball. At first, pith ball is attracted to rod due to unlike charges. When ball touches rod, it assumes negative charge of rod. Describe what occurs after ball touches rod.

_____

_____

_____

5. Move rod away from ball, then try to touch ball again in a few seconds. Explain what occurs. _____

_____

_____

6. Momentarily grasp pith balls with your hand. This discharges pith ball.
7. Repeat procedure to verify action explained in steps 4 and 6.
8. Set aside vulcanite rod and wool cloth. Pick

up glass rod and rub it with silk cloth. This action causes glass rod to develop a _____ charge by friction.

9. Using procedure outlined for vulcanite rod, touch pith ball with glass rod.

10. Explain action observed in step 9. _____

_____

_____

11. Move rod away from ball, then try to touch it again in a few seconds. What does this demonstrate about charge on ball? _____

_____

_____

12. Wait for a minute or so, then try to touch ball again. How does it respond? _____

_____

13. Disassemble wire stand and return all parts to storage cabinet.

## QUESTIONS

1. Touching the pith ball with a charged rod causes it to assume the charge of the rod by the _____ process.
2. What can be said about the length of time that the pith ball holds a charge?
3. How does this experiment demonstrate the attraction and repulsion principle of charged bodies?

# ATTRACTION AND REPULSION OF CHARGED OBJECTS

## INTRODUCTION

A number of unique things can be done with charged objects to demonstrate the principles of attraction and repulsion. Friction, you may recall, is the primary source of static electricity. The static charge assumed by an object can also be transferred to another object by either the conduction process or by induction. An interaction between charged objects may then cause attraction or repulsion according to the charge assumed by each object.

In this activity, you will see how a neutral object can be charged, then used to repel or attract a second object. A number of common daily occurrences are related to these basic principles. Some of these will be demonstrated in this experiment.

Static electricity is somewhat difficult to develop when the condition of the air is moist or of a high humidity level. Immediately after a heavy rain or snow static electricity is practically nonexistent. Conditions of this type are based upon the fact that moist air serves as a partial electrical conductor. An assumed charge on an object leaks off very quickly because of its conduction through the air. If the condition of the air in the laboratory is moist when you attempt this experiment, it may not perform very satisfactorily.

## EXPERIMENT OBJECTIVES

As a result of this laboratory experience, you should be able to accomplish the following:
1. Charge some neutral objects.
2. Learn some applications of this concept in our technological world.

## REFERENCE

Gerrish and Dugger, ELECTRICITY AND ELECTRONICS, Chapter 1, pages 10 to 13.

## MATERIALS AND EQUIPMENT

1 — Vulcanite rod
1 — Glass or lucite rod
1 — Piece of a wool cloth
1 — Piece of silk cloth
1 — Wooden base, wire stand
1 — Length of thread with pith balls at each end
1 — Balloon

## PROCEDURE

1. Assemble wire stand and place threaded pith balls over wire so that one ball is approximately 1 in. lower than other ball. Thread should be free to move so that balls readily can be placed at same level.
2. Charge vulcanite rod with wool cloth and touch it to lower pith ball. Touch second ball so it will assume same charge as lower ball.
3. Carefully slide thread through wire support so that both balls are at same level. How do they respond? _____

_____

_____

4. Discharge both pith balls by grasping them with your hand. Repeat procedure just outlined with glass rod and silk cloth. Explain what you observed. _____

_____

_____

5. Discharge both pith balls and position them so that one ball is above other ball. Charge top ball with vulcanite rod; charge bottom ball with glass rod. When they are positioned at same level, how do they respond?

_____

_____

_____

6. Disassemble wire stand and return it and threaded pith balls to storage cabinet.
7. Tear a piece of paper into several tiny pieces. Rub vulcanite rod with wool cloth and pass it over bits of paper. Describe your findings. _____

_____

_____

Paint spraying, soot removal from a smoke stack and electrostatic air cleaners operate on basic principle just demonstrated. Running a pocket comb through dry hair should also generate enough friction to charge a rubber or plastic comb.

8. Inflate a small balloon and tie it so that it remains inflated. Rub inflated balloon with a piece of wool cloth. Hold balloon against a dry, nonmetallic wall. How does it respond? _____

_____

9. With a balloon from another lab group, tie two balloons together with a piece of string. Hold string in middle, permitting two balloons to come together.

10. Rub each balloon with a wool cloth, then hold string at middle. How do the balloons respond? _____

_____

11. Deflate balloons and return all things to storage cabinet.

## QUESTIONS
1. Why does the moisture level of the air influence static electricity?
2. What are some evidences of static electricity that you have witnessed?
3. What is meant by the term coulomb?
4. How does the static field of two like charged bodies appear? Make a drawing showing the resulting field.

## INTRODUCTION

In studying static electricity, we found that friction between objects could be used to develop a static charge. Certain materials were used to produce a positive charge, while others were used to produce a negative charge. A developed charge could also be transferred to other objects by the induction process or by conduction. Generally, when a second body touches a charged object, it either causes a discharge or tends to reduce the original charge. The amount of static electricity developed by friction is almost always in a state of change. To be of value, its charge must be continually replenished. Therefore, static electricity is not a very desirable form of electricity.

Current electricity, by comparison, is a very usable form of electricity. It is rather easy to produce and readily can be controlled to do work. Current electricity is based upon the flow of electrons through a conductor. When a potential difference (voltage) is developed by an electrical source, electrons can be made to pass through conductors. The number of electrons flowing in a conductor past a given point represents an electric current. The standard unit used to measure current is the ampere. One ampere represents $6.24 \times 10^{18}$ electrons flowing past a given point in one second.

In this activity, you will study some of the basics of current electricity. These principles are extremely important because they are the basis of study for the remainder of this manual.

## EXPERIMENT OBJECTIVES

As a result of this laboratory experience, you should be able to accomplish the following:
1. Create current flow from two differently charged objects.
2. Sketch certain electrical symbols.
3. Determine the direct current flow in a schematic diagram.

## REFERENCE

Gerrish and Dugger, ELECTRICITY AND ELECTRONICS, Chapter 1, pages 12 to 14.

## PROCEDURE

1. In this activity, you will do a number of things that will help you learn some basic principles of electricity. Complete each item by supplying needed drawings, explanations or data. Be certain that you understand item in question and its answer before proceeding to next item.

2. If an electrical conductor of copper wire is connected between objects A and B of Fig. 1-5-1, what will happen? _____ _____ _____

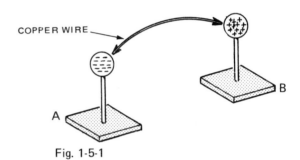

COPPER WIRE

A          B

Fig. 1-5-1

3. Before copper wire is connected between objects A and B in Fig. 1-5-1, these objects possess a difference in potential charge. How else could term "difference in potential" be expressed? _____ _____ _____

4. Explain what is meant by term "electric current?" _____ _____ _____

5. How is a "coulomb" related to electricity current? _____ _____ _____

6. What is "direction of current flow?" _____ _____ _____

7. A good conductor of electricity has

_____

_____

_____

8. What is the function of an insulating material? _____

_____

_____

9. What are some typical insulating materials?

_____

_____

_____

10. Refer to Appendix 5 in the Reference Section of ELECTRICITY AND ELEC-TRONICS and find the symbol for the following items. Then, make a sketch of the symbol for each listed item in the space provided.

| | |
|---|---|
| Battery | Ground |
| Wire (Connected) | Wire (Not Connected) |
| Meter | Incandescent Lamp |
| Resistor | Switch, SPST |

11. A meter used to measure potential difference or electromagnetic force is commonly called a _____

12. A meter used to measure current flow is commonly called an _____

13. Refer to electric circuit in Fig. 1-5-2 and indicate name of each numbered electrical symbol.

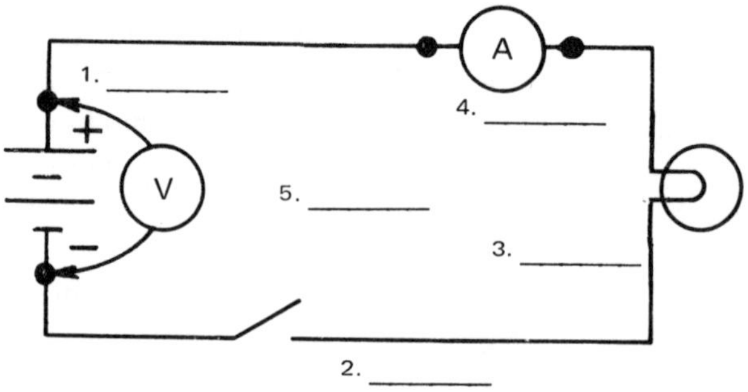

Fig. 1-5-2

14. If switch in Fig. 1-5-2 is turned on, indicate direction of current flow with arrows.

**QUESTIONS**

1. The letter symbol for current is _____

2. The letter symbol for voltage is _____

3. The purpose of an electrical switch is _____

_____

4. The battery in Fig. 1-5-2 provides _____

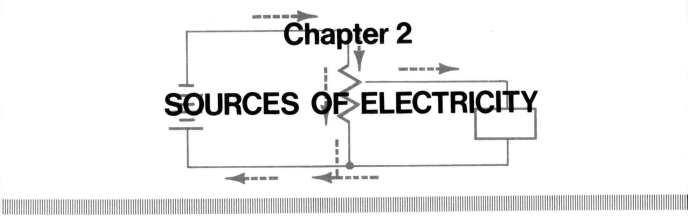

# Chapter 2

# SOURCES OF ELECTRICITY

# Experiment 2-1  VOLTMETER ORIENTATION

## INTRODUCTION

In the study of electricity and electronics, you will be called upon to measure different electrical quantities. These measurements will include values such as voltage, current, resistance and wattage. Instruments designed to measure these quantities are commonly called voltmeters, ammeters, ohmmeters and watt-meters. A meter may be designed to measure only one electrical quantity or several different quantities in a single unit. A single function meter is rather easy to use because it only measures one electrical quantity. Multifunction meters, by comparison, are somewhat more difficult to use because of the increased number of things that can be measured.

The first electrical measuring instrument you will learn to work with in the laboratory is a voltmeter. This type of meter is rather easy to use. However, the voltmeter must be connected properly each time it is used or it may be permanently damaged.

In this experiment, the basic operation of the dc function of a volt-ohm-milliampere (VOM) meter will be discussed. General voltage test procedures, connection methods and scale readings will be presented. Through this procedure, you will begin to develop some basic skill in the use of the VOM without actually connecting it into an operating circuit. Your ability to use a meter is one of the most essential skills to be developed in this study.

## EXPERIMENT OBJECTIVES

As a result of this laboratory experience, you should be able to accomplish the following:

1. Determine the proper way to set up a voltmeter.
   a. Function selection switch.
   b. Range switch.
   c. Probe connections.
2. Demonstrate how to connect a voltmeter in a circuit with correct polarity.
3. Become familiar with various voltmeter scales.

## REFERENCE

Gerrish and Dugger, ELECTRICITY AND ELECTRONICS, Chapters 1 and 2, pages 12 to 16.

## MATERIALS AND EQUIPMENT

1 — VOM or electronic multifunction meter

## PROCEDURE

1. When using a VOM to measure a specific electrical quantity, its function selector switch must be set to desired quantity. Some multifunction meters have a single dial that is used to select both functions and ranges. Other instruments employ push buttons or separate "function" and "range" selector switches. Refer to VOM at your work station and describe function selection method.

   _____

   _____

2. Set function selector switch to measure dc volts. VOMs derive their energy for operation from circuit under test. They ususally do not have an on-off switch. Electronic VOMs or multifunction meters that contain

transistors or vacuum tubes must be supplied with operating energy. These meters must employ an on-off switch.

3. First step in operating a VOM or an electronic multifunction meter includes power on and function selection. Explain how this is done with your meter.

_____

_____

4. Second operational step of a multifunction meter is range selection. What are dc voltage ranges of your meter? _____

_____

5. Third operational step deals with probe connections. On a VOM, negative or common probe usually is marked (−) or "COM." Locate (−) or "COM" meter jack and plug black test lead into it. Positive probe may be marked (+) or "VOM," according to meter design. Some meters also have separate jacks for different functions such as V dc, V ac, mA, 5000V dc or 6000V ac. Explain method of connecting positive meter probe to your meter.

_____

_____

_____

6. Fourth operational step deals with circuit connection technique. When measuring dc, polarity of meter must "match" polarity of circuit connection points to be tested. When this condition occurs, meter will make an "on scale" or "up scale" deflection of the meter hand. Reversing polarity will cause a "down scale" or "off scale" deflection. Avoid connecting meter in a reverse polarity direction.

7. Voltmeters are always connected in parallel, or across two separate connection points of a circuit. One of these points will have an excess of electrons with respect to other. Connect negative terminal of meter to this test point. Connect positive terminal of meter to test point that shows a reduced number of electrons. Connected in this manner, voltmeter will measure a difference in potential or electromotive force

(emf) between two test points.

8. Fig. 2-1-1 shows a symbol drawing of a

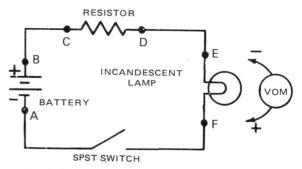

Fig. 2-1-1

simple electric circuit that is to be tested with indicated VOM.

9. To measure voltage of battery in Fig. 2-1-1, connect negative terminal of VOM to test point _____, while the positive terminal of meter would connect to test point _____

10. If range switch is set to 25V position and actual value of battery is 10V, indicate

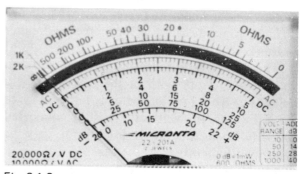

Fig. 2-1-2

where hand would appear on meter scale of Fig. 2-1-2.

11. To measure voltage across lamp, negative meter terminal would be connected to test point _____, while positive terminal would be connected to test point _____

12. A voltage reading of 6V appears across lamp. If dc range switch is in 10V position, indicate hand deflection on meter scale of Fig. 2-1-2.

13. To measure voltage across resistor, connect negative meter terminal to test point

_____ , while positive terminal would be connected to test point _____

14. A voltage reading of 4V appears across resistor. Indicate this value on 5V meter scale shown in Fig. 2-1-2.

15. When using a VOM to measure an unknown voltage, be sure to select a voltage range greater than highest voltage you might expect from circuit under test. Start at a high range and switch down to a lower range that will produce a mid-scale deflection. As a general rule, best accuracy occurs near full scale end of meter scale. Be certain that meter range is great enough to measure value under test before connecting meter to circuit.

16. VOMs or multirange meters usually are designed to have some direct reading scale ranges and some factored ranges. A direct reading scale corresponds to a specific meter range setting. The 5, 25 and 125 scales of Fig. 2-1-2 are examples of direct reading scales. Factored scales include the 500 and 1000 scales. Multiplication or division factors are used to change scale ranges. Changing 5 to 500 is achieved by multiplying the scale 5 reading by 100. Two zeros added to the scale reading easily accomplish this operation. Changing 10 to 1000 is similarly accomplished.

17. Refer to VOM or electronic multifunction meter at your work station. Which scales are direct reading and which are factored scales? _____

_____

_____

## QUESTIONS

1. What is meant by the term "observe polarity" when using a VOM to measure dc?
2. Explain how an unknown voltage is measured?
3. What is meant by the term "voltmeters are connected in parallel with the component under test?"
4. The most accurate readings of a VOM are taken at the _____

## INTRODUCTION

One very important source of electricity is the dry cell. This voltage source is composed of a carbon rod, surrounded by a paste of ground carbon, manganese dioxide and ammonium chloride, all housed in a zinc container. When the cell is initially formed, it produces a potential difference of 1.5V. After the cell has been in operation for a period of time, its active materials begin to deteriorate. This occurs to some extent even when the cell is not being used. Dry cells usually have a rather short life expectancy. Cell deterioration cannot be reversed after it has been initially formed. Weak cells are discarded when they lose their charge. A cell of this type cannot be effectively recharged. Therefore, a dry cell is classified as a primary cell because it can produce a charge of electricity only one time. The dry cell, in this case, is considered as a chemical source of electricity.

## EXPERIMENT OBJECTIVES

As a result of this laboratory experience, you should be able to accomplish the following:
1. Measure voltage produced by various dry cells.
2. Observe the various output voltages of certain cells.

## REFERENCE

Gerrish and Dugger, ELECTRICITY AND ELECTRONICS, Chapter 2, pages 15 to 17.

## MATERIALS AND EQUIPMENT

1 — Volt-ohm-milliampere (VOM) meter
1 — "D" type dry cell
1 — Assortment of dry cells, including a No. 6 dry cell, an alkaline cell, a mercury cell and several old dry cells (one assortment per class).

## PROCEDURE

1. Select a VOM from storage cabinet and set function switch to dc voltage position.
2. Connect test leads to meter. Normally, positive meter lead is red and negative lead is black when color-coded leads are used.
3. Meter should be 0 to 3V or an equivalent range.
4. Symbol for a single dry cell is ⊣|⊢——. Connect voltmeter to dry cell. Observe proper polarity between meter and dry cell. A No. 6 dry cell has negative and positive terminals at top of cell. Center terminal is positive and outer terminal is negative.
5. A standard dry cell has center connection positive and outside can negative. These cells normally are stacked together in a flashlight. Negative terminal of this type of cell usually is located at bottom of cell. Test voltage of a "D" type dry cell. Measured voltage is _____ volts. If a No. 6 cell is available, measure and record its value. Voltage of a No. 6 dry cell is _____ volts.
6. Momentarily reverse polarity of meter so that you may observe an off scale deflection. Obviously, meter does not produce a usable deflection when connected in this manner. Normally, meter is not damaged when deflected down scale. It should not be connected in this manner or permitted to remain in this condition for a prolonged period of time.
7. Connect meter for correct polarity. Again, positive meter lead is red and negative lead is black. Center terminal is positive.
8. Change voltage range of meter to next higher range position. Some meters may be designed to make this change by simply rotating a switch.
9. Measure voltage of either No. 6 dry cell or "D" type cell. Explain why this meter reading is somewhat more difficult to obtain. _____

_____

_____

10. Instructor will have a number of different primary cell types available for you to test. Test three cells listed in chart in Fig. 2-2-1. By comparing measured value with rated

CELL TEST CHART

| CELL | TYPES OF CELL | RATED VOLTAGE | MEASURED VOLTAGE | CONDITION |
|------|---------------|---------------|------------------|-----------|
| A | MERCURY CELL | | | |
| B | ALKALINE CELL | | | |
| C | OLD DRY CELL | | | |
| D | | | | |
| E | | | | |

Fig. 2-2-1

value, indicate condition of cell as good or weak. Note that a cell is usually weak or depleted when a voltage reading is less than its rated value. If time permits, you may want to test several other cells.

11. Disconnect meter and return all components to storage cabinet.

**QUESTIONS**
1. What is meant by the term "voltaic cell?"
2. The physical makeup of a LeClanche type of dry cell includes?
3. What is the major difference in a No. 6 dry cell and a "D" cell when they both produce the same voltage?

# Experiment 2-3 PRIMARY CELLS

## INTRODUCTION

A primary cell is a very unique source of electricity. It develops voltage by direct chemical action within a self-contained unit. When the cell is assembled, voltage is produced immediately. After the cell has been formed, its electrical action cannot be changed or reversed. Primary cells will only supply voltage for a rather limited length of time. When the output voltage is spent, the cell cannot be recharged.

Fundamentally, a primary cell is composed of two dissimilar materials placed in a chemical solution. The chemical solution is usually called an electrolyte. It contains positive and negative charged particles called ions. Chemically, the electolyte solution must react with at least one of the two materials placed in it. This chemical reaction causes one material to lose electrons and the other to gain electrons. As a result, a difference in potential charge is established immediately.

After a primary cell has aged or has been used, the potential charge becomes depleted. As a general rule, its charge cannot be effectively restored without replacing either the electrolyte or one of the electrode materials.

## EXPERIMENT OBJECTIVES

As a result of this laboratory experience, you should be able to accomplish the following:
1. Construct some simple primary cells.
2. Measure output voltage from these primary cells.
3. Compare various types of materials as electrodes and electrolytes in primary cells.

## REFERENCE

Gerrish and Dugger, ELECTRICITY AND ELECTRONICS, Chapter 2, pages 15 to 17.

## MATERIALS AND EQUIPMENT

1 — Experimental voltaic cell kit with three different electrode strips
1 — Volt-ohm-milliampere (VOM) meter
1 — Assortment of solutions: saltwater, alkaline and soda pop.

## PROCEDURE

1. Remove voltaic cell construction kit from storage cabinet and place it on bench top. Select carbon strip and zinc (Zn) strip from package. Attach a clamp to each strip so that it stands in an upright position. Position strips close together but not touching.
2. Prepare a solution of saltwater made of 1 teaspoon of table salt and 8 oz. of tap water. Pour saltwater solution into cell container.
3. Place metal strips into saltwater solution.
4. Connect voltmeter to two strips so as to produce an "on scale" deflection of meter. Voltage produced is _____
5. Voltmeter is also used in this case to denote polarity of cell. Carbon strip serves as _____ terminal of cell while zinc strip is _____ terminal.
6. Using same procedure, test at least four other strip combinations in experimental voltaic cell. Note that following chemical element abbreviations are stamped on each strip.

   | | | | |
   |---|---|---|---|
   | Al | = aluminum | In | = indium |
   | C | = carbon | Pb | = lead |
   | Cu | = copper | Sn | = tin |
   | Fe | = iron | Zn | = zinc |

7. Record the cell polarity and voltage for each combination in chart in Fig. 2-3-1.
8. Rinse each strip in clean water and dry them with a paper towel. Pour saltwater into a storage container or exchange it with another lab group for a container of soapy water. Repeat same test procedure using soapy water as an electrolyte for cell. Use 1/4 teaspoon of liquid detergent to 8 oz. of tap water.
9. Rinse each strip in clean water and dry them with a paper towel. Exchange soapy water solution for an 8 oz. container of carbonated soda pop. Repeat test procedure using soda pop as an electrolyte solution. Record your findings in Chart 1.
10. Clean strips and dry them with a paper towel.
11. If time permits, you may want to try other

VOLTAIC CELL CHART 1

| TRIAL TEST NO. | POSITIVE TERMINAL MATERIAL | NEGATIVE TERMINAL MATERIAL | VOLTAGE | ELECTROLYTE SOLUTION |
|---|---|---|---|---|
| 1 | | | | SALT WATER |
| 2 3 4 5 | | | | |
| 6 | | | | SOAPY WATER |
| 7 8 9 10 | | | | |
| 11 | | | | SODA POP |
| 12 13 14 15 | | | | |

Fig. 2-3-1

electrolyte solutions such as wood alcohol, turpentine, citrus fruit juice or lubricating oil. Test both alkaline and acid solutions to obtain varied results. Through this experience, you will be able to observe that voltage output of a primary cell is directly dependent upon its construction materials.

## QUESTIONS
1. Why can a primary voltaic cell only be used until its charge is depleted?
2. Describe the physical makeup of a primary cell in general terms.
3. What determines the voltage of a primary cell?

# Experiment 2-4  SECONDARY CELLS

## INTRODUCTION

Secondary cells contain two or more metal electrodes placed in an electrolyte solution. After this cell has been formed, it must go through a charging cycle. Charging current coming from an outside source causes a chemical change within the cell. One electrode takes on a positive charge; the other electrode takes on a negative charge. The physical construction of the cell dictates specific negative and positive electrodes.

When a secondary cell is connected to an electrical circuit, electrons flow from the negative terminal to the positive terminal. This action ultimately causes the cell to be discharged. Recharging the cell restores its output voltage to the rated value. Secondary cells can be charged and discharged thousands of times and still work effectively.

In this experiment, you will be able to observe the actual physical change in voltage that occurs when a nickel-cadmium cell is discharged and recharged. Through this experience, you will learn the procedure for charging a cell with a variable dc source. This procedure is similar for all rechargeable operations.

## EXPERIMENT OBJECTIVES

As a result of this laboratory experience, you should be able to accomplish the following:
1. Discharge a secondary (nickel-cadmium) cell.
2. Recharge a secondary cell.
3. Measure voltages during the discharging and recharging processes.

## REFERENCE

Gerrish and Dugger, ELECTRICITY AND ELECTRONICS, Chapter 2, pages 18 to 20.

## MATERIALS AND EQUIPMENT

1 — Volt-ohm-milliamperes (VOM) meter or equivalent
1 — 4 ohm, 1 watt resistor
1 — "C" type Ni-Cad cell, General Electric GC-2 or equivalent, and cell holder
1 — SPST switch

## PROCEDURE

1. Remove rechargeable nickel-cadmium "C" cell from storage cabinet and place it in a cell holder.
2. Connect VOM meter to cell and measure output voltage. Cell voltage is _____ volts. How does measured voltage compare with rated voltage of cell? _____
   _____
3. Prepare cell discharge circuit of Fig. 2-4-1. Turn on switch to discharge cell. Discharge cell for approximately 15 minutes. Indicate discharge current path by drawing arrows on circuit diagram.

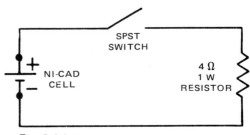

Fig. 2-4-1

4. Measure and record voltage output of cell. Discharged cell voltage is _____ volts. Compare voltage output of discharged cell with cell voltage of step 2.
5. Remove 4 ohm resistor from discharge circuit and replace it with a variable dc power supply as indicated in Fig. 2-4-2.
6. Turn on variable dc power supply and adjust it to 2V dc. Use voltmeter to observe voltage value.
7. Turn on circuit switch and charge cell for 15 minutes or longer if class time permits. Indicate direction of charging current by drawing arrows on circuit diagram.
8. Turn off circuit switch and measure cell (after 15 minutes recharge). Is there a noticeable increase in cell voltage over step 4? _____
   _____
   _____

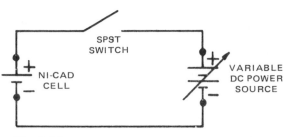

Fig. 2-4-2

9. Total cell charging time was _____ minutes.
10. Disconnect circuit, turn off power supply and return all parts to storage cabinet.

## QUESTIONS

1. Why is direction of charging current opposite to that of discharge current in this experiment?
2. What is the makeup of a Ni-Cad cell and what are some of the advantages of a Ni-Cad cell over a C-Zn cell?
3. The most common application of a rechargeable battery today is the _____

# Experiment 2-5  BATTERIES

## INTRODUCTION

The electrical output of a single cell produces a rather limited amount of voltage and ampere-hour capacity. As a general rule, the output voltage is determined by the material composition of the cell, while its capacity is based on the size of its electrodes. When two or more cells are connected together, it is possible to increase both output voltage and capacity. Cells connected in this manner usually are called "batteries."

When single cells are connected together in series, it causes an increase in output voltage. The amount of increase is based on the single cell voltage times the number of cells connected. The ampere-hour rating of this type of circuit is determined by the capacity of the smallest cell. Series connected cells do not cause an increase in capacity.

When single cells are connected together in parallel, the output voltage remains the same as that of each cell. The ampere-hour rating of this type of circuit is based directly upon the sum of individual cell capacity values. Generally, batteries with a high capacity rating are quite large physically.

To increase both output voltage and capacity, some batteries must contain series-parallel cell combinations. A wide variety of different voltage and capacity combinations are available today. These same general series and parallel rules apply to both primary and secondary cells.

In this experiment, you will connect cells in various combination circuits. Output voltages are then measured with a voltmeter and circuit capacity is calculated. Through this experience, you will see how different cell combinations can be used to produce desired voltage and capacity values of batteries.

## EXPERIMENT OBJECTIVES

As a result of this laboratory experience, you should be able to accomplish the following:
1. Connect cells in series and determine their combination voltages.
2. Connect cells in parallel and determine their combination voltages.
3. Connect cells in series-parallel and determine their combination voltages.

## REFERENCE

Gerrish and Dugger, ELECTRICITY AND ELECTRONICS, Chapter 2, pages 19 to 22.

## MATERIALS AND EQUIPMENT

4 — "C" type cells
4 — "C" cell holders
1 — Volt-ohm-milliampere (VOM) meter
1 — Assortment of connecting wires

## PROCEDURE

1. Place four "C" type dry cells in cell holders and measure voltage of each cell. Compare measured voltage with rated cell voltage.
2. Connect four cells in series as indicated in Fig. 2-5-1. Note that each symbol labeled A, B, C and D represents a single cell.

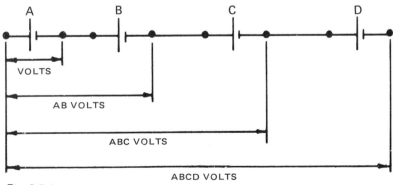

Fig. 2-5-1

3. Using formula $E_{out}$ = E of a cell x number of cells, determine voltage of each test point.

4. With a voltmeter, measure and record voltage across each test point. What can be said about voltage of series connected cells?

_____

_____

5. If ampere-hour capacity (AH) of a single "C" cell is 1.8, what is the AH rating of series circuit in Fig. 2-5-1? _____ AH.

6. Connect four cells in parallel as indicated in Fig. 2-5-2.

13. Momentarily remove cell B from circuit. How will this alter output voltage?

_____

14. Measure output voltage to verify your prediction.

15. With all four cells in original circuit, what is AH output capacity? _____ AH. Assume same 1.8 AH cell capacity used previously.

16. Without cell B, capacity is _____ AH. Without B and C, capacity is _____ AH.

17. Disconnect combination circuit and return all components to storage cabinet.

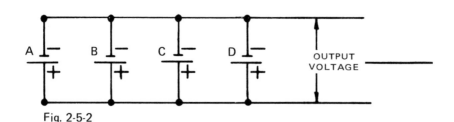

Fig. 2-5-2

7. Measure and record output of circuit in Fig. 2-5-2.

8. Remove cell A and measure output voltage. Then, remove cells A and B and measure output voltage. Finally remove cells A, B and C and measure output voltage. What conclusion about parallel connected cells can you draw from this procedure? _____

_____

_____

9. If ampere-hour rating of a "C" cell is 1.8, what is output capacity of cells A, B, C and D in parallel? _____

10. Disconnect parallel circuit and connect series-parallel combination circuit of Fig. 2-5-3.

11. Estimate output voltage of combination circuit. Output voltage is _____

12. Measure output voltage and compare it with estimated voltage.

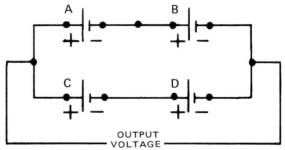

Fig. 2-5-3

## QUESTIONS

1. What would be gained in a battery by connecting several cells in a parallel combination?

2. Output voltage of a battery containing 15 carbon-zinc cells in series is _____ volts.

3. A 9V transistor radio battery contains how many carbon-zinc cells?

4. What is gained in construction of a battery when cells are connected in parallel-series combinations?

## INTRODUCTION

Today, solar power serves as a very important source of electrical energy. Light energy from the sun can be readily converted into electricity by solar cells or sun batteries. Communication satellites orbiting around the earth derive their electrical operating power by this process. Solar cells attached to the roof of a house or building also can be used as an auxiliary source of electricity during the daylight hours. This form of electricity can be effectively used to conserve the amount of electricity produced by other sources.

A solar cell is primarily classified as a photo-voltaic cell, which refers to the voltage output characteristics of the cell. When a solar cell is exposed to light, difference in potential is developed across its terminals. The physical construction of the cell includes a layer of selenium compound, a barrier layer, a transparent front and a base plate. Light striking the transparent electrode causes electrons from the selenium layer to cross the barrier and move toward the transparent electrode. Electrons crossing this barrier cannot return to the selenium. As a result, a potential difference is developed across the cell when it is exposed to light. The cell also has a current capacity rating that is primarily based on the size of the electrodes. Solar cells, as a rule, produce a rather low value of voltage and current output.

In this experiment, you will see how solar cell output can be altered to meet the demands of increased voltage and current.

## EXPERIMENT OBJECTIVES

As a result of this laboratory experience, you should be able to accomplish the following:
1. Connect a single solar cell in a circuit and test it.
2. Determine the effects of connecting series and parallel solar cells into a circuit.

## REFERENCE

Gerrish and Dugger, ELECTRICITY AND ELECTRONICS, Chapter 2, pages 23 to 25.

## MATERIALS AND EQUIPMENT

1 — Solar cell, International Rectifier B2M or equivalent
1 — Volt-ohm-milliampere (VOM) meter

## PROCEDURE

1. Connect solar cell test circuit of Fig. 2-6-1 to low voltage range of a dc voltmeter.

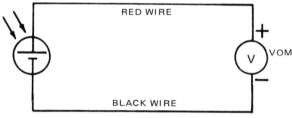

RED WIRE

BLACK WIRE

Fig. 2-6-1

2. Normal room light cell voltage is _____ volts.
3. Cover cell surface with your hand and observe output voltage. Some cells produce a very small voltage known as "dark voltage." This characteristic varies to some extent with each cell. Explain how your cell responds to this test. _____

_____

_____

4. Move test cell near an outside window and record voltage. _____ volts. How does this value compare to normal room light? Indicate status of outside light. _____

_____

5. Direct exposure to bright sunlight should produce maximum output from solar cell. If at all possible, test output of cell exposed to direct sunlight. Output voltage value is _____ volts. Why would sunlight passing through a window glass reduce output of a solar cell somewhat? _____

_____

_____

_____

6. With aid of a solar cell from another lab group, connect two cells in series as indicated in Fig. 2-6-2.

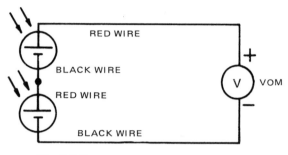

Fig. 2-6-2

7. Measure and record output voltage of series circuit for following light sources:
   Dark voltage is _____
   Normal room light voltage is _____
   Window light voltage is _____
   Direct sunlight voltage is _____

8. When solar cells are connected in series, output voltage _____ while current capacity _____

9. If current capacity of solar cell is 2 milliamperes (mA), potential current output capacity of series test circuit is _____ mA.

10. Connect two solar cells in parallel as indicated in Fig. 2-6-3.

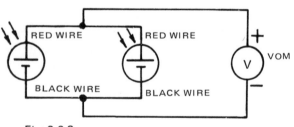

Fig. 2-6-3

11. Measure and record output voltage of parallel circuit for following light sources:
    Dark voltage is _____
    Normal room light voltage is _____
    Window light voltage is _____
    Direct sunlight voltage is _____

12. When solar cells are connected in parallel, output voltage _____ while current capacity _____

13. A solar cell has a maximum output of 0.4V at 4.6 mA. Two solar cells connected in parallel would produce an output of _____ volts at _____ mA when exposed to direct sunlight.

14. Disconnect circuit and return all components to storage cabinet.

## QUESTIONS

1. Make a sketch of the internal structure of a solar cell in the provided space.

2. Explain how direct sunlight produces a difference in potential across the cell.

# Experiment 2-7  AMMETER FAMILIARIZATION

## INTRODUCTION

In the study of electricity and electronics, there is frequently a need for the measurement of electric current. The term "ammeter" is commonly used to describe an instrument that will achieve this measurement. Ammeter is a contraction of the words ampere (unit of current) and meter.

Current flow specifically refers to the movement of electrons through the completed path of an electric circuit. When $6.24 \times 10^{18}$ electrons pass by a given point in one second, it represents one ampere of current flow. Ammeters are designed that will measure current in microamperes, milliamperes or amperes. In a volt-ohm-milliampere (VOM) meter, current is measured when the meter is switched to the ammeter function.

The current measuring function of a VOM is achieved by first selecting the appropriate function switch. VOMs with a combination range/function switch are simply positioned to the dc current position. As a general rule, a higher current range is selected first to establish an approximate current value. Then, more appropriate current range can be selected that will make an accurate deflection of the meter movement.

When a VOM is placed in the ammeter function, its internal resistance is quite low. All of the current being measured must flow through the meter and its associated parts. As a result of this, the VOM is very susceptible to damage. The lowest current range setting of the meter represents its most sensitive position.

To measure an electric current, the ammeter of a VOM must be made a part of the circuit under test. This is achieved by providing a direct path for current to pass through the meter. Therefore, an ammeter must be connected in series with the circuit to make this measurement. Fig. 2-7-1 shows the ammeter of a VOM connected to a simple circuit. The schematic drawing of the circuit represents the VOM as an ammeter symbol. Note that the meter completes the path through the circuit.

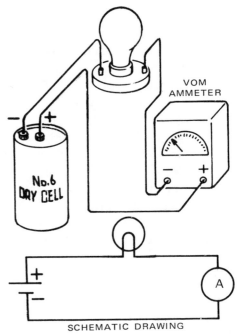

SCHEMATIC DRAWING

Fig. 2-7-1

There are a few general procedures that must be observed when initially preparing a VOM to measure an electric current. This procedure may vary somewhat with each VOM.

1. Circuit under test should be turned off before attempting to connect ammeter of VOM.

2. Set function selector switch to ammeter position. Some VOMs may include ammeter jacks instead of a selector switch.

3. Position ammeter range to its highest value initially. This may be reset to a lower range after an initial current value has been observed.

4. Typically, same meter scale is used to indicate both voltage and ampere values. Range switch determines appropriate scale selection.

5. Observe meter and circuit polarity. Most negative point should be connected to (−) or "COM," while positive point is connected to (+) or VOM terminal.

6. To connect ammeter of a VOM, break circuit flow path at a desired location and insert meter between two connections.

7. Never connect an ammeter in parallel with another circuit component.

In this experiment, you will have an opportunity to become familiar with the basic operation of the ammeter of a VOM. An inspection of the meter, its range selection switch and scale will be made first. Then, you will indicate some ammeter scale readings by marking the position of the meter hand on a scale. Through this procedure you will develop some basic skill in the use of a meter without actually connecting it into an operating circuit. Then, you will connect the meter into a simple circuit and measure an electric current. You will be called upon to make current measurements of this type throughout the remainder of this study.

## EXPERIMENT OBJECTIVES

As a result of this laboratory experience, you should be able to accomplish the following:
1. Determine the proper setup for using the ammeter section of a VOM.
   a. Function switch.
   b. Range selection switch.
   c. Probe leads.
2. Connect the ammeter properly in the circuit.
3. Read the ranges of the ammeter in a VOM.

## REFERENCE

Gerrish and Dugger, ELECTRICITY AND ELECTRONICS, Chapter 1, pages 12 and 13.

## MATERIALS AND EQUIPMENT
   1 — Multirange VOM
   1 — Variable dc power supply
   1 — No. 47 lamp
   1 — SPST toggle switch

## PROCEDURE
1. Select a VOM from storage cabinet and place it on top of workbench. Inspect meter as to location of its (—) and (+) terminals, range selection switch and meter scales.
2. Change function switch of meter to its "current" function. Select a specific current range and decide upon which scale will be used to display this value. Note that full

scale deflection of meter should correspond to range switch setting. How many complete sets of meter range numbers are included on meter scale? _____ number of sets.

3. Which meter scale is used to indicate smallest current range? _____ This scale generally is called a direct reading scale. Its full scale value also corresponds to a specific range position number. Are there other scales of this type on VOM?

_____

_____

4. Which ammeter meter scale would be best suited to indicate a current value of 100 mA? _____

5. VOMs usually have a number of factor scales. This type of scale requires multiplication or division by some factor. The 1 mA scale, for example, is used for 100 mA range. This necessitates a multiplication factor of 100. What are some other factored ranges of meters that require conversion? _____

6. Fig. 2-7-2 shows a symbol drawing of a simple electric circuit. To measure current flow at test point A, redraw circuit in blank space provided, showing ammeter properly connected. Indicate correct polarity of meter in your drawing.

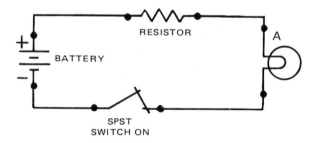

Fig. 2-7-2

Fig. 2-7-3

7. If meter of redrawn circuit indicated 4 mA with range switch in 5 mA position, where would indicating hand be deflected? Draw meter hand deflection on meter scale of Fig. 2-7-3.

8. If voltage of battery of Fig. 2-7-2 was increased, a current value of 23 mA could occur. Which range would best display this value on your VOM? _____ range. Draw hand deflection that will show this current value on correct scale of meter shown in Fig. 2-7-3.

9. If same lamp circuit had a current flow of 62 mA, which range would be used?

of 3V may be obtained from two "C" cells or from a variable dc power supply.

11. Since current value is unknown, place milliampere meter in its highest range. Turn on circuit switch and make an initial reading. If at all possible, you may need to switch to a smaller scale for increased accuracy. Turn off circuit switch while changing meter range switch positions. Current reading observed is _____ mA.

12. Turn off switch and reduce dc source voltage to 1.5V. Turn on switch and measure circuit current. Circuit current is _____ mA.

13. Turn off switch and disconnect circuit. Return all components to storage cabinet.

## QUESTIONS

1. What is the most sensitive current range that can be measured with the meter used in this experiment?

2. Why must an ammeter be made a part of the circuit under test?

3. Why are ammeters more susceptible to

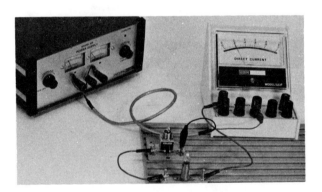

Fig. 2-7-4

_____ Mark this value on meter scale of Fig. 2-7-3.

10. Connect circuit of Fig. 2-7-4. Power source

damage than a voltmeter?

4. How does a direct reading scale differ from one with a multiplier factor?

# Experiment 2-8 ELECTRICITY FROM HEAT

## INTRODUCTION

When two different pieces of wire are commonly joined at one end and heated, electricity is produced across the free ends. A device that operates in this capacity is commonly called a "thermocouple." These devices are typically used to regulate automatic shutoff valves in gas-fired hot-water heaters and furnaces. When the pilot light of a gas-fired device goes out, a thermocouple senses the change in heat and shuts off the gas jet.

Commercially prepared thermocouples are made of special metal alloys such as iron-constantan and chromel-alumel. Rather substantial amounts of dc current and voltage are produced by these alloy combinations. This output can be amplified to control automatic circuit operations, or it may be used directly as an electrical source to energize specific components.

As an energy source, several thermocouples may be connected together in series and parallel circuit configurations. The same basic principles of other series and parallel connected sources apply to the thermocouple. In series, the output voltages are additive with the current the same as that of a single unit. In parallel, voltage does not increase, but current output is additive.

In this experiment, you will build a thermocouple, test it with a VOM and observe how electrical energy is produced by heat.

### EXPERIMENT OBJECTIVES

As a result of this laboratory experience, you should be able to accomplish the following:
1. Construct a thermocouple.
2. Measure output voltage and current from the thermocouple.
3. Experiment with connecting thermocouples in series and parallel.

### REFERENCE

Gerrish and Dugger, ELECTRICITY AND ELECTRONICS, Chapter 2, page 25.

### MATERIALS AND EQUIPMENT

1 — Volt-ohm-milliampere (VOM) meter
1 — 6 in. length of iron-constantan wire
1 — 6 in. length of copper wire
1 — Source of heat (matches or lighter)

## PROCEDURE

1. Construct a thermocouple by twisting together a length of iron-constantan wire and copper wire at one end. Twist two wires together for approximately 1 in. as indicated in Fig. 2-8-1.

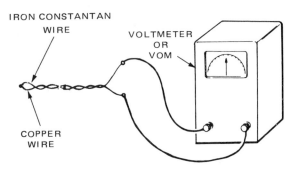

Fig. 2-8-1

2. Prepare VOM to measure dc voltage and connect it to thermocouple. Select a low voltage range.
3. Connect VOM to free ends of thermocouple. Polarity of meter is not important. It is used here to determine polarity of thermocouple according to direction of deflection.
4. Heat joined ends of thermocouple with a match or lighter. If an up-scale deflection occurs, polarity of thermocouple and meter are the same. A down-scale deflection indicates reversed polarity.
5. Iron wire has a _____ polarity, while copper wire is of _____ polarity.
6. Output voltage of thermocouple is _____ volts.
7. Observing polarity, prepare VOM to measure current flow. As a general rule, current output of thermocouple is quite small.
8. Heat joined end of thermocouple again and record output current flow: _____ mA.
9. With a thermocouple from another lab group, connect two thermocouples together in series. Procedure is the same as

connecting dry cells in series.

10. Position twisted end of each thermocouple so that both ends may be heated by the same flame. Free ends should not touch.

11. Heat twisted lead ends. Measure and record output voltage of the series structure: _____ volts.

12. Using the same procedure, connect two thermocouples together in parallel. Note that parallel connected devices have both negative and both positive leads commonly connected together.

13. Heat joined ends and measure resulting current output of this parallel circuit: _____ mA.

14. Disconnect thermocouple and VOM. Return all parts to storage cabinet.

## QUESTIONS

1. Define the term "thermocouple."
2. How does the basic principle of thermocouple connected in series compare with other series connected sources?
3. How does the basic principle of thermocouples connected in parallel compare with other parallel connected sources?

## INTRODUCTION

When direct current (dc) is measured with a VOM, polarity must be observed because dc flows at a constant rate in one direction. The steady value of current and voltage are important characteristics of direct current.

Alternating current (ac) deals with voltage and current values that are in a constant state of change. A dc meter cannot be used to measure ac unless it is modified. VOMs are designed to measure either dc or ac voltages by employing a rectifying device known as a diode. This device simply changes ac, which flows first in one direction then in the other, into a single direction current flow. The resulting output of the rectifier is read on a special scale and labeled ac. Diodes and rectification will be investigated in succeeding chapters.

In this experiment, you will become familiar with the functional operation of a VOM as an ac voltmeter, then measure some actual voltage values. The technique of measuring ac voltage will be used throughout this study.

### EXPERIMENT OBJECTIVES

As a result of this laboratory experience, you should be able to accomplish the following:
1. Learn how to set up a VOM to measure ac voltage.
2. Determine how to read a VOM scale for ac voltage.
3. Measure ac from a power supply output (or a transformer).

### REFERENCE

Gerrish and Dugger, ELECTRICITY AND ELECTRONICS, Chapter 2, pages 25 and 26.

### MATERIALS AND EQUIPMENT

1 — Volt-ohm-milliampere (VOM) meter
1 — Power supply with 12.6V CT

### PROCEDURE

1. Select a VOM from storage cabinet and place it on top of workbench. Inspect meter and locate (−) and (+) terminal connections, range selector switch and ac voltage scales.
2. Change function switch to ac voltage function. Select a specific voltage range and decide which meter scale will be used to display it. Note that full scale deflection of meter hand should correspond to range switch setting. How many ac range positions does VOM have? _____
3. How many direct reading ac scales are there? _____ Does this meter have any factored scales where multiplication or division must be performed? _____
4. When measuring ac voltage, meter polarity is not observed. This is due to nature of ac which is in a continuous state of value and direction change. The ac scale of a VOM usually is printed in red or another color to distinguish it from the dc scale. Total length of an ac scale area is also somewhat shorter than a corresponding dc scale. The ac measurements generally are not quite as accurate as dc values because of this difference in scale size.
5. When measuring ac voltage, voltmeter of a VOM is simply connected across (in parallel with) circuit under test. Procedure is identical to that of measuring ac voltage. You will find ac voltage easier to accomplish, however, because the polarity is not observed.
6. A schematic drawing of a simple ac circuit is shown in Fig. 2-9-1. Note the ac voltage that appears across each component. Indicate which VOM range would be most desirable to read these voltage values. A-B is _____ C-D is _____ E-F is _____

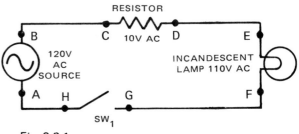

Fig. 2-9-1

7. Complete ac scale of Fig. 2-9-2 so that it corresponds to scale of your VOM. It is not necessary to indicate all meter graduations. Only major voltage values are needed to indicate voltages of step 6.

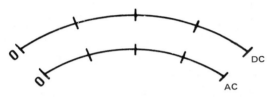

Fig. 2-9-2

8. Draw meter hand deflection that will indicate voltage values at points A-B, C-D and E-F of step 6. Label each indication accordingly.
9. Turn on power supply at your work station. Locate low voltage ac filament source.
10. Prepare VOM to measure an unknown ac voltage value. Select a meter range that will make a satisfactory indication of voltage at filament source terminals. The ac filament source is _____ volts.
11. If your work station has a variable ac voltage source or an alternate low voltage source, measure and record its output. Alternate ac source produces _____ volts.
12. Turn off power supply and disconnect VOM. Return all components to storage cabinet.

## QUESTIONS
1. Why is ac voltage measured on a different scale than dc voltage?
2. What are the primary differences between measuring ac and dc voltages?

# ⫿⫿⫿⫿⫿⫿⫿ Experiment 2-10  PRESSURE SOURCES OF ELECTRICITY ⫿⫿⫿⫿⫿⫿

## INTRODUCTION

Certain crystal substances such as Rochelle salts have an unusual property. When mechanical pressure is applied to the surface of a crystal, it will produce a corresponding voltage across its surface. This property is called the Piezoelectric effect. Crystal microphones and phonograph cartridges utilize this principle in their operation.

When the physical shape of a crystal is distorted, it produces a voltage across its front and back surface. The output voltage changes polarity in step with the applied pressure. As a result, the output voltage possesses an alternating current (ac) characteristic. An ac voltmeter must be used to test the output voltage of a phonograph cartridge or a crystal microphone. Normally, the output voltage is quite small. It must be increased in value through amplification to be of any significant value.

In this experiment, you will test voltage output of a phonograph cartridge and a crystal microphone. The ac voltage will be measured with a VOM and sound output will be tested with an earphone. Fig. 2-10-1 shows a typical phonograph cartridge and a crystal microphone.

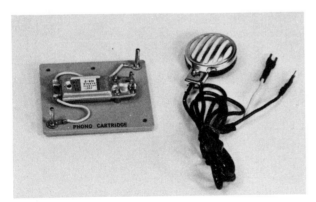

Fig. 2-10-1

## EXPERIMENT OBJECTIVES

As a result of this laboratory experience, you should be able to accomplish the following:

1. Generate ac from a phonograph cartridge assembly by pressure.
2. Generate ac by pressure from a crystal microphone.
3. Produce electricity by pressure from a crystal earphone.

## REFERENCE

Gerrish and Dugger, ELECTRICITY AND ELECTRONICS, Chapter 2, pages 25 and 26.

## MATERIALS AND EQUIPMENT

1 — Volt-ohm-milliampere (VOM) meter
1 — Phonograph cartridge assembly
1 — Crystal microphone
1 — Crystal earphone

## PROCEDURE

1. Select mounted phonograph cartridge from storage cabinet and place it on workbench.
2. Prepare VOM to measure a dc voltage of approximately 2V. Connect meter leads to cartridge terminals.
3. Some cartridge units may have a protective cover placed over needle. If so, remove cover and set it aside until you have completed experiment. Other cartridge units may require that a phonograph needle be placed in the holder. A knurled screw usually holds needle in place. Loosen screw, insert needle, then gently tighten screw until needle is held firmly in place.
4. Carefully apply pressure first to one side of needle, then to other side while observing meter reading. Describe your observations.

_____

_____

_____

5. Change function switch of VOM so that it will measure a low voltage ac. Using same procedure as step 4, observe meter while applying pressure to needle. How does this operation compare with procedure step 4?

_____

_____

6. Carefully draw a rough-surfaced material (coarse file or strip of sandpaper) across needle. How does meter respond to this

test? _____

_____

7. Disconnect phonograph cartridge from meter and exchange it with a crystal microphone.

8. Gently blow into microphone while observing meter. How does meter respond to this action? _____

_____

9. Try whistling or talking into crystal microphone while observing meter. How does it respond? _____

_____

10. If a sensitive earphone is available, disconnect meter from microphone and connect earphone in its place. Have on person blow or whistle into microphone while a second person listens to resulting output.

11. If time permits, you may want to use earphone to test output of phonograph cartridge used in step 3 of experiment. Move a rough textured surface and a smooth surface over needle and test its output. Describe your findings. _____

_____

12. Disconnect components and return everything to storage cabinets.

## QUESTIONS

1. Explain how the crystal microphone produces electricity.
2. Explain how the phonograph cartridge produces electricity.
3. What is meant by the term piezoelectric effect?

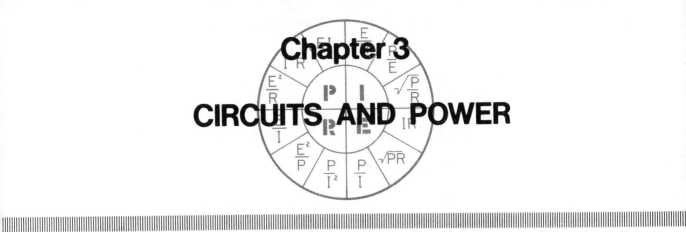

# Chapter 3
# CIRCUITS AND POWER

## Experiment 3-1 DETERMINING WIRE SIZES

### INTRODUCTION

In an electrical circuit, current is made to flow through a conducting material or wire. Large diameter conductors provide a better path for electrons to flow than smaller conductors. The resistance of a wire conductor varies inversely with its size or cross-sectional area.

In order to have some degree of standardization, wire conductors are arranged according to specific numbered sizes. No. 0 wire is the largest size indicated on an American Standard Wire Gauge. The smallest size wire indicated on this gauge is No. 36. Periodically, a person working with electrical circuits is called upon to measure different wire sizes. In this experiment, you will have an opportunity to develop some skill in the use of an American Standard Wire Gauge.

### EXPERIMENT OBJECTIVES

As a result of this laboratory experience, you should be able to accomplish the following:
1. Measure various sizes of wire.
2. Become familiar with different sizes of solid and stranded wire used in electrical circuit applications.

### REFERENCE

Gerrish and Dugger, ELECTRICITY AND ELECTRONICS, Chapter 3, pages 28 to 31.

### MATERIALS AND EQUIPMENT

1 — American Standard Wire Gauge
1 — Assortment of solid and stranded wires

### PROCEDURE

1. Instructor will provide your lab group with three short lengths of solid electrical wire. Select largest diameter piece of wire from assortment.
2. Obtain a wire gauge from storage or tool cabinet and place it at your work station.
3. To determine size of wire, hold gauge in one hand and select a numbered slot stamped around outer edge of gauge that will accept wire sample. Wire must pass through flat part of slot without any play. Do not force wire through slot hard enough to mar or scratch sides of wire.
4. Try several different size slots before deciding upon size of wire. Record determined size of largest wire. _____ AWG.
5. Reverse side of wire gauge indicates thickness of gauge size in thousandths of an inch. Record thickness of wire size determined in step 4. _____ in.
6. To change thickness of a wire size in thousandths of an inch to mils of diameter, simply move decimal point three places to right. Diameter of wire size of step 6 in mils is _____
7. Circular mil cross-sectional area of a conductor is equal to square of its diameter in mils. Cross-sectional area of wire size of step 6 is _____ circular mils.
8. Determine wire size of smallest piece of wire in assortment. Wire size is _____ AWG. Thickness is _____ in. Diameter is _____ mils. Cross-sectional area is _____ circular mils.
9. Measure remaining wire. Wire size is

_____ AWG. Thickness is _____ in. Diameter is _____ mils. Cross-sectional area is _____ circular mils.

10. Instructor also will provide you with a piece of stranded wire. Remove approximately 1/2 in. of insulation from one end of wire. Count number of solid wires in stranded cable. Determine wire size of one solid wire. _____ AWG.

11. Twist individual strands of wire together to reform stranded cable. Measure composite size of wire. _____ AWG.

12. Return lengths of wire to instructor and return gauge to storage cabinet.

## QUESTIONS

1. What is an advantage of stranded wire over solid wire?

2. In a home, one circuit is connected with No. 12 AWG and one with No. 14 AWG. Which circuit will provide the largest amount of current flow? Why?

3. What four factors determine the resistance of a conductor?

## INTRODUCTION

An ohmmeter is an important test instrument designed to measure the dc resistance of a circuit or electrical component. This type of meter is quite unique when compared with voltmeters and ammeters. Voltmeters and ammeters, derive their energy for operation from the circuit being tested. An ohmmeter has a built-in power source that supplies its own voltage to the components under test. Therefore, ohmmeters are used to test only unenergized components.

When the two test leads of an ohmmeter are touched together, current flows from the meter power source through the ohmmeter circuit. The meter is designed to show zero resistance on its scale when this operation occurs. When a resistance is placed between the two test probes, current flow is reduced according to the value of the added resistance. The deflection hand of the meter movement then displays this value on a scale calibrated in ohms.

Resistance measuring is one of the three primary functions of a VOM. To prepare the VOM to measure resistance, set its function switch to the ohms position. Then, position range switch to one of three or four possible resistance positions. Resistance of a component is determined by connecting it between ohmmeter test leads. To avoid unnecessary battery deterioration, do not leave VOM in resistance testing position when not in use.

In this experiment, you will prepare a VOM to measure resistance, then develop some skill in the basic operation of the ohmmeter. This test instrument is extremely helpful in locating faulty circuit components or measuring component values.

## EXPERIMENT OBJECTIVES

As a result of this laboratory experience, you should be able to accomplish the following:
1. Determine the proper way to set up an ohmmeter.
   a. Function and range switch.
   b. Probe connections.
2. Zero an ohmmeter.

3. Read the scale of an ohmmeter.
4. Measure continuity, using a VOM.

## REFERENCE

Gerrish and Dugger, ELECTRICITY AND ELECTRONICS, Chapter 3, pages 28 and 29.

## MATERIALS AND EQUIPMENT

1 — Volt-ohm-milliampere (VOM) meter
4 — No. 47 incandescent lamps
1 — SPST toggle switch

## PROCEDURE

1. Prepare VOM to measure resistance.
   a. Place function selector switch in ohms position. For VOMs with a combination function/range switch, simply adjust switch to one of the ohm or R positions. See Fig. 3-2-1. For VOMs with a separate

Fig. 3-2-1

function selector switch, place this switch in "ohms" position first. See Fig. 3-2-2. Then, select appropriate range switch position.

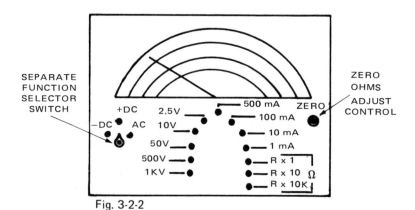

Fig. 3-2-2

b. Set ohms range switch to R x 1 position. If meter indicating hand is pointing to infinite or highest resistance position at this time, meter is ready for testing. If VOM being used has two adjust controls, one is designed to change position of deflection hand at infinite end of scale. Term "infinite adjust" or " ∞ adjust" is a label normally associated with this control. Do not confuse this with "ohms adjust" control which alters position of

to infinite resistance position. Touch probes together again, then separate them to see if deflection hand is properly set to infinite and zero. As a general rule, meter zeroing should occur each time range switch is changed to a different ohms position.

d. Set range selector switch to a different range and zero meter. How many range positions does this VOM have? What are they? _____

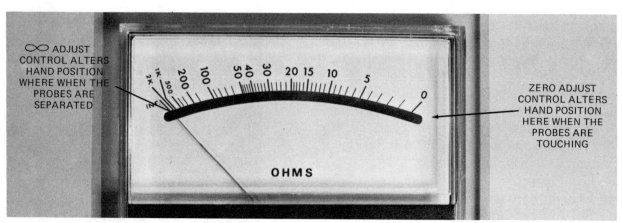

Fig. 3-2-3

deflection hand at zero end of scale. See Fig. 3-2-3.

c. Touch two test probes together. If everything is properly set, meter hand should deflect to zero position. Adjust zero position control so that hand deflects to zero position on ohms scale. When internal battery of ohmmeter is weak, meter may not zero properly. Separating two test probes will cause hand to return

_____

_____

e. When range switch is in R x 1 position, resistance is read directly from ohms scale. Other ohmmeter ranges include a multiplication factor of R x 10, R x 100, R x 1K, R x 10K, etc. To find a resistance value when these ranges are being used, simply read position of meter hand on ohms scale and multiply it by range position factor. Range factors of a VOM vary with different meter manufacturers.

2. When measuring resistance with an ohmmeter, component or circuit under test must not be energized by an electrical source. Ohmmeters, as a general rule, employ batteries to produce meter deflection. An outside source of energy added to that of built-in source would cause a very large meter current that could destroy meter movement. Never connect an ohmmeter to a device or circuit that has power applied to it.

3. One important use of an ohmmeter is testing for a continuous electrical path through components of a circuit. This frequently is called a continuity test. A test of this type will show where a break or open condition occurs.

4. Select a SPST toggle switch from storage cabinet. A continuity test of switch will show if it is operating properly. Connect probes of ohmmeter to two terminals of switch. When switch is turned on, it completes a path between two terminals. This should cause a very low resistance indication on meter. When switch is in off position, its resistance is infinite. How would continuity of a faulty switch test? _____

_____

_____

5. Remove four lamps from storage cabinet and test them for continuity. Approximate resis-

tance of each lamp is _____ ohms. How would an open lamp test?

6. Ohmmeters are also used to determine actual circuit or component resistance values. Actual component value is then compared with its intended value to determine conditioning of component. A test of this type could be applied to lamps of step 5 if their normal operating resistance was known. Resistors are tested in this to see if their value is within designed tolerance range.

7. After using an ohmmeter, prepare it properly for storage. Following this procedure will permit it to function accurately when time arises for it to be used again.

   a. Place function switch in off position. If VOM does not have an off position, set function switch to a high valued voltage position.

   b. Then remove test leads from their jacks. They may be wrapped around meter or stored in small bundle near meter.

8. Prepare VOM for storage and return all components to storage cabinet.

## QUESTIONS

1. Why must an ohmmeter be used only to test a de-energized circuit or component?

2. What does a continuity test show about a component?

3. What is the consequence of using a meter that has not been properly zeroed to measure resistance?

# Experiment 3-3  COLOR-CODED RESISTORS

## INTRODUCTION

Resistors are purposely placed in electric circuits to reduce voltage values and limit current flow. They come in a wide variety of types and sizes, depending upon their intended function in a circuit. Resistance value of low wattage resistors from 1/8 watt to 4 watts are purposely marked by color-coded bands painted on the body of the resistor. A person working with electrical and electronic circuits must be able to recognize resistor values by their color coding.

Fig. 3-3-1 shows the placement of color bands on the body of a resistor. Note that the four bands are offset to the left when reading the coded value. Bands A and B represent the first and second digits of the representative number value. Band C indicates the multiplier value of the number. Digits indicated by the colors of bands A and B are multiplied by the color-coded value of band C. Band D indicates the tolerance range of the resistor. This band represents a percentage that the actual value of the resistor will fall with respect to its color-coded value. A 1000 ohm 10 percent tolerance resistor can have an actual value 900 to 1100 ohms and still be in tolerance.

The color code table in Fig. 3-3-2 is used to determine the value of a resistor.

In this experiment, you will use a VOM to determine whether color-coded resistors are good or bad, according to readings shown on the ohmmeter.

## EXPERIMENT OBJECTIVES

As a result of this laboratory experience, you should be able to accomplish the following:
1. Read the color-coded values of various resistors.
2. Measure the actual resistance of these color-coded resistors, using a VOM.
3. Compute tolerance ranges of various resistors.

## REFERENCE

Gerrish and Dugger, ELECTRICITY AND ELECTRONICS, Chapter 3, pages 36 to 38 and 306.

## MATERIALS AND EQUIPMENT

1 — Volt-ohm-milliampere (VOM) meter
10 — Selected color code resistors

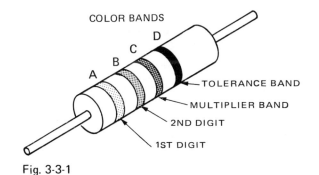

COLOR BANDS

D
C
B
A

TOLERANCE BAND

MULTIPLIER BAND

2ND DIGIT

1ST DIGIT

Fig. 3-3-1

RESISTOR COLOR CODE TABLE

| COLOR BANDS | NUMERICAL VALUE 1ST DIGIT | NUMERICAL VALUE 2ND DIGIT | DECIMAL MULTIPLIER | TOLERANCE PERCENTAGE |
|---|---|---|---|---|
| BLACK | — | 0 | 1 | |
| BROWN | 1 | 1 | 10 | |
| RED | 2 | 2 | 100 | |
| ORANGE | 3 | 3 | 1000 | |
| YELLOW | 4 | 4 | 10,000 | |
| GREEN | 5 | 5 | 100,000 | |
| BLUE | 6 | 6 | 1,000,000 | |
| VIOLET | 7 | 7 | 10,000,000 | |
| GRAY | 8 | 8 | 100,000,000 | |
| WHITE | 9 | 9 | 1,000,000,000 | |
| SILVER | — | — | 0.01 | ± 10% |
| GOLD | — | — | 0.1 | ± 5% |
| NONE | — | — | — | ± 20% |

Fig. 3-3-2

## PROCEDURE

1. Select several different resistors from storage cabinet. Indicate four color-coded bands of each resistor in table shown in Fig. 3-3-3.

2. Using number assigned each resistor in left hand column of Fig. 3-3-3, indicate color-coded value of each resistor in Fig. 3-3-4. Refer to Appendix 2, page 306 of the text for an explanation of the resistor color code.

3. Using color-coded tolerance percentage, cal-

| NO. | COLOR-CODED BANDS | 1ST DIGIT | 2ND DIGIT | MULTIPLIER | TOLERANCE |
|---|---|---|---|---|---|
| 1 | | | | | |
| 2 | | | | | |
| 3 | | | | | |
| 4 | | | | | |
| 5 | | | | | |
| 6 | | | | | |
| 7 | | | | | |
| 8 | | | | | |
| 9 | | | | | |
| 10 | | | | | |

Fig. 3-3-3

Fig. 3-3-4. Record measured value in appropriate column.

5. Indicate good or bad status of each resistor according to measured value and color-coded tolerance range.

6. Prepare VOM for storage and return all resistors to storage cabinet.

## QUESTIONS

1. What is meant by the tolerance as applied to

culate resistance plus or minus range for each resistor. Record this value in tolerance range column of the table in Fig. 3-3-4.

4. Prepare VOM to measure resistance, then measure actual value of each resistor listed in

RESISTOR VALUES

| NO. | COLOR-CODED VALUE | TOLERANCE RANGE | MEASURED VALUE | STATUS |
|---|---|---|---|---|
| 1 | | | | |
| 2 | | | | |
| 3 | | | | |
| 4 | | | | |
| 5 | | | | |
| 6 | | | | |
| 7 | | | | |
| 8 | | | | |
| 9 | | | | |
| 10 | | | | |

Fig. 3-3-4

a color-coded resistor?

2. Why are resistors purposely placed in an electric circuit?

3. What does the physical size of a color-coded resistor denote?

# Experiment 3-4  OHM'S LAW VERIFICATION

## INTRODUCTION

In 1828, George Simon Ohm, a German scientist, derived a set of fundamental laws by experimentation that serve as the basis of electrical theory today. Ohm's Law states that: "The current flow of an electric circuit is directly related to the voltage and inversely related to the resistance." Mathematically, this relationship is expressed by the formulas:

$$I = \frac{E}{R} \qquad E = I \times R \qquad R = \frac{E}{I}$$

In this experiment, you will construct an electrical circuit, test it with a VOM, then verify component values through measurement or calculation. You will also develop more skill in the use of the VOM as an electrical measuring instrument. Finally, you will verify Ohm's Law through experimentation and learn how to transpose a simple equation when solving for an unknown value.

## EXPERIMENT OBJECTIVES

As a result of this laboratory experience, you should be able to accomplish the following:
1. Construct some simple series circuits and use a VOM to measure voltage, current and resistance.
2. Use Ohm's Law to verify measured values.
3. Use Watt's Law to calculate power in a circuit.

## REFERENCE

Gerrish and Dugger, ELECTRICITY AND ELECTRONICS, Chapter 3, pages 31 to 35.

## MATERIALS AND EQUIPMENT

1 — Volt-ohm-milliampere (VOM) meter
1 — No. 47 lamp and holder
1 — 100 ohm, 1/4 watt, 10 percent tolerance resistor
1 — SPST toggle switch
1 — Variable dc power supply

## PROCEDURE

1. Select components needed to construct a dc lamp circuit as in Fig. 3-4-1.

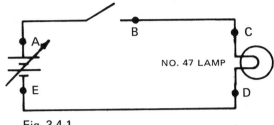

Fig. 3-4-1

2. Prepare VOM to measure dc voltage. Connect it across output terminals of a variable dc power supply. Turn on power supply and adjust it to produce 5V. Circuit switch should be in off position at this time.

3. Turn on circuit switch and energize lamp. If lamp turns on, continue to step 4. If it does not turn on, disconnect power supply and test continuity of circuit between points A and G with the ohmmeter of a VOM. An "open" lamp is a typical problem. Test points A-B, B-C, C-D and D-E are used to determine continuity of specific circuit components and connecting wires. After finding faulty connection or component, correct problem. Return connection A-E to power supply, turn on circuit switch and observe operating lamp circuit.

4. Turn off circuit switch, and disconnect connecting wire between points D-E. Prepare VOM to measure dc current and connect it into circuit at these points. Turn on circuit switch. Measure and record dc circuit current flow. _____

5. Remove VOM from circuit and return connecting wire between points D-E.

6. According to Ohm's Law, resistance (R) of this circuit can be determined by the formula:

$$R = \frac{E}{I}$$

Calculate resistance of circuit, using applied circuit voltage and measured current. R is _____ ohms.

7. Prepare ohmmeter to measure dc resistance. Disconnect circuit from power supply at test points A-E. Measure and

record total resistance of circuit. How closely does measured resistance compare with calculated resistance? _____

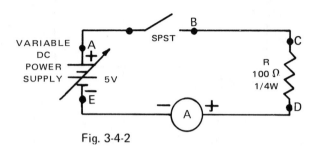

VARIABLE
DC
POWER
SUPPLY

Fig. 3-4-2

8. Turn off circuit switch and remove lamp from circuit. In place of lamp, insert a 100 ohm 1/4 watt resistor. Fig. 3-4-2 shows a schematic diagram of the modified circuit.

9. Calculate circuit current flow using Ohm's Law. Calculated current flow is _____ mA.

10. Turn off circuit switch and remove connecting wire between points D-E. Prepare

VOM to measure dc current and insert ammeter into circuit between points E-D.

11. Turn on circuit switch. Measure and record circuit current flow. I is _____ mA.

12. With circuit in operation for approximately three minutes, feel 100 ohm resistor. What causes resistor to become warm? _____

_____

13. Calculate power rating or wattage of resistor, using either E, I or R. Power is _____ watts. How close is 1/4 watt resistor to its maximum power rating?

14. Turn off power supply and disconnect circuit. Return all components to storage cabinet.

## QUESTIONS

1. Explain Ohm's Law by words.
2. What is electrical power?
3. If voltage in Fig. 3-4-2 was increased to 8V dc, how would it alter the circuit?

# Experiment 3-5  SERIES DC CIRCUITS

## INTRODUCTION

In a series circuit, current flows in a single path from the negative side of the source through the components to the positive side of the source.

A series circuit has unique operating characteristics. Total resistance is based on the sum of the individual component resistances. Mathematically: $R_{Total} = R_1 + R_2 + R_3$ + etc. Additional resistors will increase total circuit resistance; fewer resistors will decrease total resistance.

Current characteristics are quite simple. With one path, current flow is the same throughout the circuit. Increased total resistance, however, causes a corresponding reduction in circuit current. Likewise, when total resistance is decreased, current increases. An "open" or "break" in the circuit path at any point will disable the entire circuit.

Voltage characteristics are unusual. Voltage drop, for example, across each resistive component is equal to the current passing through the component times its resistance. Therefore, the sum of all voltage drops around a series circuit equals the value of the applied source voltage.

In this experiment, you will test basic E, I and R characteristics of a series dc circuit. The experiment is divided into three distinct parts.

## EXPERIMENT OBJECTIVES

As a result of this laboratory experience, you should be able to accomplish the following:

Part A—Series Resistance Characteristics
1. Construct a series circuit with three fixed resistors and measure the total resistance in the circuit.
2. Measure resistance of a potentiometer.
3. Construct a series circuit with fixed and variable resistors and determine total resistance in circuit.

Part B—Series Current Characteristics
1. Calculate current flow in a dc series circuit.
2. Measure current flow in a dc series circuit using a VOM.

Part C—Series Voltage Characteristics
1. Calculate voltage in a dc circuit.
2. Measure voltage in a dc series circuit using a VOM.

## REFERENCE

Gerrish and Dugger, ELECTRICITY AND ELECTRONICS, Chapter 3, pages 38 and 39.

## MATERIALS AND EQUIPMENT

1 — Volt-ohm-milliampere (VOM) meter
1 — Variable power supply
1 — 5K, 2 watt potentiometer
1 — Resistor decade module-Hickok ETC-10 or the following resistors:
    1 — 47 ohm, 1/4 watt resistor
    1 — 100 ohm, 1/4 watt resistor
    1 — 470 ohm, 1/4 watt resistor

## PROCEDURE
## PART A—SERIES RESISTANCE CHARACTERISTICS

1. Connect a dc series circuit as shown in Fig. 3-5-1A, using a resistor decade module or discrete resistors.

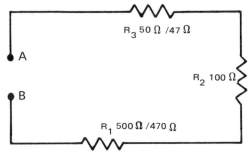

Fig. 3-5-1A

2. A resistor decade module has values printed on each resistor. When using individual resistors, employ resistor color code of Experiment 3-3 to select proper resistor values.
3. Calculate total resistance of series circuit, using circuit resistance values. Calculated resistance of circuit is _____ ohms.
4. Prepare VOM to measure resistance. Mea-

sure and record total resistance of circuit between test points A and B in Fig. 3-5-1A. Total resistance ($R_T$) is _____ ohms. If this value is significantly smaller or larger than calculated value of step 3, measure each resistor to see if it is intended value. Make necessary changes to correct circuit.

5. Tolerance range of resistance is _____ ohms.

6. Variable resistors are frequently used to alter total resistance of a circuit. A potentiometer (one form of variable resistor) will be used to demonstrate this characteristic of a series circuit.

7. Select a 5K resistor from storage cabinet and place it near constructed circuit.

8. Use VOM to measure resistance of potentiometer between test points A and C in Fig. 3-5-2A. Fill in measured value as A-C ohms.

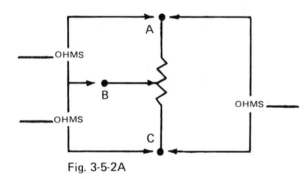

Fig. 3-5-2A

9. Adjust shaft of potentiometer through its full clockwise and counterclockwise range. Does resistance of A-C change? _____

_____

10. Connect VOM between test points A-B and adjust shaft of potentiometer through its range. Fill in resistance value in ohms between test points A-B in Fig. 2-5-2A.

11. Connect VOM between test points B-C and adjust shaft of potentiometer through its range. Fill in resistance value in ohms between test points B-C.

12. What is the difference between A-B and B-C resistance and shaft rotation of potentiometer? _____

_____

13. Connect potentiometer into a series circuit as shown in Fig. 3-5-3A.

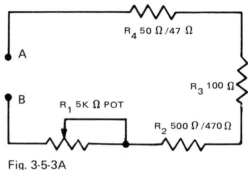

Fig. 3-5-3A

14. Connect VOM across test points A-B to measure total resistance of the series circuit. Adjust potentiometer to its full clockwise position. $R_T$ is _____ ohms.

15. Adjust potentiometer to its extreme counterclockwise position and measure total resistance of circuit. $R_T$ is _____ ohms.

16. Total resistance range of circuit is _____ to _____ ohms.

17. Disconnect circuit and return all parts to storage cabinet.

## QUESTIONS

1. In a series circuit, the total resistance of the circuit is determined by _____

2. In Fig. 3-5-3A, if the circuit was broken between $R_2$ and $R_3$, total resistance of the circuit would be _____

3. If you connect a jumper wire across $R_3$, shorting it out, total resistance would be

_____

## PROCEDURE
## PART B—SERIES CURRENT CHARACTERISTICS

1. Connect series dc circuit as in Fig. 3-5-1B. Use individual resistors of those mounted on resistor decade module.

2. Before turning on circuit switch, turn on variable dc power supply. Prepare VOM to measure dc voltage and connect it to test points A-H in Fig. 3-5-1B. Adjust power supply to produce 10V dc.

3. Using indicated values of resistors, deter-

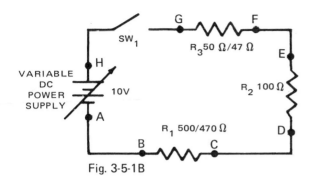

Fig. 3-5-1B

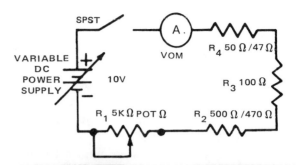

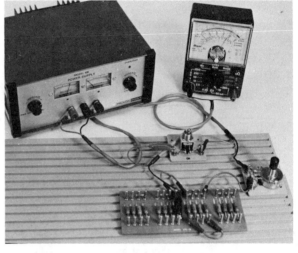

Fig. 3-5-2B

mine total resistance of circuit. Using total circuit resistance and applied source voltage, calculate total current flow of circuit. Calculated current flow is _____ mA.

4. Prepare VOM to measure current flow. Remove connecting wire between test points A-B and connect meter into circuit at this location.

5. Turn on circuit switch and record measured total current flow. $I_T$ is _____ mA.

6. How do measured and calculated values compare? _____

_____

7. Turn off circuit switch. Remove VOM from test points A-B and return connecting wire between these two points. Measure circuit current flow at test points E-F, following same procedure outlined for points A-B. How does this value compare with A-B? _____ What conclusion can be made about current flow of a series circuit?

_____

_____

_____

8. Turn off circuit switch and add a 5K potentiometer to circuit between points A-B as indicated in Fig. 3-5-2B.

9. Turn on circuit switch and adjust potentiometer through its resistance range. Total current flow of circuit ranges from _____ _____ to _____ mA. This means that when resistance of $R_1$ increases, the $I_T$ _____, or when resistance of $R_1$ decreases, the $I_T$ _____.

10. With circuit switch on and a current indication on VOM, break current path between $R_3$ and $R_2$ momentarily. What

influence does this have on $I_T$? _____

_____

Describe this characteristic of a series circuit. _____

11. Let circuit operate for approximately five minutes without turning it off. Touch each resistor to see if there is a noticeable change in temperature. Explain how temperature of resistors respond. _____

_____

_____

12. Carefully increase voltage of power supply to produce 20 mA of $I_T$. Touch each resistor to determine if there is a noticeable change in temperature. Power consumed by each resistor is directly related to current flow. With 20 mA of current flow through $R_4$, power consumed is _____ watts. Total power consumed by a series circuit is the sum of power consumed by each resistive component.

13. Turn off circuit switch and power supply. Disconnect circuit and return all parts to storage cabinet.

## QUESTIONS

1. Current flow of a series circuit is the _____ through each component.
2. Current flow of a series circuit is _____ related to source voltage applied to total circuit resistance.
3. Total current flow of a series circuit is _____ related to total resistance when a dc voltage is applied.
4. The sum of power consumed by individual resistors of a series circuit is equal to _____ power consumed by the circuit.
5. When the same current flows through a series circuit, greatest power is consumed by the _____ resistor.

## PROCEDURE
## PART C—SERIES VOLTAGE CHARACTERISTICS

1. Construct series circuit as in Fig. 3-5-1C.
2. Before turning on circuit switch, turn on variable dc power supply. Prepare VOM to measure dc voltage and connect it to test points A-H. Adjust power supply to 12V.
3. Prepare VOM to measure current flow, then insert it into circuit at test points A-B. Turn on circuit switch and measure current flow of circuit. $I_T$ is _____ mA.
4. Remove VOM from circuit and restore connecting wire.

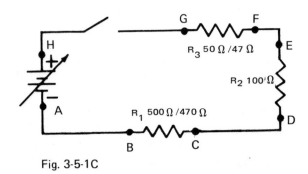

Fig. 3-5-1C

5. Using measured circuit current of step 3, calculate voltage drop across each resistor. $E_{R_1}$ is _____ volts, $E_{R_2}$ is _____

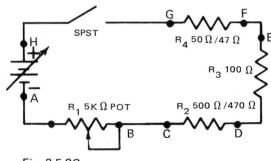

Fig. 3-5-2C

volts, $E_{R_3}$ is _____ volts.

6. Prepare VOM to measure dc voltage, then measure voltage drop across each resistor. $E_{R_1}$ is _____ volts, $E_{R_2}$ is _____ volts, $E_{R_3}$ is _____ volts.
7. Turn off circuit switch and add a 5K potentiometer to circuit at test points A-B as shown in Fig. 3-5-2C.
8. Turn on circuit switch. Place VOM across potentiometer, then adjust it to 6V dc. Measure and record voltages across remaining resistors. $E_{R_1}$ is 6V, $E_{R_2}$ is _____ volts, $E_{R_3}$ is _____ volts, $E_{R_4}$ is _____ volts. How does the sum of these voltages compare with applied source voltage? _____

_____

9. Turn off circuit switch. Prepare VOM to measure resistance. The resistance of potentiometer $R_1$ is _____ ohms. In a series circuit, a _____ (small or large) resistance value will produce greatest voltage drop.
10. Connect VOM across $R_2$ and adjust $R_1$ through its resistance range. Voltage across $R_1$ varies from _____ to _____ volts. $V_{R_2}$ is largest when $R_1$ is _____
11. Turn off circuit switch and power supply. Disconnect circuit and return all parts to storage cabinet.

## QUESTIONS

1. The sum of the voltage drops across each resistor of a series circuit equals _____
2. As current passes through a resistor, a certain amount of energy is used which causes a

_____

3. Explain the relationship of resistor size of a series circuit and voltage drop.

# PARALLEL DC CIRCUIT CHARACTERISTICS

## INTRODUCTION

A parallel dc circuit is connected so that the same voltage from the source is applied to each resistive branch. Alternate values of current flow through each parallel branch according to its resistance. The current starts at the negative side of the source and divides into each branch path. The output of each branch then combines and returns to the positive side of the source. Circuits of this type are commonly used to supply electrical energy to the lights of a home or industrial building.

The characteristics of a parallel circuit are quite unique in a study of electricity and electronics. These characteristics apply to circuit resistance, current, voltage and power. The total resistance of a parallel circuit, for example, is based upon the formula:

$$R_T = \frac{R_1 \times R_2}{R_1 + R_2} \text{ or}$$

$$\frac{1}{R_T} = \frac{1}{R_1} + \frac{1}{R_2} + \frac{1}{R_3} \ldots$$

When an additional resistor is placed in a parallel circuit, total resistance decreases. Removing a resistor from a parallel circuit causes total resistance to become larger.

The current characteristics of a parallel circuit are somewhat more unusual than the other characteristics. Each parallel path or branch has its own unique current flow based upon the value of its resistance. If all resistors are of the same value, the current will be the same in each branch path. The total current flow $I_T$ is equal to the sum of the branch current flow values. A "break" or "open" in a parallel branch only applies to that specific branch. Therefore, the operation of each branch path is independent of other branches of the circuit.

The voltage characteristic of a parallel circuit is quite simple. The same voltage is applied to each resistance path or branch. A value change in the source voltage does, however, alter the current and power characteristics of a parallel circuit.

Each branch of a parallel circuit consumes or uses a certain amount of power. This is based specifically upon the E, I or R values of each circuit branch. The total power ($P_T$) used by a parallel circuit is based on the sum of the power consumed by each branch. Mathematically the formula $P_T = P_1 + P_2 + P_3 + $ etc. shows this relationship.

In this experiment, you will test some of the basic E, I and R characteristics of a parallel dc circuit. The experiment is divided into three distinct parts dealing with these characteristics. Each part will take approximately 35 to 40 minutes to complete. If your class period is longer than an hour, you should have time to complete two parts in one period. For 50 to 60 minute periods, it is best to do one part of the experiment each class period.

## EXPERIMENT OBJECTIVES

As a result of this laboratory experience, you should be able to accomplish the following:

Part A—Parallel Resistance Characteristics
1. Construct a parallel circuit.
2. Calculate total resistance in the circuit.
3. Measure total resistance in the circuit using a VOM.

Part B—Parallel Current Characteristics
1. Calculate current in various parts of a parallel circuit.
2. Confirm these current calculations by measuring them with a VOM.
3. Calculate total power in the parallel circuit.

Part C—Parallel Voltage Characteristics
1. Confrim with the VOM that voltage is equal through a parallel circuit.

## REFERENCE

Gerrish and Dugger, ELECTRICITY AND ELECTRONICS, Chapter 3, pages 40 to 42.

## MATERIALS AND EQUIPMENT

1 — Volt-ohm-milliampere (VOM) meter

1 — SPST toggle switch
1 — Variable power supply
2 — No. 47 lamps and sockets
1 — Resistor decade module, Hickok ETC-10 or the following resistors:
    1 — 47 ohm, 1/4 watt
    2 — 220 ohm, 1/4 watt
    1 — 470 ohm, 1/4 watt
    1 — 1K, 1/4 watt
    1 — 2.2K, 1/4 watt

## PROCEDURE
## PART A—PARALLEL RESISTANCE CHARACTERISTICS

1. Connect two 200 ohm resistors of the resistor decade module or two 220 ohm resistors in parallel. Calculate the total resistance. $R_T$ is _____ ohms.
2. Prepare VOM to measure resistance. Measure resistance of parallel resistors. Resistance is _____ ohms.
3. Using same procedure, connect a 100 ohm resistor and a 500 ohm resistor in parallel with decade module. If separate resistors are being used, connect a 100 ohm and a 470 ohm resistor in parallel. Calculate total resistance ($R_T$) of parallel combination. $R_T$ is _____ ohms.
4. Measure total resistance of the parallel combination with a VOM. Measured $R_T$ is _____ ohms.
5. Using resistor combination of step 3, connect a 10 ohm resistor in parallel with the combination. Calculated total resistance is _____ ohms. Measured resistance of the combination is _____ ohms.
6. What conclusion can be drawn about total resistance of a parallel circuit and individual resistor values? _____

_____

7. Remove two No. 47 lamps from storage cabinet and position them together on workbench. Measure resistance of each lamp and record its value. $L_1$ is _____ ohms. $L_2$ is _____ ohms.
8. Connect two lamps in parallel and measure total resistance. Parallel lamp resistance is _____ ohms.

9. With VOM connected to parallel circuit, carefully remove one lamp. How does this alter total resistance of circuit? _____

_____

10. Disconnect lamps and return all parts to storage cabinet.

## QUESTIONS
1. When resistors of the same value are connected in parallel, the total resistance is determined by _____
2. Using the product/sum method, determine total resistance of a 40 ohm and a 60 ohm resistor connected in parallel.
3. Using the sum of conductance method, the total resistance of 1K, 2K and 5K resistors connected in parallel is _____
4. When the resistors are in parallel, the total resistance will always be (greater or smaller) than smallest individual resistor value.

## PROCEDURE
## PART B—PARALLEL CURRENT CHARACTERISTICS

1. Connect parallel dc circuit as in Fig. 3-6-1B. Use individual resistors or those mounted on resistor decade module.
2. Before turning on circuit switch, prepare VOM to measure dc voltage. Turn on variable dc power supply and adjust it to produce 5V dc as indicated by VOM.
3. Calculate total resistance of circuit using diagram values of $R_1$, $R_2$ and $R_3$. $R_T$ is _____ ohms.
4. Assuming that 5V will be applied to parallel circuit, calculate total current. $I_T$ is _____ amps.
5. Prepare VOM to measure total current of parallel circuit between points A-B. Turn on switch, then observe and record total current of circuit. $I_T$ is _____ mA.
6. Momentarily turn off circuit switch and break circuit between B-C. Remove VOM from points A-B and connect it between B-C. Place a connecting wire between points A-B.
7. Turn on switch. Measure and record current flow through $R_1$. $I_{R_1}$ is _____ mA.

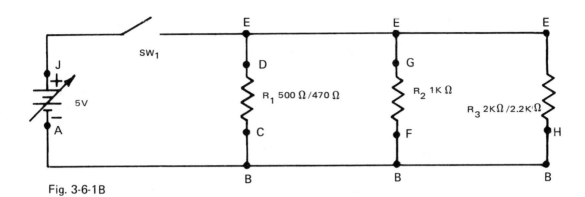

Fig. 3-6-1B

8. Using same procedure outlined in steps 6 and 7, measure and record $I_{R_2}$ and $I_{R_3}$. $I_{R_2}$ is _____ mA. $I_{R_3}$ is _____ mA.

9. Total current flow of parallel circuit using measured values of $I_{R_1}$, $I_{R_2}$ and $I_{R_3}$ equals an $I_T$ of _____ mA. How do measured and calculated values of $I_T$ compare? _____

10. Calculate total power consumed by circuit using measured $I_T$ and V values. $P_T$ is _____ watts.

11. Calculate power consumed by each resistor of circuit. $P_1$ is _____ watts, $P_2$ is _____ watts, $P_3$ is _____ watts.

12. Turn off circuit and remove VOM from circuit. Remove connecting wire from points A-B and place VOM back into circuit to measure $I_T$.

13. Turn on circuit switch and note $I_T$ of circuit. Momentarily remove $R_3$ from circuit. $I_T$ is _____ mA. Return $R_3$ to circuit and disconnect $R_1$. $I_T$ is _____ mA. The $I_T$ of a parallel circuit is in-

fluenced more by the value of its _____ (largest or smallest) resistor.

14. Turn off circuit switch and power supply. Disconnect circuit and return all parts to storage cabinet.

## QUESTIONS

1. If three 100 ohm resistors are connected in parallel and a fourth 100 ohm resistor is added to the circuit in parallel, how would this addition change $I_T$?

2. In a parallel circuit, the largest amount of current flows through which resistor value?

3. The total current flow of a parallel circuit is determined by _____
_____

## PROCEDURE
## PART C—PARALLEL VOLTAGE CHARACTERISTICS

1. Connect a parallel dc circuit as in Fig. 3-6-1C. Use individual resistors or those mounted on a resistor decade module.

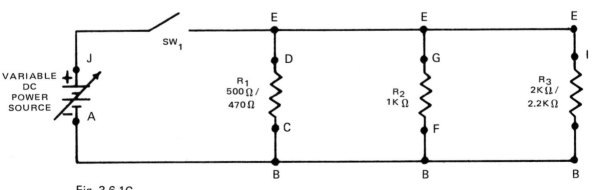

Fig. 3-6-1C

2. Before turning on circuit switch, prepare VOM to measure dc voltage. Turn on power supply and adjust it to 5V across test points A-J.

3. Turn on circuit switch and measure voltage across each resistor. $E_{R_1}$ is _____ volts, $E_{R_2}$ is _____ volts, $E_{R_3}$ is _____ volts.

4. Turn on circuit switch and prepare VOM to measure current flow between points B-C. Connect VOM and turn on circuit switch. $I_{R_1}$ is _____ mA.

5. Using measured $I_{R_1}$ and diagram value of $R_1$, calculate voltage across $R_1$. Calculated $E_{R_1}$ is _____ volts.

6. Using procedure outlined in steps 4 and 5 calculate value of $E_{R_2}$ and $E_{R_3}$. $I_{R_2}$ is _____ mA. $I_{R_3}$ is _____ mA. $E_{R_2}$ is _____ volts. $E_{R_3}$ is _____ volts.

7. Remove VOM from circuit and return all connecting wires.

8. Turn off circuit switch. Prepare VOM to measure dc voltage across points A-J. Adjust power supply to 10V. Then, turn on circuit switch and measure voltage across each resistor. Voltage across each resistor of a parallel circuit is equal to the _____

9. Connect VOM across $R_2$ and observe voltage. Momentarily disconnect resistor $R_3$ from circuit. What influence does this have on voltage of a parallel circuit? _____

10. Return $R_3$ to circuit and momentarily disconnect resistor $R_1$. What influence does this have on voltage of a parallel circuit? _____

11. Reduce source voltage to 3V dc and repeat steps 9 and 10. Explain this voltage characteristic of a parallel circuit. _____

12. Turn off circuit switch and power supply. Return all parts to storage cabinet.

## QUESTIONS

1. If the voltage applied to three different resistor values in parallel is the same, what are the characteristic differences of the circuit?

2. When a resistor is added to or removed from a parallel circuit, the voltage _____

3. The voltage across each resistor of a parallel circuit is _____ dependent upon the value of the source voltage.

# Experiment 3-7 SERIES-PARALLEL DC CIRCUITS

## INTRODUCTION

Series-parallel combination circuits are used more frequently today than either a straight series or parallel circuit alone. The basic characteristics of both the series and parallel circuit are considered in a combination circuit. As a general rule, the combination circuit must be simplified somewhat before calculations can be applied. Parallel branches usually are combined to form an equivalent single resistor. Ultimately, series resistors and equivalent resistors are added together to determine total circuit resistance.

In this experiment, you will construct and test the E, I, R and P characteristics of a combination circuit. Calculated values and measured values are then compared while analyzing circuit operation. The number of different combination circuits in operation today is quite

## REFERENCE

Gerrish and Dugger, ELECTRICITY AND ELECTRONICS, Chapter 3, pages 43 to 45.

## MATERIALS AND EQUIPMENT

1 — Volt-ohm-milliampere (VOM) meter
1 — Resistor decade module, Hickok ETC-10, or the following resistors:
   1 — 100 ohm, 1/4 watt
   2 — 220 ohm, 1/4 watt
   1 — 470 ohm, 1/4 watt
1 — SPST toggle switch
1 — Variable power supply

## PROCEDURE

1. Connect series-parallel circuit as in Fig. 3-7-1, using a resistor decade module or individual resistors.

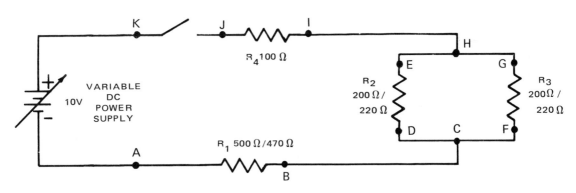

Fig. 3-7-1

large. The circuit used in this experiment is representative of only one type. The basic principles used to simplify this circuit can be applied to other combination circuits regardless of the complexity.

## EXPERIMENT OBJECTIVES

As a result of this laboratory experience, you should be able to accomplish the following:
1. Construct a combination (series-parallel) circuit.
2. Calculate, measure and compare values of E, I, R and P in this combination circuit.

2. Calculate total resistance of circuit. Calculated $R_T$ is _____ ohms.
3. Prepare a VOM to measure resistance, then connect it to test points A-K. Measured $R_T$ is _____ ohms.
4. Measure and record circuit resistance at A-B, C-H and I-J. A-B is _____ ohms. C-H is _____ ohms. I-J is _____ ohms.
5. Prepare VOM to measure dc voltage, then connect it to output of dc power supply. Turn on power supply and adjust it to produce an output of 10V.

6. Connect power supply to circuit at points A-K. Turn on VOM circuit switch and measure voltage at points A-B, C-H and I-J. A-B is _____ volts. C-H is _____ volts. I-J is _____ volts.

7. Calculate total current flow of circuit using measured value of $R_T$ and E. $I_T$ is _____ mA.

8. Prepare VOM to measure $I_T$ at K-J. This can be achieved by connecting meter across switch and turning switch off. $I_T$ is _____ mA.

9. Measure and record current flow at points B-C, C-D, C-F and H-I. B-C is _____ mA. C-D is _____ mA, C-F _____ mA, and H-I is _____ mA. Explain why there is a difference in the measured current flow. _____

   _____

10. Using measured values of E and I, calculate total power used by circuit. $P_T$ is _____ watts. Power consumed by $R_1$, $R_2$, $R_3$ and $R_4$ is equal to $P_T$. Calculate power used by each resistor. $P_1$ is _____ watts, $P_2$ is _____ watts, $P_3$ is _____ watts and $P_4$ is _____ watts.

11. Turn off circuit switch and power supply. Disconnect circuit and return all parts to storage cabinet.

## QUESTIONS

1. What are some general procedures to consider when determining the total resistance of a series-parallel combination circuit?

2. What should be taken into account when measuring the voltage of a series-parallel combination circuit?

3. Give some general considerations regarding the current flow in a series-parallel combination circuit?

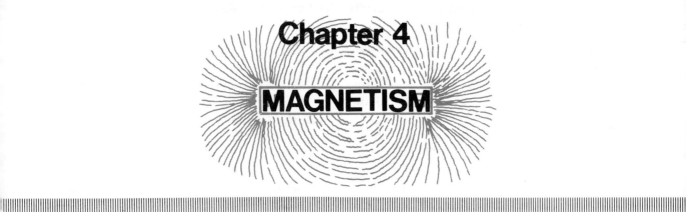

# Chapter 4

# MAGNETISM

## Experiment 4-1  PERMANENT MAGNETS

### INTRODUCTION

A permanent magnet is made of a substance that will attract iron, steel and other magnetic materials. Invisible lines of force produced by a permanent magnet are concentrated at the ends of the magnet. These concentrations are called the magnetic poles. Each magnet has a north pole and a south pole. Magnetic lines of force travel from the north pole to the south pole outside of the magnet. Inside of the magnet, the force lines travel from south to north.

By experimentation, it was found that poles of a permanent magnet will either attract or repel the poles of a similar magnet. The first two laws of magnetism are: Like poles repel one another. Unlike poles attract each other. These two laws apply to all permanent magnets.

A third law of magnetism refers to the distance between magnet poles. The repelling or attracting action is strongest when the poles are close together. The action is reduced as magnets are moved apart. This law also applies to all magnetic fields.

In this experiment, you will work with a compass and a set of permanent magnets, which will permit you to see the direction of the external and internal lines of force.

### EXPERIMENT OBJECTIVES

As a result of this laboratory experience, you should be able to accomplish the following:
1. Use a compass to determine the polarity of a permanent magnet.
2. Use a compass to plot the field pattern around a permanent magnet.
3. Make a compass from a permanent magnet.

### REFERENCE

Gerrish and Dugger, ELECTRICITY AND ELECTRONICS, Chapter 4, pages 49 to 52.

### MATERIALS AND EQUIPMENT

1 — Set of permanent magnets
1 — Compass
1 — Support stand

### PROCEDURE

1. Remove compass from storage and place it on bench top. Indicator hand of compass is a small magnet that is free to pivot. Pointer end of compass is called north-seeking pole or simply north or N pole of magnet.
2. Place a sheet of paper under compass and mark direction of magnetic north pole indicated by compass.
3. Move compass well out of the way or return it to storage until needed again.
4. Remove set of permanent magnet rods from storage cabinet. Separate two rods and return one to storage.
5. Make a small sling out of a piece of scrap wire or a paper clip (to hold magnet). See Fig. 4-1-1. Tie a piece of string to sling and attach it to a support stand. Place bar magnet in sling.

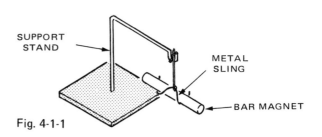

SUPPORT STAND

METAL SLING

BAR MAGNET

Fig. 4-1-1

6. After a few seconds, bar magnet should align itself as the compass did with one end pointing toward north. Mark an N on north-seeking pole with a piece of chalk or pencil.

7. To test polarity, place magnet on bench top. With compass, determine N pole. Since like poles repel, the north-seeking pole of magnet will repel N pole of compass.

8. Place bar magnet on a sheet of paper on bench top, as indicated in Fig. 4-1-2.

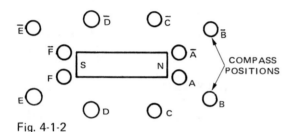

Fig. 4-1-2

9. Position compass at point A and indicate direction compass hand is pointing. Then, moving in a clockwise direction, mark direction of compass hand for points B, C, D, E and F on the paper.

10. Starting at point A, move counterclockwise to indicate direction of compass hand for points B, C, D, E and F.

11. Magnetic lines of force from bar magnet follow a pattern as indicated by compass. Mark this pattern with arrows from A to F and $\bar{A}$ to $\bar{F}$.

12. Return compass to storage cabinet or position it out of the way at this time.

13. Remove second bar of magnet set from storage cabinet.

14. Determine N and S poles of second bar with marked magnet.

15. Note that unlike poles will attract and like poles will repel.

16. Place two magnets together and return them to storage cabinet. Some magnet sets may include a metal keeper for each end of set. If included, attach keepers to magnet set.

**QUESTIONS**

1. If the N pole of a compass seeks or points toward the north, what is the actual polarity of the north pole?

2. The direction of a magnetic field or invisible lines of force is from _____ to _____ outside of the magnet as observed in this experiment.

3. What are the first two primary laws of permanent magnetism?

4. What is the third law of magnetism?

## INTRODUCTION

The ability of permanent magnets to attract or repel certain metals or other magnets demonstrates that an invisible field surrounds the magnet. The force developed around the magnet is called its magnetic field. The direction of the field and its path can be plotted with a compass.

The magnetic field of a single bar magnet starts at the north pole and travels in a loop pattern to the south pole. It then travels from S to N within the bar magnet, making a complete path. When like poles of two magnets are brought together, each magnet produces the same type of field. The resulting field (where like poles are opposing each other) is compressed somewhat before it returns to the opposite pole.

When unlike poles of two magnets are brought together, the fields combine. Lines of force readily travel between N of one magnet and S of the second magnet. As a result, the lines of force are very concentrated in this area. Some lines also travel between the N and S of the opposite ends of the two magnets.

When two magnets are brought together by attraction, the resulting field is similar to that of a single magnet. The outward field is from N to S. The internal path of the two magnets is S to N to S to N, which responds as a single magnet with an S and N pole.

In this experiment, you will trace the field path of attracting and repelling magnets with a compass, then plot the path on a sheet of paper. Through this experience, you will actually see a representative field path of the invisible lines of force of resulting magnetic fields.

## EXPERIMENT OBJECTIVES

As a result of this laboratory experience, you should be able to accomplish the following:
1. Trace the field pattern of two magnets (poles unlike) with a compass.
2. Trace the field pattern of two magnets (poles alike) with a compass.
3. Trace the field pattern of two magnets together with a compass.

## REFERENCE

Gerrish and Dugger, ELECTRICITY AND ELECTRONICS, Chapter 4, pages 49 to 52.

## MATERIALS AND EQUIPMENT

1 — Set of permanent magnets
1 — Compass

## PROCEDURE

1. Remove set of permanent magnets from storage cabinet and separate two bars.
2. With one bar held in each hand move two bars together. Like poles will produce a repelling action that will not permit bars to go together. Unlike poles will attract each other immediately when bars are brought together. Note that it is rather difficult to hold the bar ends of the magnets apart when they are brought close together.
3. Position two magnets so that unlike poles are separated by approximately 4 in., as in Fig. 4-2-1.

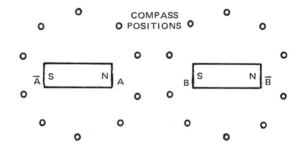

Fig. 4-2-1

4. Starting at position A and moving to $\overline{A}$, plot direction of magnetic field with compass at indicated locations. Starting again at point A, move in counterclockwise direction to $\overline{A}$ by locating compass at indicated positions.
5. Plot field of right hand magnet in a similar manner, starting at position B and moving to $\overline{B}$.
6. Make a sketch of resulting magnetic fields on a separate sheet of paper.
7. Using procedure outlined in steps 3 to 6,

locate the two magnets as indicated in Fig. 4-2-2.

Fig. 4-2-3

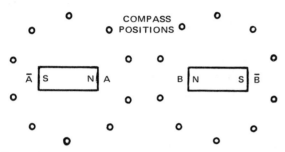

Fig. 4-2-2

8. Plot magnetic field with a compass, starting at point A and moving to Ā. Using same procedure, plot direction of field of right hand magnet.
9. Make a sketch of resulting field on a separate sheet of paper.
10. Using same procedure outlined previously, position magnets as indicated in Fig. 4-2-3.

11. Plot magnetic field with a compass, starting at point A and moving first clockwise to Ā, then counterclockwise from A to Ā.
12. Make a sketch of resulting field on a separate sheet of paper.
13. Place two magnets together for storage. Return magnet set and compass to storage cabinet.

## QUESTIONS
1. Describe the resulting magnetic fields of Fig. 4-2-1.
2. Describe the resulting magnetic field of Fig. 4-2-2.
3. How does the resulting field of the attracting magnets compare with that of a single magnet?

# Experiment 4-3 ELECTROMAGNETS

## INTRODUCTION

When an electric current passes through a conductor, it produces a magnetic field. If this conductor is wound into a loop or coil, the strength of the resulting electromagnetic field is increased. The field produced by each conductor adds to the fields produced by the other coiled conductors. Therefore, the strength of a coil is directly dependent upon the number of turns of the coil. In addition to this, the amount of current passing through a conductor is a determining factor in electromagnet field strength. The product of coil current flow "I" and the number of turns "N" is called the ampere-turns ratio or "IN" of a coil.

In this experiment, you will build an electromagnet and test its ability to pick up small pieces of metal. You will change the core material from air to metal, and increase the current to see how these factors affect the strength of an electromagnet. You will see how the strength of an electromagnet can be stopped by turning off the energy source. Electromagnets, coils and solenoids are found in electrical appliances, instruments, motors-generators, and industrial control equipment.

## EXPERIMENT OBJECTIVES

As a result of this laboratory experience, you should be able to accomplish the following:
1. Construct a simple electromagnet.
2. Test different core materials in electromagnet.
3. Notice how different current in electromagnet affects the field.

## REFERENCE

Gerrish and Dugger, ELECTRICITY AND ELECTRONICS, Chapter 4, pages 52 to 56.

## MATERIALS AND EQUIPMENT

1 — 30 ft. length of magnet wire
1 — 3/4 in. D x 2 1/2 in. L metal core
1 — Variable dc power supply
1 — SPST toggle switch
1 — Volt-ohm-milliampere (VOM) meter
1 — Assortment of straight pins

## PROCEDURE

1. Remove 30 ft. length of enamel magnet wire from storage cabinet. With wire gauge, determine size of wire. AWG is _____

2. Using copper wire table on page 30 of the text, ELECTRICITY AND ELECTRONICS, determine resistance of 1000 ft. of wire. You will find that 30/1000 or 3 percent of this resistance is _____ ohms.

3. Clean approximately 1/2 in. of enamel insulation from each end of length of wire.

4. Loosely wind magnet wire around 3/4 in. diameter metal bar. Bar should slide freely in and out of coil when winding is completed. See Fig. 4-3-1.

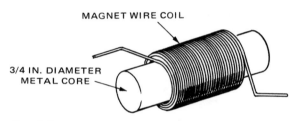

MAGNET WIRE COIL

3/4 IN. DIAMETER METAL CORE

Fig. 4-3-1

5. Remove metal core from coil. Connect coil to variable dc power supply, as indicated in Fig. 4-3-2. VOM is used to measure circuit current flow.

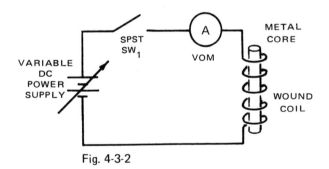

Fig. 4-3-2

6. Adjust power supply to 0 volts initially before turning it on. Turn on circuit switch and carefully adjust power supply to produce 500 mA of current flow.

7. Hold coil in your hand and see if it will pick up a few straight pins, or small nails.

Does it have enough strength to pick up small nails? _____

8. When circuit switch is turned off, electromagnet field is turned off. Turn off circuit switch.

9. Often, to increase strength of electromagnet, a metal core is used. The metal core, in this case, will provide a better path for magnetic lines than air core. Insert 3/4 in. metal bar into electromagnet. Test its ability to pick up same straight pins or small nails.

10. Strength of an electromagnet can also be increased by changing ampere turns (IN) characteristic of coil. Since number of turns of coil cannot be changed, current will be increased to test this theory.

11. Carefully adjust power supply to produce 1 ampere of current flow. Test ability of coil to pick up same nails, or scraps of metal, as

in step 9. There should be a noticeable increase in magnetic field strength. As a general rule, coil may begin to get warm in short time. Do not leave coil circuit energized for more than a few seconds at any one time.

12. Turn off circuit switch and power supply. Disconnect coil and circuit components. Unwind coil and wrap wire around your hand, forming a coil for storage. Return all components to storage cabinet.

## QUESTIONS

1. What determines the strength of an electromagnetic coil?
2. What are the unique advantages of an electromagnet over a permanent magnet?
3. Why does a metal core alter the strength of an electromagnet when compared with an air core?

# Experiment 4-4 ELECTROMAGNETIC FIELDS

## INTRODUCTION

An electromagnet is a pre-wound solenoid coil with a soft iron core in its center. When current is applied, the coil produces an electromagnetic field which passes readily through the soft metal core. The strength of the resulting electromagnetic field is determined by the ampere-turns or IN of the coil and its core material. When the field is strong, its influence extends quite a distance from the core. Weaker fields do not extend very far.

An electromagnet is a rather unique device when compared with a permanent magnet. Its field strength for example, can be increased according to the IN ratio. The polarity of the field can be reversed by simply changing the direction of current flow. Also, the field of an electromagnet can be turned on and off whenever desired. Because of these special characteristics, an electromagnet has a number of useful applications today.

In this experiment, you will work with a commercially wound device called a "gilley coil." This type of coil has many layers of turns wound on top of each other. The first layer is rather small in diameter, while the outermost layer has a larger diameter. Through these experiences with a gilley coil, you will be able to observe some of the more important principles of electromagnetism.

## EXPERIMENT OBJECTIVES

As a result of this laboratory experience, you should be able to accomplish the following:
1. Test a commercial electromagnet (gilley coil).
2. Determine the polarity of the electromagnet.
3. Plot the direction and strength of the electromagnetic field at various distances from the coil.

## REFERENCE

Gerrish and Dugger, ELECTRICITY AND ELECTRONICS, Chapter 4, pages 54 to 56.

## MATERIALS AND EQUIPMENT

1 — Volt-ohm-milliampere (VOM) meter

1 — Gilley coil
1 — 5/8 in. D and 2 1/2 in. L soft iron core
1 — Compass
1 — Variable dc power supply

## PROCEDURE

1. Remove mounted gilley coil from cabinet and connect coil circuit as in Fig. 4-4-1.

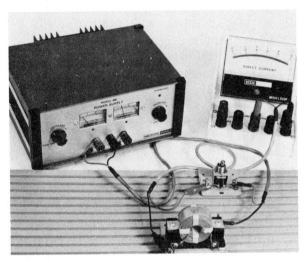

Fig. 4-4-1

2. Before applying power to circuit, carefully examine coil. Note which side of coil is connected to negative polarity of the power supply. Apply "left-hand coil rule" and determine "N" polarity of coil. Mark this on coil in Fig. 4-4-1.
3. Before turning on circuit switch, adjust power supply to 0 volts output position. Turn on power supply and circuit switch. Carefully adjust power supply to produce 1 ampere of current on ammeter of VOM.
4. With a compass, determine polarity of coil.
5. On a separate sheet of paper, make a drawing of coil near center of sheet. Label north and south poles of coil.
6. With a compass, plot magnetic field of gilley coil. Starting at N pole, plot field by moving compass in a clockwise direction to S pole. Indicate direction of field on this sheet of paper with arrows.
7. Starting again from N pole, plot direction

of field with compass moving in a counter-clockwise direction. Indicate direction of field on sheet of paper with arrows.

8. Momentarily turn circuit switch on and off while observing polarity of coil. What influence does this action have upon polarity of field? _____

9. Turn off circuit switch and remove VOM. Complete circuit by placing a connecting wire between switch and coil terminal.

10. Reverse negative and positive leads of power supply.

11. Turn on circuit switch and test polarity of coil with compass. How does it compare with step 4? _____

12. Place 2 1/2 in. metal core in coil and again test polarity. Plot field with compass again, only this time see how far compass can be positioned away from coil and still be influenced.

13. Remove core from coil and plot field. How does position of magnetic field compare with step 12? _____

_____

14. Turn off circuit switch and power supply. Disconnect circuit and return all parts to storage cabinet.

## QUESTIONS

1. What influence does the direction of current flow have upon the polarity of an electromagnet?

2. When the strength of an electromagnetic field is increased, how does it alter the influence of the field distance-wise?

3. Apply "left-hand rule" to Fig. 4-4-2. Show its polarity. Mark N and S on coil at correct location.

Fig. 4-4-2.

# Experiment 4-5  ELECTROMAGNETIC RELAYS

## INTRODUCTION

A relay is a unique device assigned to control an electric circuit by electromagnetic action. When the coil of a relay is energized, it produces an electromagnetic field. Action of the field, in turn, causes a soft iron piece, called an "armature," to move physically. Movement of the armature then causes contact points of a switch to open and close accordingly.

Advantages of a relay are numerous: Safety to the operator by controlling large voltages by harmless low voltages. Remote control of heavy current machines without running costly heavy gauge wires. Numerous electric circuits can be easily controlled by one heavy-duty relay. Applications of the relay are found in automobiles, home appliances, radio transmitters and motor control equipment.

In this experiment, you will examine a relay, test it with an ohmmeter and observe its operation in a control circuit. The relay used in this experiment is only one of an extremely large variety of types available.

## EXPERIMENT OBJECTIVES

As a result of this laboratory experience, you should be able to accomplish the following:

1. Examine the parts of a relay.
2. Test the on-off operation of a relay.
3. Use a relay to turn a lamp on and off.

## REFERENCE

Gerrish and Dugger, ELECTRICITY AND ELECTRONICS, Chapter 4, pages 56 and 57.

## MATERIALS AND EQUIPMENT

1 — Volt-ohm-milliampere (VOM) meter
1 — 10V dc relay (Sigma 11F 100g 1A) or equivalent
1 — Variable dc power supply
2 — No. 47 lamps and sockets
1 — SPST toggle switch

## PROCEDURE

1. Remove mounted relay from storage cabinet and place it on a circuit construction board as in Fig. 4-5-1.

Fig. 4-5-1

2. Carefully examine relay. Note that there are two coil terminals and three switch terminals.
3. Prepare VOM to measure resistance and connect it across coil terminals. Measure resistance of coil. _____ ohms.
4. Connect one probe of ohmmeter to center terminal of three switch terminals. With other probe of ohmmeter, touch left switch terminal. If continuity occurs between terminals, this represents normally closed (N.C.) part of switch. If VOM does not indicate continuity, these terminals are normally open (N.O.).
5. Label these two terminals. Fig. 4-5-1 as N.O. or N.C.
6. Using same procedure outlined in step 4, test center and right switch terminals with VOM. Label these terminals N.O. or N.C.
7. If your testing procedure is correct, one side will be N.O. and other side N.C. If not, test switch terminals again. It is possible for relay points to be forced together or stuck in one position. A faulty relay would show this condition.
8. With point of a pencil or pen, gently push down on armature of relay. It mechanically moves up and down, and spring tension causes it to come to rest in one position (unenergized state). Pressing down on armature simulates state of relay when it is energized.
9. Again test N.O. and N.C. condition of switch terminals with an ohmmeter. De-

pressing armature should cause a condition change between switch terminals if relay is working properly. If not, contact points may be bent out of position. Your instructor will help you correct this.

10. Construct relay circuit as in Fig. 4-5-2.

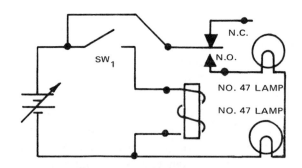

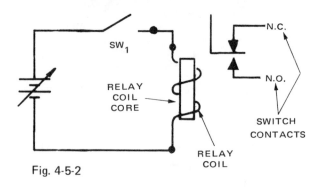

Fig. 4-5-2

11. Before connecting power supply to circuit, turn it on and adjust output to 10V dc, as indicated by dc voltmeter of VOM.

12. Turn on circuit switch, then turn it off. When relay is energized, it usually produces a clicking sound. You should be able to see armature move when coil is energized.

13. With ohmmeter of VOM, test state change of relay switch terminals between energized and nonenergized conditions of operation. If relay is functioning properly, add lamp control circuit as in Fig. 4-5-3. If not, ask your instructor for help.

14. Turn on circuit switch to energize relay. When energized, relay should turn on series lamp circuit.

15. Change lamp connection to N.C. terminal instead of N.O. terminal. How does this circuit operation differ from that of step 14? _____

_____

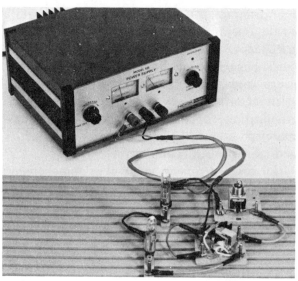

Fig. 4-5-3

16. Turn off power supply and circuit switch. Return all parts to storage cabinet.

## QUESTIONS

1. What type of switch is included in the relay?
2. Give some advantages of using a relay instead of a plain switch to control a circuit.
3. What makes the armature of the relay move physically?

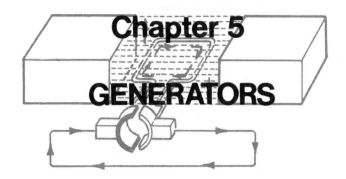

# Chapter 5
# GENERATORS

## Experiment 5-1  GENERATOR PRINCIPLES

### INTRODUCTION

In order to generate electricity, a coil of wire must pass through a magnetic field or a magnetic field must pass through a coil of wire. Motion is of primary importance in the generation of electricity.

The strength of voltage induced in a coil is based upon two primary factors:
1. The number of lines of force cut by the coil.
2. The speed at which the coil moves through the field.

By experimentation, it was found that one volt is induced in a single conductor when it cuts across 100,000,000 or $10^8$ lines of force per second. The amount of induced voltage can be increased by adding more conductors and cutting the field at a faster rate.

In this experiment, you will pass a magnet in and out of a coil of wire to find that electricity flows first in one direction, then in the opposite direction. This type of electricity is called alternating current or ac. The value of this generated voltage is in a constant state of change, and it periodically reverses polarity. One positive alternation plus an equal negative alternation produces one cycle of ac. The method of producing electricity in this experiment is not very practical. It is only used here to demonstrate the basic principles of generation.

### EXPERIMENT OBJECTIVES

As a result of this laboratory experience, you should be able to accomplish the following:
1. Generate ac by means of a magnet and a coil in a closed circuit.
2. See what magnet polarity does to the direction of the generated current.

### REFERENCE

Gerrish and Dugger, ELECTRICITY AND ELECTRONICS, Chapter 5, pages 64 to 66.

### MATERIALS AND EQUIPMENT

1 — Volt-ohm-milliampere (VOM) meter
1 — Gilley coil
1 — Set of permanent magnets
1 — Compass

### PROCEDURE

1. Remove mounted gilley coil from storage cabinet and place it on circuit construction board.
2. Prepare VOM to measure an ac current of approximately 0.5 mA. Connect meter to coil as indicated in Fig. 5-1-1.
3. Remove permanent magnet set and compass from storage cabinet. Separate two bar magnets and return one to storage cabinet or position it well away from other magnet.
4. With compass, determine polarity of magnet. Then, set compass well away from magnet.
5. Position magnet so that S pole will easily slide into gilley coil as indicated.
6. Slowly move S pole of magnet into coil and explain how meter responds. _____

_____

7. Then, pull magnet from coil. Explain how meter responds. _____

_____

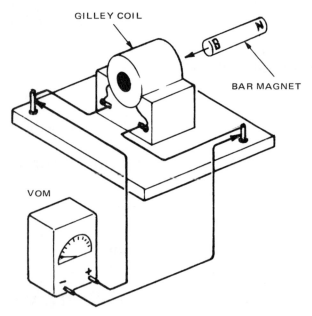

GILLEY COIL

BAR MAGNET

N

B

VOM

+

−

Fig. 5-1-1

8. Using same procedure, move magnet in and out of coil somewhat faster than in steps 6 and 7. What does this indicate about polarity of generated current? _____

_____

9. Reverse polarity of magnet so that N pole goes into coil.

10. Repeat steps 6 and 7 and explain how meter responds to this change. _____

_____

11. As an alternative, hold magnet in a fixed

position. Slide coil over magnet, then pull it away from magnet.

12. Slide magnet inside of coil and let it come to rest. Since magnetic field is still present, why is there no generation taking place?

13. Prepare VOM to measure a low voltage dc. Connect it to coil as indicated in Fig. 5-1-1.

14. Slowly move magnet in and out of coil while observing meter. How does meter respond? _____

_____

15. Prepare VOM to measure a low voltage ac with it connected as in step 13.

16. Slide magnet in and out of coil as quickly as you desire while observing meter. How does it respond? _____

_____

17. Disconnect coil and VOM. Place magnets together in a set for storage. Return all parts to storage cabinet.

**QUESTIONS**

1. What type of electricity is generated in this experiment?

2. What determines the strength of the voltage induced in the coil?

3. What is necessary to produce one volt of generated electricity?

4. Explain what is meant by the term alternating current or ac?

# Experiment 5-2 ROTATING ELECTRIC GENERATORS

## INTRODUCTION

In experiment 5-1, we produced electricity by moving a permanent magnet near or around a coil of wire. The amount of voltage generated was directly dependent upon the speed at which the magnet moved in and out of the coil of wire. Obviously, electric generators of this type are not very practical.

Rotating generators use the same basic principle of the coil-magnet generator, only in a more practical way. Generators of this type employ a rotating coil of wire called an armature. When the armature coils pass through a magnetic field, voltage is produced by the induction process. Sliding brush contacts remove generated voltage from the rotating armature.

In a functional generator, the armature rotates in a single direction. This means that the coils of the armature are continually changing positions from one side to the other in a rotary motion. When the coils are parallel with the permanent magnet field, the largest number of force lines are being cut. The generated output voltage is at its greatest level at this position. When the coils are at right angles to the magnetic field, practically no force lines are being cut. At this position, the output is very small or 0. One complete revolution of the armature causes the output voltage to start a 0, rise to a peak value, fall to 0, rise to a reverse polarity peak, then return to 0. A voltage value change of this type produces a sine curve during one complete cycle of operation.

In this experiment, you will construct a simple rotating electric generator and observe the influence that speed and direction of rotation has upon its output. This generator has a stationary permanent magnetic field and a rotating coil. Generators of this type have a rather limited output and are not commonly used today. However, this experimental unit effectively demonstrates the operating principles of a rotary generation.

## EXPERIMENT OBJECTIVES

As a result of this laboratory experience, you should be able to accomplish the following:
1. Construct a simple ac electric generator.
2. Observe the basic parts.
3. Use a VOM to measure output voltage of the ac generator.

## REFERENCE

Gerrish and Dugger, ELECTRICITY AND ELECTRONICS, Chapter 5, pages 66 to 68.

## MATERIALS AND EQUIPMENT

1 — Volt-ohm-milliampere (VOM) meter
1 — Modified St. Louis motor-generator unit (Hickok)

## PROCEDURE

1. Obtain a St. Louis motor-generator unit from the instructor and place it at your work station.
2. Modify motor-generator unit to prepare it for the experiment. See Fig. 5-2-1.

Fig. 5-2-1

3. Rotating member of generator is called a slip ring armature or rotor. It has two complete metal rings placed on an insulated piece attached to a shaft. A wire from the coil is attached to each slip ring.
4. Place slip ring armature between centers of frame unit. Avoid bending thin metal brushes during assembly. Position brushes on slip rings. Adjust end pressure of bearing so that armature rotates freely, but does not wobble between centers.
5. Insert permanent magnets into holders so

that N and S poles are near armature. Position magnets as close to armature as possible, but not touching it during rotation.

6. Prepare VOM to measure dc current. Start at a high mA range. Connect test probes to two output terminals of generator unit.

7. Rotate slip ring armature slowly while observing mA indication on VOM. Change setting to a range that will indicate exact current output of generator.

8. Position armature at right angles to permanent magnets, as in Fig. 5-2-2. Rotate armature one half revolution clockwise. Describe how meter responds. _____

Fig. 5-2-2

9. Rotate armature remaining one half revolution in same direction as in step 8. Describe how meter responds. _____

10. Explain how one complete revolution of slip ring armature causes meter to deflect?

_____

_____

11. Prepare VOM to measure ac voltage and connect meter to output terminals of generator.

12. Rotate armature as rapidly as you can with your fingers. Measured ac output voltage is _____ volts.

13. Reverse direction of armature rotation and measure ac output voltage. _____ volts.

14. Disconnect VOM from generator unit and return all parts to proper storage place.

## QUESTIONS

1. What effect does armature speed have upon generated output voltage?
2. Why does armature speed influence generator output voltage?
3. One complete revolution of the St. Louis generator produces _____ of ac.
4. The generated output voltage is greatest when the armature is _____ with the permanent magnetic field.

# Experiment 5-3 ROTATING DC GENERATOR

## INTRODUCTION

When the rotating armature coil of a generator cuts through the field of a permanent magnet, voltage is induced in the coil. When the output of this armature is removed from brush contacts that ride on slip rings, alternating current electricity is produced. If the commutator of the armature is changed to a split ring structure, the output will be direct current. This type of dc generator usually produces fluctuating direct current instead of pure dc.

In this experiment, you will build a simple dc generator with a permanent magnetic field and test output with a VOM. Through this experience, you will be able to examine the split ring commutator of the armature and test its continuity. You will also be able to observe the influence that armature speed and direction of rotation has upon dc output.

The generator used in this experiment has a stationary field and a rotating coil. Generators of this type have a rather limited amount of output and are not in common use today. However, the operation of nearly all dc generators is directly related to the basic principles demonstrated by this unit.

## EXPERIMENT OBJECTIVES

As a result of this laboratory experience, you should be able to accomplish the following:
1. Construct a simple dc generator.
2. Become familiar with the basic parts.
3. Measure output voltage of the dc generator.

## REFERENCE

Gerrish and Dugger, ELECTRICITY AND ELECTRONICS, Chapter 5, pages 66 and 67.

## MATERIALS AND EQUIPMENT

1 — Volt-ohm-milliampere (VOM) meter
1 — Modified St. Louis motor-generator unit (Hickok)

## PROCEDURE

1. Obtain a St. Louis motor-generator unit from the instructor and place it on the bench top of your work station.

2. Modify unit to prepare it for an experiment. See Fig. 5-3-1.

Fig. 5-3-1

3. Select split ring armature from storage box. Carefully examine physical structure of coil and its commutator. Note that each side of coil is connected to a segment of commutator.

4. Prepare VOM to measure resistance. Measure resistance of armature coil between two segments of commutator. Coil resistance is _____ ohms.

5. Remove any previously assembled rotating member from base frame of generator unit. Insert split ring armature between centers of base. Avoid bending thin metal brushes during assembly. Position brushes so they ride evenly on commutator. Adjust end pressure of bearing so that armature rotates freely but does not wobble between centers.

6. Connect ohmmeter probes to output terminals and spin armature. If brushes are properly seated, there should be a resistance indication at any armature position. Disconnect ohmmeter.

7. Insert permanent magnets into holders so that N and S poles are as close to armature as possible but not touching it during rotation.

8. Prepare the VOM to measure dc current. Start at a high mA range. Connect test

probes to two output terminals of generator unit.

9. Rotate armature in a trial test to see if an output is produced. Change range of VOM to obtain an exact output indication. If no output occurs, test brush assembly and armature coils again.

10. Position armature coils at a right angle to permanent magnetic field, Fig. 5-3-2.

Fig. 5-3-2

11. Rotate armature one half revolution clockwise. Describe how meter responded to this action. _____

_____

12. Rotate armature remaining half revolution

in same direction as in step 11. Describe how meter responded to this action.

_____

_____

13. Rotate armature as rapidly as you can with your fingers. Maximum output is _____ mA.

14. Prepare VOM to measure dc voltage. Connect meter test probes to generator output terminals.

15. Rotate armature in a clockwise direction with your fingers. Maximum output voltage is _____ volts dc.

16. Rotate armature in a clockwise direction with your fingers. How does meter respond? _____

17. Disconnect VOM from generator unit and return all parts to proper storage place.

## QUESTIONS

1. What is the primary difference between an ac generator and a dc generator?

2. Why does the output of a dc generator only flow in one direction?

3. The output of this dc generator is not smooth. Describe its shape.

4. To increase voltage output of a dc generator, you could _____

_____

# Experiment 5-4 FIELD COIL GENERATORS

## INTRODUCTION

Field coil generators are in greater use today than the permanent magnet field generators of the preceding experiments. Electromagnetic field generators provide a number of advantages over PM field generators. By changing the strength of the electromagnetic field, a field coil generator can have a variable output. The field strength of this generator also can be turned off when it is not being used, and its polarity can be reversed when a change in output is desired.

The basic operating principle of a field coil generator is similar to that of a PM field generator. Current from an outside source applied to the field coil causes it to produce an N and S polarity due to electromagnetism. Also, the core of an electromagnetic field can be shaped into concentrated pole areas more so than that of a PM field. Therefore, field coil generators usually are more efficient than a PM generator.

Independently excited field coil generators derive their energy for field excitation from an outside source. Batteries and variable dc power sources are typical. Large scale field coil generators are used in industry to produce dc for metal refining and electroplating.

In this experiment, you will build an independently excited generator and observe how its output can be altered by changes in field strength. Also, how an ohmmeter can be used to measure field and armature continuity. This technique is commonly used to test a generator with faulty output.

## EXPERIMENT OBJECTIVES

As a result of this laboratory experience, you should be able to accomplish the following:
1. Construct and test an independently excited generator.
2. Observe how the generator output can be changed by field strength.
3. Test field and armature continuity.

## REFERENCE

Gerrish and Dugger, ELECTRICITY AND ELECTRONICS, Chapter 5, pages 67 to 69.

## MATERIALS AND EQUIPMENT

1 — Volt-ohm-milliampere (VOM) meter
1 — Modified St. Louis motor-generator unit (Hickok)
1 — Compass

## PROCEDURE

1. Obtain a St. Louis motor-generator unit from the instructor and place it at your work station.
2. Modify previous unit to prepare it for the experiment. Refer to assembled dc generator unit in Fig. 5-4-1.

Fig. 5-4-1

3. Remove two permanent magnets from holders. Turn magnet holder pieces inward toward armature frame. Attach electromagnetic field winding in two holes under magnet holders. Assembled views of electromagnet attachment are shown in Figs. 5-4-2 and 5-4-3.

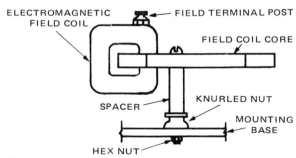

Fig. 5-4-2

4. Place split ring armature in frame and adjust bearing so that armature rotates without wobbling.

5. Position brushes to ride smoothly on commutator. After assembly, test continuity of brush-commutator unit with ohmmeter of VOM. Rotate armature while observing continuity. Armature resistance is _____ ohms.

6. Measure resistance of electromagnetic field coil with ohmmeter of VOM. Field coil resistance is _____ ohms.

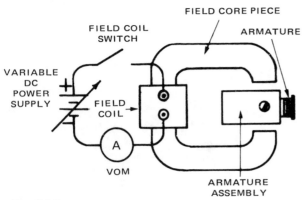

Fig. 5-4-3

7. Using left-hand rule of magnetism, determine polarity of electromagnetic field coil. Mark your predicted polarity on field core in Fig. 5-4-3.

8. With field coil switch off, adjust dc power supply to its "0" output position. Turn on power supply and field coil switch. Adjust power supply to produce 500 mA of current on ammeter of VOM.

9. With a compass, determine polarity of field core. Does it agree with your predicted polarity? _____

10. Turn off field coil switch and remove VOM. Place a connecting wire in its place

to complete field current.

11. Connect ammeter of VOM to output terminals of armature. Turn on field coil switch and spin armature with your fingers. Output current developed is _____ mA.

12. Change VOM to measure dc voltage at output terminals of armature. Spin armature with your fingers while observing output. Maximum dc voltage developed is _____ volts.

13. Turn off field coil switch and carefully remove split ring commutator armature. In its place, slide in slip ring armature. Adjust brushes to make good contact when armature is rotated.

14. Prepare VOM to measure ac voltage at slip ring brush output terminals.

15. Turn on field coil switch and spin armature with your fingers. Maxmium ac voltage produced is _____ volts.

16. Reduce power supply voltage to approximately 50 percent of its original value. Spin armature again and measure output voltage. The ac voltage is _____
How does this voltage value compare with that of step 15? _____

17. Turn off field coil switch and power supply. Return all parts to storage cabinet and return generator unit to instructor.

## QUESTIONS

1. What are some of the advantages of an electromagnetic field generator over a PM field generator?

2. If the armature speed of the dc generator of this experiment were turning at a constant speed, how could the voltage output be altered?

3. What is meant by the term "independently excited generator?"

# Experiment 5-5   AC AND DC GENERATOR OUTPUT

## INTRODUCTION

The voltage or current output of either an ac or dc generator has different values. For example, an ac waveform gradually changes value and periodically changes polarity. The dc generator output likewise changes value but flows in only one direction.

A wave that gradually increases in value to a peak, then decreases to zero in the same way is commonly called a "sine curve." Alternating current has a similar sine curve for both its positive and negative alternations. The positive alternation is displayed above the zero reference line and negative alternation is displayed below it. The output of a dc generator is commonly displayed as two sine curves either above or below the zero reference line.

In the study of electricity, the sine wave outputs of ac or dc generators are in a constant state of change. Because of this, the sine waves are frequently described by different values. The maximum or extreme part of a sine wave usually is called the "peak value." This part of the wave occurs when a maximum number of force lines are being cut by the armature. If 0 deg. is the starting point, one fourth of a revolution or 90 deg. is where the peak of the wave occurs. The sine of 90 deg. is 1.0. From 0 deg. to 90 deg., sine values range from .0 to 1.0. In a similar manner from 90 deg. to 180 deg., the sine values range from 1.0 to 0. An "instantaneous value" at any point along the curve can be determined by multiplying the sine of the degree angle by the peak value.

The "average value" of a sine curve is determined by adding the sine degree angle values (at specific equal intervals) together and dividing by the number of values used. A typical average value of a sine curve is 0.637. In ac, the true value is zero because the positive alternation is cancelled by the negative alternation. The average value of dc generator output is an important value consideration because the waveforms are of the same polarity.

"Effective values" are commonly used to demonstrate the work producing capability of alternating current. This value essentially indicates the effective amount of work done by ac compared to an equivalent amount of dc. It has been established that 120V of effective value or rms (root-mean-square) ac will produce the same amount of heat as 120V of dc. The effective value of ac is calculated by squaring instantaneous values, averaging or taking the mean of these values, then extracting the square root. Typically, ac voltmeters indicate rms or effective values unless indicated otherwise. An accepted effective value of ac is 0.707 of the peak value. The peak value of an rms reading can be determined by multiplying the rms value by 1.414.

In this experiment, you will determine the different values of a sine wave and see how typical conversion values are derived. Larger instantaneous degree angle values could be made very exacting to accepted standard values.

## EXPERIMENT OBJECTIVES

As a result of this laboratory experience, you should be able to accomplish the following:
1. Calculate rms instantaneous and average values for an ac sine wave.
2. Determine average values for pulsating dc waves.

## REFERENCE

Gerrish and Dugger, ELECTRICITY AND ELECTRONICS, Chapter 5, pages 67 and 72 to 74.

## PROCEDURE

1. Refer to ac sine wave in Fig. 5-5-1. Mark positive and negative parts of wave on drawing.
2. Indicate specific degree divisions into which sine curve is divided. Mark these divisions on curve.
3. If peak value of waveform is 100 volts, calculate instantaneous voltage for each degree angle listed by using formula: e = peak value x sin of the angle. Appendix 4, pages 308 to 309 of text, lists necessary trigonometry functions to make these calculations. Mark calculated instantaneous

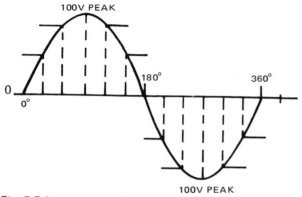

Fig. 5-5-1

values of waveform at appropriate blanks in Fig. 5-5-1.

4. Calculate average value of first half of waveform by adding instantaneous values of each listed angle. Divide this value by number of angle values used. In practice, an average value of 0.637 x 100 is accepted. How close is your calculated average value?

_____

5. Effective value or rms of a sine wave is calculated by first determining instantaneous values of entire wave. Calculate instantaneous values for second half of wave and record values on waveform.

6. Square each instantaneous value and mark this value next to instantaneous value.

7. Determine mean or average of wave by adding all squared values and dividing by number of values used. Mean of squared values is _____

8. Extract square root of squared mean value. Calculated rms value is _____
(Typically an accepted rms value is 0.707 of the peak value.)

9. The "peak-to-peak" value is another important ac value consideration. This value represents total amplitude change between positive peak and negative peak. A peak-to-peak ac value is simply twice peak value.

10. Peak-to-peak value of ac waveform in Fig. 5-5-1 is _____ volts.

11. A dc waveform taken from output of a generator could appear as wave shown in Fig. 5-5-2. This wave changes value at a rate based upon rotational speed of armature. The term "fluctuating dc" usually is used to describe this type of wave.

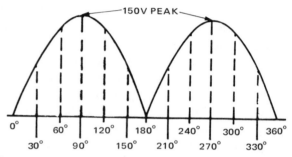

Fig. 5-5-2

12. A dc voltmeter or ammeter connected to output of generator producing this waveform would indicate average value of wave. Using same procedure outlined for ac wave in steps 3 and 4, calculate average value of fluctuating dc wave. Complete following value chart.

## QUESTIONS

1. Explain what is meant by the term rms or effective value ac.
2. What is true average value of an ac wave?
3. If an ac voltmeter were connected to an electrical receptacle in a home, it could read 120V ac. What value of ac does this represent?
4. What is an instantaneous value voltage?
5. What determines peak-to-peak ac voltage?

| SINE | | INSTANTANEOUS VALUE |
|---|---|---|
| 0 DEG. | = | |
| 30 DEG. | = | |
| 60 DEG. | = | |
| 90 DEG. | = | |
| 120 DEG. | = | |
| 150 DEG. | = | |
| 180 DEG. | = | |

| SINE | | INSTANTANEOUS VALUE |
|---|---|---|
| 180 DEG. | = | |
| 210 DEG. | = | |
| 240 DEG. | = | |
| 270 DEG. | = | |
| 300 DEG. | = | |
| 330 DEG. | = | |
| 360 DEG. | = | |

AVERAGE DC VALUE IS _____

## INTRODUCTION

An oscilloscope is designed to measure and display a variety of electrical waveforms. This instrument changes electrical energy into light energy and displays it on a phosphorescent screen similar to a television receiver.

The display area of an oscilloscope is achieved by a cathode ray tube or CRT. Electrons, released by an element known as the cathode, form a concentrated beam and travel to the face of the CRT. These electrons are attracted to the viewing area by a high positive potential. Upon striking the phosphor coating on the inside of the CRT, a characteristic glow is produced.

The electron beam is moved or deflected by voltage applied to metal plates within the tube. Horizontal deflection or "sweep" moves the electron beam from left to right on the face of the CRT. Vertical deflection or sweep moves the electron beam up and down. When a wave is displayed on the viewing area, it has both vertical and horizontal sweep voltages applied to the deflection plates. See Fig. 5-6-1.

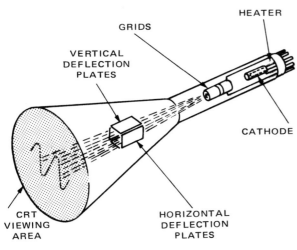

Fig. 5-6-1

Oscilloscope operation is quite simple. The controls are similar to those on a TV receiver and more conveniently located. The name of each control generally defines its operation. Before attempting to do the experiment, see Chapter 19 of the text ELECTRICITY AND ELECTRONICS for a list of typical oscilloscope controls and their function.

In this experiment, you will begin to develop some basic skill in the use of the oscilloscope. The oscilloscope will be used throughout the remainder of this study to view waveforms and measure voltages.

## EXPERIMENT OBJECTIVES

As a result of this laboratory experience, you should be able to accomplish the following:
1. Become familiar with certain controls on the oscilloscope.
2. Set up the oscilloscope to display an ac wave.
3. Use the oscilloscope to observe dc voltage changes.

## REFERENCE

Gerrish and Dugger, ELECTRICITY AND ELECTRONICS, Chapter 19, pages 286 and 287.

## MATERIALS AND EQUIPMENT

1 — A triggered oscilloscope
1 — An ac voltage source 6.3V
2 — "D" cells

## PROCEDURE

1. Plug oscilloscope line cord into an ac outlet and position it so you can easily reach controls and see viewing area.
2. Locate on and off switch. In some instruments, this switch is part of intensity control. Turn on switch. A power indicating lamp usually is energized when switch is in ON position.
3. Within a few seconds, a trace of light should appear on CRT. While waiting, make following control adjustments:
   a. Brightness or intensity . . . to mid-range or reasonable viewing level.
   b. Focus . . . to produce a shape trace.
   c. Vertical position or centering . . . trace to center of CRT.

d. Horizontal position or centering . . . trace to center of CRT.

e. Vertical polarity . . . to positive or positive-up.

f. Vertical input . . . to ac position.

g. Sync or trigger source . . . to internal sync or interval trigger source.

4. If you have not been able to produce a horizontal line on CRT by this time, ask your instructor for assistance.

5. Locate vertical input probe and ground lead of oscilloscope. Connect these two leads to a 6.3V ac source.

6. Make following control adjustments:

a. Horizontal time/cm or sweep frequency . . . to 5m sec or 10 to 100 Hz.

b. Vertical volts/cm or vertical input range . . . to 10V/cm or X10 position.

c. Vertical variable . . . calibrate (Cal).

d. Horizontal time/cm variable . . . calibrate or adjust to produce two sine waves.

7. If you have not been able to produce a distinct sine wave on CRT by this time, ask your instructor to assist you in getting a display.

8. Change horizontal time/cm variable control or horizontal sweep frequency control while observing display. How does this alter display? _____

_____

9. Alter vertical volts/cm or vertical input range control. How does this adjustment alter display? _____

10. Disconnect vertical probes from ac input signal. How does this alter display?

_____

11. If your oscilloscope has a dc vertical input, plug vertical probe into it. If it has a switch, change it to dc input position.

12. Adjust vertical volts/cm or vertical input to 1V/cm or X1 range.

13. Connect ground probe to negative terminal of a dry cell and vertical probe to positive terminal. What influence does 1.5V dc have upon vertical position of the trace?

_____

14. Change polarity by switching ground and vertical probes. How does this modification change display? _____

15. Connect two dry cells in series and repeat steps 14 and 15 for 3V dc. How could trace of an oscilloscope be used to indicate different voltage values? _____

_____

16. Turn off oscilloscope and return all parts to storage cabinet.

## QUESTIONS

1. What is a cathode ray tube or CRT?

2. Explain the function of the CRT deflection plates?

3. What is meant by the terms horizontal sweep and vertical sweep?

# Chapter 6

# INDUCTANCE AND RL CIRCUITS

## Experiment 6-1  DC RL CIRCUITS

### INTRODUCTION

Inductance is the property of an electric circuit to oppose a change in current flow. This opposition to a change in current is primarily due to energy stored in the magnetic field of a coil. A coil that will produce one volt of induced emf when the current is changing at a rate of one ampere per second is rated at one henry of inductance.

When dc is applied initially to an inductor, a magnetic field will build up when the circuit is energized. Expansion of the magnetic field cutting across other coil windings causes a counter emf to be induced into the coil. This counter emf tends to oppose the original current flow. When the current ultimately reaches it maximum level, it is only limited to the resistance of the wire coil.

When the dc source applied to a coil is turned off, inductance occurs again. In this case, the magnetic field surrounding an operating coil collapses. This action causes a continuation of the current flow a short time after the source has been disconnected. In a dc circuit, inductance is only present when the circuit is turned on and when it is turned off.

In this experiment, you will apply dc to an inductor-lamp circuit. With the inductor in the circuit, you will be able to see the delay in lamp brilliance when the circuit is first turned on and when it is disconnected. You will also be able to observe how delay is changed by adding resistance when forming an RL circuit.

### EXPERIMENT OBJECTIVES

As a result of this laboratory experience, you

should be able to accomplish the following:
1. Observe time delay lamp brilliance in an resistance-inductance (RL) circuit.
2. Test the effect of the core on an RL circuit.
3. Experiment with different resistance in an RL circuit.

### REFERENCE

Gerrish and Dugger, ELECTRICITY AND ELECTRONICS, Chapter 6, pages 78 to 80.

### MATERIALS AND EQUIPMENT

1 — Inductor-coil No. 1 of transformer assembly unit (Hickok 3320-383; with laminated core 12180-38)
1 — No. 47 lamp with socket
1 — SPST toggle switch
1 — Variable dc power source
1 — 47 ohm, 1/4 watt resistor or 50 ohm, 1/4 watt resistor from resistor decade

### PROCEDURE

1. Connect lamp test circuit of Fig. 6-1-1.

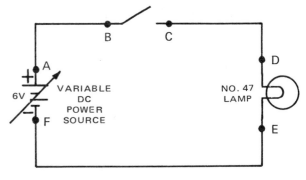

Fig. 6-1-1

2. Turn on circuit switch and test operation of lamp. Observe brightness level of lamp and speed it takes to reach full brightness. Turn circuit switch on and off a few times while making these observations.

3. Turn off circuit switch and insert coil No. 1 between points C and D, as indicated in Fig. 6-1-2.

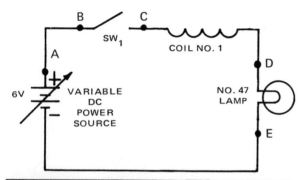

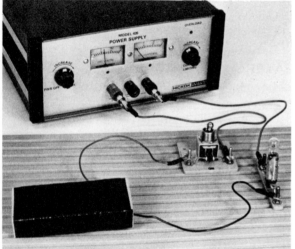

Fig. 6-1-2

4. Turn on circuit switch while observing brightness level of lamp and time it takes to reach full brightness. How does appearance of lamp compare with step 2? _____

5. Carefully slide laminated core piece into coil No. 1 while observing lamp. How does this change lamp brightness and time it takes to reach full brightness? _____

6. Turn off circuit switch and add a 47 or 50 ohm resistor in series with coil and lamp, as shown in Fig. 6-1-3.

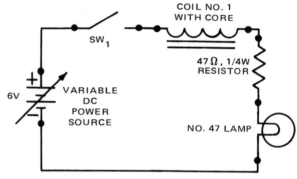

Fig. 6-1-3

7. Turn on circuit switch and notice delay time it takes lamp to reach its operating brilliance. Test this several times.

8. Turn off circuit switch and connect a jumper wire across resistor. Turn on switch and observe delay time.

9. Alternately place resistor in circuit and test its delay time, then use jumper to test delay time with resistor out of circuit.

10. Turn off circuit switch and disconnect circuit. Return all parts to storage cabinet.

## QUESTIONS

1. What causes the delay of brightness in the circuit in Fig. 6-1-3?
2. What is an inductor or an inductance?
3. Explain the effects of inductance on an operating circuit?

# Experiment 6-2  AC RL CIRCUITS

## INTRODUCTION

When alternating current or ac is applied to circuits containing inductance, the effect is quite different than that of the previous dc circuit. For example, ac is in a continuous state of change. This means that any counter emf developed by an inductor is constantly opposing the applied current. The opposition offered by an inductor to ac is called "inductive reactance." The letters $X_L$ are commonly used to denote inductive reactance. In a formula, for example: $X_L = 2 \pi \; fL$.

The inductive reactance of a coil causes the current flow of an ac circuit to lag behind the voltage by as much as 90 deg. This effect is measureable, with the opposition offered to ac in ohms.

## REFERENCE

Gerrish and Dugger, ELECTRICITY AND ELECTRONICS, Chapter 6, pages 80 and 81, 89 to 91.

## MATERIALS AND EQUIPMENT

- 1 — Inductor-coil No. 1 of transformer assembly unit (Hickok 3320-383)
- 1 — No. 47 lamp
- 1 — SPST toggle switch
- 1 — 6.3V, 60 Hz ac source (filament transformer)
- 1 — 47 ohm, 1/4 watt resistor or a 50 ohm resistor decade

## PROCEDURE

1. Construct lamp test circuit shown in Fig. 6-2-1.

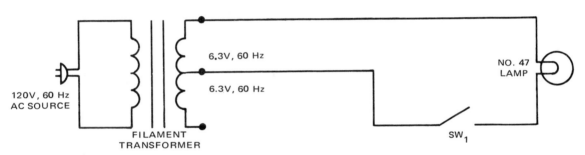

Fig. 6-2-1

In this experiment, you will apply ac to an inductor-lamp circuit and observe the outcome. With the inductor in the circuit, you will be able to see some delay in lamp brilliance. The time constant of this type of circuit is expressed by the formula t = RL. When resistance is added to the circuit, it decreases lamp brilliance and reduces the delay time.

## EXPERIMENT OBJECTIVES

As a result of this laboratory experience, you should be able to accomplish the following:

1. Experiment with the effect of ac in an RL circuit.
2. Note the effect of resistance on the time delay on the brilliance of a lamp in an RL circuit.

2. Turn on circuit switch and test operation of lamp. Particularly note brightness level of lamp and speed that it takes to reach full brightness. Turn switch on and off a few times while making these observations.
3. Turn off circuit switch and insert coil No. 1 into circuit between switch and lamp as indicated in Fig. 6-2-2.
4. Turn on circuit switch while observing brightness level of lamp and time it takes to reach full brightness. How does appearance of lamp compare with step No. 2?

_____

_____

5. Carefully slide laminated core piece into coil No. 1 while observing lamp. How does this affect lamp brightness and time it takes

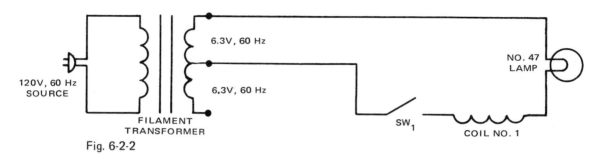

Fig. 6-2-2

to reach full brightness? _____

_____

6. Turn off circuit switch and add a 47 ohm resistor or a 50 ohm resistor to circuit as shown in Fig. 6-2-3. Obtain a 50 ohm resistor from resistor decade box.
7. Turn on circuit switch and observe delay

9. Alternately place resistor in circuit, then use jumper to test delay time. How does resistor alter delay time? _____

_____

10. Turn off circuit switch and 6.3V ac source. Disconnect circuit and return all parts to storage cabinet.

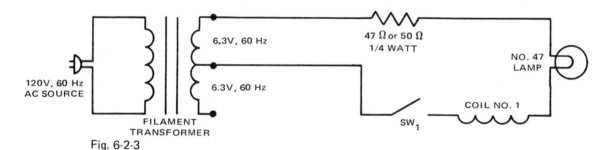

Fig. 6-2-3

time it takes lamp to reach its operating brilliance. It may be necessary to slide laminated core partially from coil to improve lamp brilliance.
8. Turn off switch and connect a jumper wire across 50 ohm resistor. Then, turn on switch and observe lamp delay time without resistor in circuit.

## QUESTIONS

1. If the inductor in Fig. 6-2-3 is approximately 0.38 H, what is the time constant of the RL circuit?
2. If the inductor used in this experiment is 0.38 H, what is its $X_L$?
3. How does the core of coil No. 1 influence its inductance?

## INTRODUCTION

When the magnetic field of one coil cuts across another coil and induces a voltage, the two coils have mutual inductance. Closeness of the coils, core material and position of the resulting field determine the amount of linkage between the two coils. If all of the lines of force of one coil cut across the second coil, there is unity coupling. Varying degrees of coupling can be achieved by the placement of mutual coils.

A transformer is the best example of an application of mutual inductance. Transformers are designed to transfer energy from one circuit to another by electromagnetic induction. A transformer is constructed so that it has two or more coils wound on common core. The amount of coupling in this device approaches unity.

The primary winding of a transformer receives the initial energy from the source. Current flow through this winding causes the magnetic field to expand when it is first applied. When the magnetic field is stationary, energy is not transferred. A collapsing magnetic field occurs when source energy is reduced or turned off. The magnetic field of the primary winding must, therefore, be in a state of motion in order to initiate an energy transfer to the secondary winding.

In this experiment, you will build a simple transformer. With dc applied to the primary, you will see the transfer of energy to the secondary by deflection of a VOM. No energy transfer occurs when the switch remains in the ON position. Turning the primary switch off will permit you to see how a collapsing field causes a transfer of energy. An oscilloscope will show the resulting output waveform of the transformer.

## EXPERIMENT OBJECTIVES

As a result of this laboratory experience, you should be able to accomplish the following:
1. Construct a simple transformer.
2. Measure the induced secondary voltage.
3. Observe the secondary waveforms with an oscilloscope.

## REFERENCE

Gerrish and Dugger, ELECTRICITY AND ELECTRONICS, Chapter 6, pages 82 and 83.

## MATERIALS AND EQUIPMENT

1 — Transformer (Hickok coil 1 - 3320-383; coil 2 - 3320-393; core - 12180-38)
1 — Volt-ohm-milliampere (VOM) meter
1 — Oscilloscope
1 — SPST toggle switch
1 — "D" cell

## PROCEDURE

1. Connect transformer assembly unit as shown in Fig. 6-3-1.

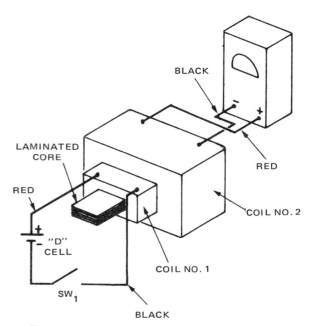

Fig. 6-3-1

2. Prepare VOM to measure a dc current of approximately 1 mA. Connect VOM to coil No. 2 as indicated.
3. Close circuit switch of coil No. 1 while observing VOM. After a couple of seconds, open switch. Explain how VOM responds to on-off action of switch. You may want to run two or three trials to be certain of action.
4. Place coil No. 1 inside of coil No. 2, then

89

slide laminated core into coil No. 1. With VOM connected to coil No. 2, repeat step 3. How does meter response of this step differ from step 3?

5. Prepare oscilloscope for operation with a vertical volts/cm of 10V or with vertical attenuator control in X10 range. Horizontal time/cm should be set to 1m sec or 100 to 1000 Hz horizontal sweep range. With nothing applied to the oscilloscope, it should produce a single horizontal sweep line.

6. Connect oscilloscope to output wires of coil No. 2 as indicated in Fig. 6-3-2. Remove VOM from coil No. 2.

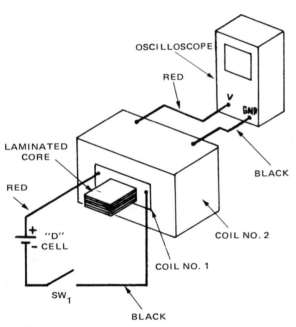

Fig. 6-3-2

7. Turn circuit switch on and off several times while observing oscilloscope viewing area. You may need to adjust vertical input variable control to alter waveform size to where it can be properly viewed. If horizontal sweep rate is too high or fast, trace

will be compressed. A slower sweep rate will spread trace across entire screen. Adjust horizontal sweep to produce a good view of waveform.

8. Make a sketch of observed waveform in space provided in Fig. 6-3-3.

0 _____

OBSERVED OSCILLOSCOPE WAVEFORM
Fig. 6-3-3

9. Disconnect oscilloscope from coil No. 2. Turn off oscilloscope.

10. Hold two lead wires of coil No. 2 in one hand so that one lead touches your thumb and second lead touches a finger.

11. Close switch, then open it. You should be able to feel transfer of energy between two coils.

12. Disconnect circuit and return all components to storage cabinet.

## QUESTIONS

1. Why does the meter hand deflect when the switch is closed initially, but return to zero when the circuit remains in the ON condition?

2. What are the two distinct times during the operation cycle of this transformer unit when energy passes between coils?

3. What must happen for ac to be transferred through a device of this type?

4. Electrical energy is applied to which transformer winding?

5. The output of a transformer is developed across which winding?

## INTRODUCTION

When electrical energy is applied to the primary winding of a transformer, it causes the magnetic field to expand initially. This expanding field cuts across the secondary winding, causing a voltage to be induced into it. By this action, the polarity of the induced voltage becomes opposite to that of the original energy source. Then, when the magnetic field is turned off, the lines of force collapse and return to the core material with a corresponding change in polarity. You will find that the polarity of the secondary winding is always opposite to that of the primary, regardless of status of the magnetic field.

In this experiment, you will build a transformer and test its polarity with neon lamps. A neon lamp contains two electrodes which, in response to voltage, produce illumination. When dc is applied to this type of lamp, only the negative electrode is illuminated. By observing the illuminated electrode of a neon lamp connected to a transformer coil, the polarity of the coil can be determined.

When ac is applied to a neon lamp, its electrodes will alternately illuminate with each direction change in current flow. When 60 Hz of ac is applied, both electrodes will appear to be illuminated because of the rapid change in polarity. Determining transformer polarity is a very important consideration when connecting them in power supplies and in transformer coupled amplifier circuits.

### EXPERIMENT OBJECTIVES

As a result of this laboratory experience, you should be able to accomplish the following:

1. Test transformer secondary polarity with neon lamps.
2. Note how the core affects output voltage.

### REFERENCE

Gerrish and Dugger, ELECTRICITY AND ELECTRONICS, Chapter 6, pages 85 to 89.

### MATERIALS AND EQUIPMENT

1 — Transformer assembly unit (Hickok)
2 — NE-2 Neon lamps
1 — SPST toggle switch
2 — "C" or "D" type dry cells with holders
1 — 15K, 1/4 watt resistor
1 — Variable dc power supply, 0-100V (optional)

### PROCEDURE

1. Remove NE-2 neon lamp from storage cabinet. Carefully examine internal structure of lamp. As a general rule, two flexible lead wires can be seen through glass connecting to two electrodes.
2. Prepare VOM to measure resistance and connect it to two lamp lead wire terminals. A good lamp should show infinite resistance between two electrodes.
3. Neon lamp will illuminate when 68 volts or more is applied to lamp in series with a 15K resistor. Electrode of neon lamp connected to negative side of dc voltage source will produce a characteristic orange glow when energized. Optional: If a 100V variable dc power supply is available, test voltage needed to illuminate a neon lamp.
4. Connect transformer polarity test circuit as in Fig. 6-4-1. Voltage induced into a coil by collapsing field of an inductor is generally twenty or more times greater than applied voltage. Voltage of this type reaches it peak value for only a short time.
5. Close switch that applies voltage from dc source to coil. Then, open switch while

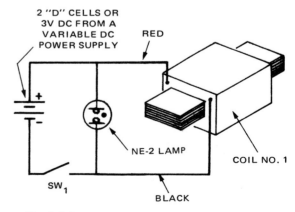

2 "D" CELLS OR 3V DC FROM A VARIABLE DC POWER SUPPLY

RED

+

−

NE-2 LAMP

COIL NO. 1

SW$_1$

BLACK

Fig. 6-4-1

observing NE-2 lamp. Negative side of source is connected to black coil wire and one side of lamp when energized. When switch is turned off, lamp electrode connected to red coil wire flashes. What causes this reverse in polarity of voltage applied to lamp? _____

6. Next, reverse polarity of two cells so that black wire is positive and red wire is negative. Repeat step 5 again. How does lamp respond to circuit change? _____

_____

7. Disconnect inductor test circuit and connect transformer polarity test circuit shown in Fig. 6-4-2. Test leads of coils No. 1 and No. 2 must come from same end of assembled transformer.

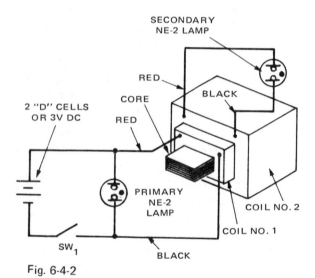

Fig. 6-4-2

8. Momentarily turn on circuit switch while observing primary NE-2 lamp. Which lead causes lamp to illuminate? _____ lead. Polarity of this lead is _____

Be certain that switch is left in OFF position to conserve battery power.

9. Momentarily turn on primary circuit switch while observing secondary NE-2 lamp. Which lead causes lamp to illuminate? _____ lead. Polarity of this load is

_____

What does this test indicate about polarity of primary and secondary windings of transformer? _____

_____

10. Reverse polarity of two dry cells connected to coil No. 1. Repeat steps 8 and 9 again. Does your polarity conclusion still agree after input reversal of this step? _____

11. Remove laminated core from transformer unit. Momentarily turn circuit switch on and off while observing lamps. How do lamps respond in transformer with core removed? _____

_____

12. What accounts for this change? _____

_____

13. Disconnect circuit and return all components to storage cabinet.

## QUESTIONS

1. Why does the collapsing field of an inductor produce more induced voltage than the expanding field?
2. What causes energy to be transferred between the primary and secondary windings of a transformer?
3. When ac is applied to the primary winding of a transformer, what is the polarity of the secondary winding?

# Experiment 6-5  TRANSFORMERS

## INTRODUCTION

A transformer is a device designed to transfer energy from one circuit to another by electromagnetic induction. The amount of output energy developed by a transformer is determined by the turns-ratio of the primary and secondary windings. If the primary winding has more turns than the secondary winding, primary voltage is "stepped down." Secondary voltage will be greater than primary voltage if the turns-ratio favors the secondary winding.

When a transformer is designed to "step up" the primary voltage, the secondary current is reduced by an equal ratio. For example, stepping up the voltage 1:3 times reduces the secondary current by a ratio of 3:1. By stepping down the voltage by a 10:1 ratio, the secondary current is increased 1:10. Therefore, the resulting current capability of a transformer is inversely related to the voltage ratio.

In this experiment, you will wind a secondary coil on the primary coil of the transformer assembly unit. Then, you will measure and record voltages. Next, calculate the number of primary turns, using the voltage/turns ratio formula. Through this experience, you will be able to see how a manufacturer can design transformers that will either step up or step down the primary voltage. You will also use the transformer unit to build a step down transformer and test its output.

## EXPERIMENT OBJECTIVES

As a result of this laboratory experience, you should be able to accomplish the following:
1. Construct and test a transformer secondary winding around a prewound primary winding.
2. Calculate primary turns in the transformer, using the voltage/turns ratio formula.
3. Build a step down transformer and test its output.

## REFERENCE

Gerrish and Dugger, ELECTRICITY AND ELECTRONICS, Chapter 6, pages 83 to 86.

## MATERIALS AND EQUIPMENT

1 — Volt-ohm-milliampere (VOM) meter
1 — Transformer (Hickok coil 1 - 3320-383; coil 2 - 3320-393; core - 12180-38)
1 — SPST toggle switch
1 — 6.3V, 60 Hz ac source
1 — 30 ft. length of No. 22 magnet wire

## PROCEDURE

1. Connect coil No. 1 of transformer assembly unit to 6.3V ac source as indicated in Fig. 6-5-1. Slide laminated core piece into coil.

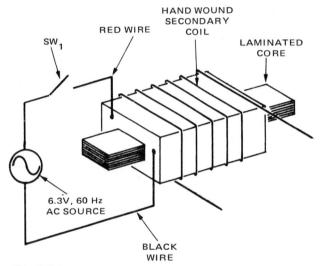

Fig. 6-5-1

2. Coil No. 1 will serve as primary winding of transformer test unit.
3. Remove 30 ft. length of No. 22 copper magnet wire from storage cabinet. Wind a coil around outside of coil No. 1 with magnet wire. Wrap turns close together and avoid overlapping them as much as possible. Number of turns wound on secondary coil is _____
4. Prepare VOM to measure ac voltage and connect it to hand wound secondary coil. Measured output voltage is _____ volts.
5. With VOM, measure and record voltage applied to primary winding. Primary winding voltage is _____ volts.
6. Use turns-ratio formula:

$$\frac{E_{primary}}{E_{secondary}} = \frac{N_{primary}}{N_{secondary}}$$

Calculate number of turns in primary winding.

7. Turn off circuit switch and remove wound secondary coil from coil No. 1. Wind length of wire into a loose coil around your hand and tie it together with loose end. Return coil to storage cabinet.

8. Slide coil No. 2 of transformer assembly unit over coil No. 1. Coil No. 2 will serve as secondary winding with coil No. 1 primary winding.

9. Turn on circuit switch and use VOM to measure secondary voltage of coil No. 2. Secondary voltage is _____ volts. This represents a step _____ (up or down) type of transformer.

10. In order for this transformer to develop measured secondary voltage, there must be _____ (more or less) secondary turns than primary turns.

11. Turn off circuit switch and remove laminated core from coil No. 1. Turn on circuit switch and use VOM to measure secondary voltage. Secondary voltage without laminated core is _____ volts.

12. Turn off circuit switch and disconnect coil No. 1 from 6.3V ac/60 Hz source. Connect coil No. 2 to 6.3V source. Now, coil No. 2 will serve as primary winding for this part of experiment.

13. Assemble remainder of transformer by sliding coil No. 1 into center of coil No. 2. Then, slide laminated core into coil No. 1.

14. Turn on circuit switch and prepare VOM to measure voltage of coil No. 1. Secondary voltage of coil No. 1 is _____ volts.

15. Measure and record primary voltage applied to coil No. 2. Primary coil voltage is _____ volts. Comparing measured primary voltage with measured secondary voltage of step 14, this experimental transformer is a step _____ (up or down) unit.

16. Turn off circuit switch and disconnect transformer assembly unit. Return all parts to storage cabinet.

## QUESTIONS

1. The primary winding of a given transformer has 1000 turns of wire and 120V ac/60 Hz applied to the primary. If a secondary voltage of 12V is desired, how many secondary windings would be needed?

2. Using the same primary winding from question 1, how many secondary turns are needed to produce 360V?

3. How could the core of the experimental transformer be changed to improve the operating efficiency of the unit?

# Experiment 6-6 TRANSFORMER WINDINGS

## INTRODUCTION

A wide variety of transformers are used in electrical and electronic circuits today. Those with a single primary and a single secondary winding are very common. In addition, a single secondary winding can be divided or tapped into two windings with a common connection. This type of winding provides two voltages with reference to center tap that are 180 deg. out of phase. Transformers with tapped primary windings permit different source voltages to be applied to input. Multiple secondary winding transformers are frequently used in television receivers. Multiple winding transformers usually have the same general appearance as other transformers. The only apparent difference is the number of winding terminals or lead wires.

In this experiment, you will see how transformers are tested to determine faulty conditions. A low voltage, center tapped secondary winding transformer will be used. The operating principle of this device is basically the same as the type of transformer used to deliver energy to homes and commercial buildings. This same type of transformer is also used in rectifier power supplies.

## EXPERIMENT OBJECTIVES

As a result of this laboratory experience, you should be able to accomplish the following:
1. Calculate the voltage and resistance of a center tapped transformer.
2. Observe the phase relationship in the secondary windings of a center tapped transformer.

## REFERENCE

Gerrish and Dugger, ELECTRICITY AND ELECTRONICS, Chapter 6, pages 82 to 86.

## MATERIALS AND EQUIPMENT

1 — Volt-ohm-milliampere (VOM) meter
1 — Oscilloscope
1 — 12.6V CT filament transformer
2 — SPST toggle switches
2 — No. 47 lamps and sockets
1 — 2200 ohm, 1/4 watt resistor or resistor decade

## PROCEDURE

1. Prepare VOM to measure secondary voltage of a low voltage transformer, which may be housed in a power supply or mounted as a separate unit.
2. Turn on power supply or plug transformer into primary ac power source. Measure output voltage across test points indicated in Fig. 6-6-1. Record each value.
3. Center tapped transformer in Fig. 6-6-1 is similar to transformer that supplies electrical power to your home, only on a smaller scale. Terminal B is representative of neutral connection or common ground. Terminals A and C are representative of hot leg of source which, typically, is protected by a fuse or circuit breaker.
4. Connect circuit shown in Fig. 6-6-2, using lamps and switches. Note that ground symbol is used to indicate commonly connected components.
5. Lamps in Fig. 6-6-2 are representative of separate ac circuits in a home. The resistor denotes a heating element in an electric range or clothes dryer. Typical voltages of 208/120 or 240/120 are supplied by transformers connected in this manner.
6. Turn lamps on and off with appropriate switch. Note that they are completely

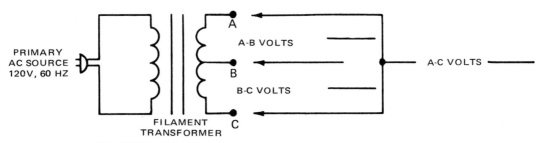

Fig. 6-6-1

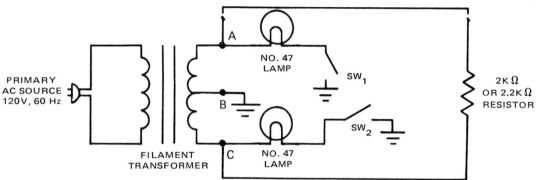

Fig. 6-6-2

independent of each other but derive circuit power from same source.

7. Prepare oscilloscope for operation and make following adjustments:
   Sweep frequency – 5m sec/cm or 10 to 100 Hz.
   Vertical input range – 10V/cm or X10
   Trigger or sync source – Line

8. Connect common lead of oscilloscope to point B. Connect vertical probe to point A. Two or three sine waves should be displayed on CRT. If necessary, adjust vertical input range and horizontal sweep frequency to produce an appropriate display. If a display cannot be obtained, ask your instructor to assist you.

9. Adjust horizontal position control so beginning edge of waveform is displayed on left side of viewing area. Note polarity of first alternation of wave. It is of a positive or negative polarity. _____ polarity.

10. Move vertical probe to test point C on transformer with common lead to point B. Display produced should be of a polarity opposite to that of step 9. Polarity of waveform is of a _____ polarity. If there is no polarity change, set trigger source or sync switch to something other than line trigger or sync position.

11. Turn off circuit switches and power supply. If a transformer unit is used, unplug it from ac source.

12. Prepare VOM to measure resistance. Measure and record resistance between A-B, B-C and A-C of transformer. A-B is _____ ohms. B-C is _____ ohms. A-C is _____ ohms. How would these values appear if secondary winding is faulty? _____

13. If you are using a discrete transformer unit instead of a power supply, measure resistance of primary winding. _____ ohms.

14. Test resistance of transformer between primary and secondary windings. Use highest resistance range of VOM. A good transformer should indicate infinite resistance for this test. How does transformer tested respond? _____

15. Return all component parts to storage cabinet.

## QUESTIONS

1. What is the phase relationship between the secondary windings A-B and B-C of the transformer used in this experiment?

2. What is the phase relationship between the primary and secondary windings of a transformer?

3. If a transformer has a center tapped secondary winding, what voltage output can be obtained from the terminal combinations?

# Experiment 6-7  INDUCTIVE REACTANCE

## INTRODUCTION

When alternating current is applied to an inductor, the resulting magnetic field is in a constant state of change. The opposition offered by an inductor to ac is called "inductive reactance" or $X_L$. The amount of opposition offered by an inductor is directly dependent upon the frequency of the ac source. The formula $X_L = 2 \pi fL$ shows this relationship. With an inductor of a constant value, a change in frequency will cause a corresponding change in $X_L$.

An ohm is the fundamental unit of inductive reactance. However, inductive reactance cannot be measured directly with an ohmmeter. $X_L$ is calculated by measured values of inductor voltage $E_L$ and inductor current $I_L$.

In this experiment, you will build a series RL circuit and connect it to a high frequency ac voltage source. Then, measure $E_L$ and $E_R$ voltages across the inductor and resistor with a VOM. These values cannot be added together to equal source voltage because they are not in phase. Prepare a graph using measured values of $E_L$ and $E_R$ voltages to determine circuit impedance voltage $E_Z$. You will see phase relationship between these voltage values directly on the graph.

Through this experiment, you will observe the influence of frequency on $E_L$ and $E_R$. You will also determine the phase angle of the circuit by calculation or by measurement with a protractor. Inductive circuits are commonly used in filtering out unwanted frequencies.

## EXPERIMENT OBJECTIVES

As a result of this laboratory experience, you should be able to accomplish the following:
1. Construct a series RL circuit.
2. Calculate the total circuit voltage, using $E_L$ and $E_R$.
3. Observe the influence of frequency on $E_L$ and $E_R$.

## REFERENCE

Gerrish and Dugger, ELECTRICITY AND ELECTRONICS, Chapter 6, pages 89 to 94.

## MATERIALS AND EQUIPMENT

1 — Volt-ohm-milliampere (VOM) meter
1 — Signal generator or function generator
1 — 25 mH inductor
1 — 2.2K, 1/4 watt resistor or 2K resistor from resistor decade
1 — SPST toggle switch

## PROCEDURE

1. Construct inductive resistance test circuit shown in Fig. 6-7-1. Note that ac source has a frequency of 50 KHz. This must be obtained from an ac signal generator or function generator.

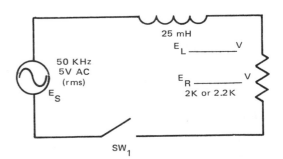

Fig. 6-7-1

2. Turn on signal generator and prepare VOM to measure ac voltage. Before turning on circuit switch, adjust generator output to 50 KHz with a voltage level of 5V ac. Close circuit switch and measure source voltage again. If voltage has changed, adjust it to produce 5V ac.
3. With VOM, measure and record voltage across inductor ($E_L$) and resistor voltage ($E_R$).
4. In a series dc circuit, sum of all voltage drops equals source voltage. Why does $E_L + E_R = E_S$?
5. To add values of $E_L$ and $E_R$, use graph in Fig. 6-7-2.
6. Select $E_L$ value on vertical or Y axes and $E_R$ value on horizontal or X axes of graph.
7. Project value of $E_L$ to right where it intersects with a line projected up from $E_R$

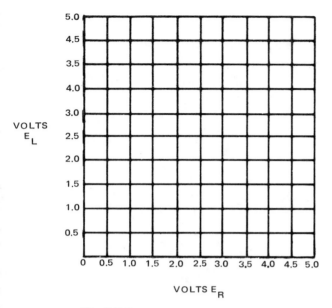

VOLTS $E_L$

5.0
4.5
3.5
4.0
3.0
2.5
2.0
1.5
1.0
0.5

0   0.5  1.0  1.5  2.0  2.5  3.0  3.5  4.0  4.5  5.0

VOLTS $E_R$

Fig. 6-7-2

value. Mark intersection point $E_z$.

8. With a straightedge, draw a line that will connect $E_z$ and 0 points.

9. Measure length of $E_z$ line, using same scale as $E_L$ and $E_R$. Voltage value of $E_z$ is _____ volts. $E_z$ should equal value of $E_s$. How close does measured value of $E_s$ compare with graphed value of $E_z$? _____

10. Connect VOM across inductor in circuit. Change frequency of source to 5 KHz, 500 Hz while observing $E_L$ voltage. Repeat this test at 50 Hz and observe $E_L$. How does frequency of source influence value of $E_L$?

_____

_____

11. Return frequency of source to 50 KHz. Connect VOM across resistor and measure $E_R$. Change frequency of source to 5 KHz, 500 Hz and 50 Hz while observing the value of $E_R$. How does the frequency of source influence value of $E_R$? _____

_____

12. Turn off circuit switch and ac signal source. Disconnect circuit and return all parts to storage cabinet.

**QUESTIONS**

1. How does the $X_L$ of an inductor change with respect to frequency?
2. Why is an inductor frequency dependent?
3. Determine phase angle of $E_R$ and $E_z$, using either a protractor or the formula: Phase angle = cos of $E_R / E_z$.
4. What is the phase angle relationship between I and E due to L in an ac circuit?

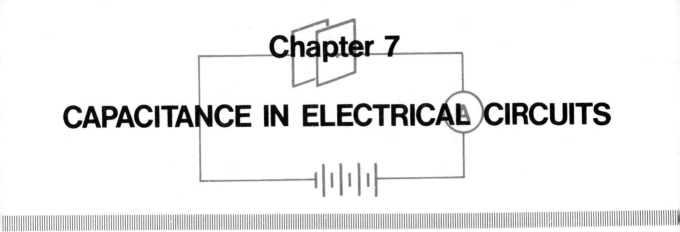

# Chapter 7
# CAPACITANCE IN ELECTRICAL CIRCUITS

## Experiment 7-1  CAPACITOR TESTING

### INTRODUCTION

A capacitor is an electrical device that has two or more conductor plates separated by a dielectric material. When dc is applied to a capacitor, a momentary current flow occurs. The capacitor plate connected to the negative side of the source takes on a negative charge; the other plate takes on a positive charge. After the capacitor plates have been charged, current flow ceases. A capacitor supposedly blocks the flow of dc other than what takes place when it is being charged.

The charging action of a capacitor can be demonstrated by observing the response of an ohmmeter connected across its terminals. When the capacitor is charging to the voltage source of the ohmmeter, its resistance is low. The ohmmeter initially deflects or "kicks" to the low resistance part of the scale. As the capacitor begins to accumulate a charge, its resistance begins to swing toward the high resistance end of the scale.

The "kick test" of a capacitor, then, is a quick and easy method used to determine the capacitor's condition. A large value capacitor makes an obvious low resistant deflection, then a high resistance kick when it is good. An open capacitor, by comparison, usually indicates high or infinite resistance at all times. The same test applied to a shorted capacitor indicates a rather low resistance at all times. "Leaky" capacitors generally charge rather slowly, which is indicated by a slow high resistance swing. The value of a capacitor also has a great deal to do with the "kick test" response indicated by the ohmmeter.

In this experiment, you will apply the ohmmeter of a VOM to a capacitor to see its charging action. As a general rule, a good capacitor of a similar value should be compared with the questionable capacitor until you become more familiar with specific charging action times.

### EXPERIMENT OBJECTIVES

As a result of this laboratory experience, you should be able to accomplish the following:
1. Use an ohmmeter to observe the charging action of a capacitor.
2. Notice the effect of time on the charge of a capacitor.
3. Learn how to test a capacitor for a short, open or leaky condition.

### REFERENCE

Gerrish and Dugger, ELECTRICITY AND ELECTRONICS, Chapter 7, pages 96 and 97.

### MATERIALS AND EQUIPMENT
    1 — Volt-ohm-milliampere (VOM) meter
    1 — 680 $\mu$F, 50V dc capacitor
    1 — 0.22 $\mu$F, 100V dc capacitor
    1 — 0.01 $\mu$F, 100V dc capacitor
    1 — SPST toggle switch

### PROCEDURE
1. Capacitors may be mounted individually on separate strips or may be a part of power supply module.
2. Examine 680 $\mu$F, 50V dc capacitor. It is a polarized unit with a + and − printed on housing. Negative end of capacitor may

have a printed band around it instead of a negative sign. Polarized capacitors must be connected correctly to voltage source. Non-polarized capacitors can be connected to voltage source in either direction without being damaged.

3. Prepare VOM to measure resistance in 1K (kilohm) range. Connect meter-capacitor test circuit as in Fig. 7-1-1.

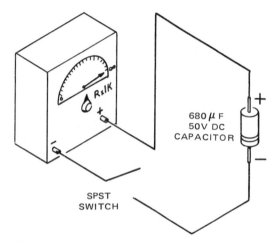

Fig. 7-1-1

4. Turn on SPST switch while observing meter. Describe reaction of meter. _____

_____

_____

5. Turn off SPST switch and discharge capacitor by connecting a jumper wire momentarily between two capacitor terminals. Then, remove jumper wire and retest capacitor as in step 4.

6. A good capacitor will cause ohmmeter to deflect to a low resistant value instantly, then gradually increase in resistance until infinity is reached. An open capacitor will not deflect ohmmeter at all. A shorted capacitor will show a continuous low resistance reading. A "leaky" (partially shorted) capacitor will show a normal charge deflection to low resistant end of scale, but is

very slow moving in high resistant direction.

7. How would you classify capacitor tested in step 4? Good _____ Open _____ Shorted _____ Leaky _____

8. A small valued capacitor responds same way as large capacitor of step 4, except action is not as pronounced.

9. Remove 680 $\mu$F capacitor from test circuit and place a 0.22 $\mu$F capacitor in its place. Change ohmmeter to 100K or an equivalent range.

10. Turn on SPST switch. Observe charging action of capacitor. Explain this action as compared with step 4. _____

_____

11. Turn off switch and discharge capacitor by momentarily connecting a jumper wire between two terminals. Repeat step 10 to verify your observation.

12. Remove 0.22 $\mu$F capacitor and place a 0.01 $\mu$F capacitor in its place. Change ohmmeter to its highest resistance range. Turn on switch and observe charging action of capacitor. Then, momentarily turn off switch and discharge capacitor with a jumper wire. Remove jumper wire and retest capacitor. Explain how meter responds in this test. _____

_____

13. How would you classify condition capacitor? Good _____ Open _____ Shorted _____ Leaky _____

14. Disconnect circuit and return all parts to storage cabinet.

### QUESTIONS

1. Explain what occurs during the "kick test" of a capacitor.
2. Why is a jumper wire connected across a capacitor after the ohmmeter test has been applied?
3. When an ohmmeter is used to test a capacitor, where is the source of energy derived?

# CAPACITOR CHARGING AND DISCHARGING ACTION

## INTRODUCTION

A capacitor has the unusual property of being able to hold an electrical charge after being connected to a source of electrical energy. Because of this ability, a capacitor is used to smooth out or filter variations in the amplitude of a dc power supply. In this way, dc power supplies can be designed to have very pure dc output.

When dc is initially applied to a capacitor, electrons flow from the negative side of the source to one of the plates, causing it to develop a negative charge. The other plate of the capacitor has electrons removed from it at the same time. Ultimately, this plate becomes electron deficient or positively charged. Initial current flow at this time is at a maximum level. The voltage across the capacitor initially is zero.

When the potential voltage across a charging capacitor begins to rise, its charging current decreases in value. A charge capacitor ultimately reaches the full voltage value of the charging source with current flow falling to zero. A capacitor has the ability to hold this charge for a certain length of time, according to its dielectric material.

The discharging action of a capacitor causes a direction change in the current flow compared with its charging current. Electrons initially flow away from the negative plate and toward the positive plate which is electron deficient. This discharge current is of a maximum value and quickly drops to zero. The voltage change of a charged capacitor is directly opposite to that of the charging cycle. Initially, it is at a maximum value and drops to zero when completely discharged.

In this experiment, a capacitor test circuit will permit you to see its charge and discharge action, while a VOM shows voltage and current values. A lamp circuit will allow you to observe the direction change that occurs in voltage and current during the charge and discharge of a capacitor. This is known as rise and decay of voltage and current.

## EXPERIMENT OBJECTIVES

As a result of this laboratory experience, you should be able to accomplish the following:
1. Build a test circuit that will charge and discharge capacitors.
2. Use a VOM to test voltage and current values in a capacitor.
3. Construct a lamp circuit and observe the transient response with a capacitor in the circuit.

## REFERENCE

Gerrish and Dugger, ELECTRICITY AND ELECTRONICS, Chapter 7, pages 100 to 102.

## MATERIALS AND EQUIPMENT

1 — Volt-ohm-milliampere (VOM) meter
1 — 680 $\mu$ F, 50V dc capacitor
1 — SPST toggle switch
1 — SPDT toggle switch
1 — Power source, 0-15V, 1A dc
1 — No. 47 lamp with socket

## PROCEDURE

1. Connect capacitor test circuit of Fig. 7-2-1. A 680 $\mu$ F, 50V dc capacitor may be found on power supply module board or connected to a single mounting strip.
2. Pivot point (P) of SPDT switch must be determined with ohmmeter of VOM.
3. Before turning on circuit switch, turn on power supply and adjust it to 10V dc. VOM may be used to measure this adjustment.
4. Prepare VOM to measure a charging current of approximately 10 $\mu$ A and connect it into circuit. Be certain to observe polarity of meter and capacitor.
5. With charge-discharge switch in charge position, turn on circuit switch while observing ammeter. A momentary up-scale current indication should occur. Describe your observation. _____

_____

_____

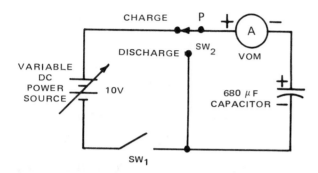

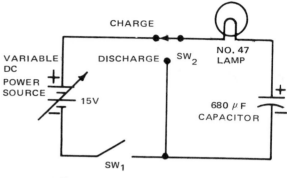

Fig. 7-2-2

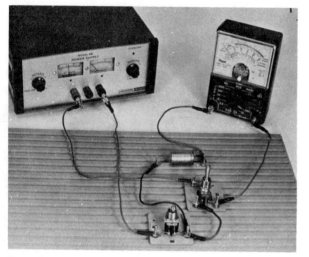

Fig. 7-2-1

6. Place charge-discharge switch in discharge position while observing meter. Describe response of meter. _____

_____

7. Turn off circuit switch and disconnect VOM from circuit. Complete circuit by attaching a connecting wire in place of VOM.

8. Prepare VOM to measure dc voltage and connect it across capacitor. Be sure to observe capacitor and meter polarity.

9. With charge-discharge switch in charge position, turn on circuit switch while observing VOM. Then, place switch in discharge position. Try this charge-discharge

action a few times to see transient response of capacitor. How would you describe transient response time? _____

_____

10. Turn off circuit switch and change circuit to conform with Fig. 7-2-2. Note that power supply has been changed to 15V dc.

11. Lamp of this circuit is used to visually reveal charge and discharge transient time. Resistance of lamp delays transient time somewhat.

12. Turn on circuit switch. Charge capacitor, then discharge it. How would you describe transient time of this circuit? _____

_____

13. Turn off circuit switch, discharge capacitor and turn off power supply. Disconnect circuit and return all components to storage cabinet.

## QUESTIONS

1. Explain what happens when a capacitor is charged from a dc source.
2. Assume that a capacitor has been fully charged from a dc source. What occurs when the source is removed and the capacitor is discharged?
3. What does the term "transient response" of a capacitor mean?

# ▥▥▥▥▥▥▥▥▥▥▥▥▥ Experiment 7-3  RC TIME CONSTANT ▥▥▥▥▥▥▥▥▥▥▥▥▥

## INTRODUCTION

When dc is applied directly to a capacitor, it immediately charges to the value of the source voltage. However, if a resistor is placed in series with the capacitor, charging occurs at a different rate of time. A circuit of this type is described as having an RC time constant. An RC time constant refers to a predictable charging rate based upon the value of R x C. Likewise, a fully charged capacitor discharging through a resistor also drops its voltage at a predictable rate according to the RC time constant. Universal charge and discharge rates of an RC circuit are commonly used to shape waveforms and in timing circuits that control machine operations.

In this experiment, you will build an RC circuit, calculate the time constant and see the change that takes place when a capacitor is charged and discharged through a resistor.

## REFERENCE

Gerrish and Dugger, ELECTRICITY AND ELECTRONICS, Chapter 7, pages 101 and 102.

## MATERIALS AND EQUIPMENT

1 — Volt-ohm-milliampere (VOM) meter
1 — Variable power supply, 0-10V, 1A dc
1 — 680 $\mu$ F, 50V dc capacitor
1 — 5K, 1/4 watt resistor from resistor decade or 1-4700 ohm, 1/4 watt resistor
1 — SPST toggle switch
1 — SPDT toggle switch

## PROCEDURE

1. Connect RC circuit shown in Fig. 7-3-1. A 680 $\mu$ F capacitor may be mounted separately on a strip or obtained from power supply module.

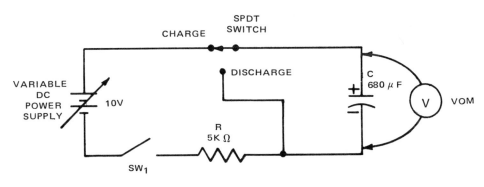

Fig. 7-3-1

Rather long time constants are used so that the voltage values can be easily predicted and measured.

## EXPERIMENT OBJECTIVES

As a result of this laboratory experience, you should be able to accomplish the following:
1. Build an RC circuit.
2. Calculate the time constant in the RC circuit.
3. Predict the charging and discharging voltage in the RC circuit.

2. Prepare VOM to measure dc voltage and connect it across a variable dc power supply. With circuit switch in OFF position, turn on power supply and adjust it to 10 volts.

3. Calculate time constant (t) for charging part of circuit. One time constant ($t_1$) is _____ seconds. Referring to time constant chart in Fig. 7-3-2, fill in time in seconds and predicted charge voltage for each time constant.

4. If a watch or clock with a sweep hand is

| TIME CONSTANT | R X C TIME IN SECONDS | PERCENT OF VOLTAGE | PREDICTED CHARGE VOLTAGE WITH 10V APPLIED |
|---|---|---|---|
| 1 | | 63.2 | |
| 2 | | 86.5 | |
| 3 | | 95.0 | |
| 4 | | 98.0 | |
| 5 | | 99.9+ | |

Fig. 7-3-2

available, test accuracy of the RC circuit. Place charge-discharge switch in charge position. Turn on circuit switch for one calculated time constant, then turn it off and quickly read VOM.

5. If a watch or clock is not available, try counting one thousand one, one thousand two, etc., for each second. Turn off circuit switch at end of one time constant and quickly read charge voltage on C. Note that meter value changes gradually. What causes this? _____

_____

6. Using time method or counting method, test out other time constants and voltage values in chart. Note that $t_1$ and $t_2$ are

rather accurate but $t_3$, $t_4$ and $t_5$ are less predictable. Is there any reason for this inaccuracy? _____

_____

7. Change RC circuit in Fig. 7-3-1 to conform with circuit shown in Fig. 7-3-3. Capacitor in this circuit charges instantly, but discharges through a resistor.

8. Calculate time constant of discharge part of circuit. One discharge time constant ($t_1$) is _____ seconds. Referring to discharge time constant chart in Fig. 7-3-4, fill in RC time in seconds and predicted amount of discharge voltage for each time constant.

9. To test discharge characteristic of RC circuit, place charge-discharge switch in

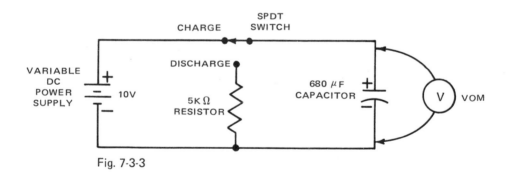

Fig. 7-3-3

DISCHARGE TIME CONSTANT

| TIME CONSTANT | R X C TIME IN SECONDS | PERCENTAGE OF VOLTAGE DISCHARGE | PREDICTED DISCHARGE VOLTAGE |
|---|---|---|---|
| 1 | | DOWN 63.2 | |
| 2 | | DOWN 86.5 | |
| 3 | | DOWN 95.0 | |
| 4 | | DOWN 98.0 | |
| 5 | | DOWN 99.9+ | |

Fig. 7-3-4

charge position and turn on circuit switch. This action causes C to charge to source voltage. Then, switch to discharge position and time discharge or count for on time constant. Open circuit switch and read volts scale immediately and compare your measured value with your predicted value.

10. Using same procedure, test remaining time constants of chart. How closely do your predicted values and measured values compare? _____

_____

11. Turn off circuit switch and power supply. Disconnect circuit and return all parts to storage cabinet.

## QUESTIONS

1. How many time constants are needed to fully charge a capacitor?
2. If more source voltage is applied, how would it change the time constant?
3. If a 50K resistor were used in the two circuits of this experiment instead of 5K, how would it change the operation?

# Experiment 7-4  CAPACITOR CIRCUITS

## INTRODUCTION

When selecting a capacitor for a specific application, you must consider the type of source energy being used. If dc is used as a source, current flow only occurs when the energy is initially applied to the circuit. The capacitor ultimately charges to the value of the source. During the remainder of the time, dc does not pass through a circuit.

When ac is applied to a capacitor, it charges to the peak value of the first half cycle. When the source voltage begins to drop in value, the capacitor discharges back toward the source, causing a continuation of current flow for the remainder of the cycle. When the alternate half cycle occurs, the capacitor charges to the peak value again. It likewise discharges back into the source when the peak value is reduced. This causes a current flow for the remainder of the alternation. In essence, ac will pass and dc is blocked when applied to a series capacitor.

The value of a capacitor has a great deal to do with the opposition it offers to ac. When capacitors are connected in parallel, the total capacitance is the sum of the individual values. Large valued capacitors offer a minimum of opposition to low frequency ac circuits.

When capacitors are connected in series, total capacitance is reduced. Total capacitance can be determined by finding the product of the two values, then dividing by the sum of the values. Or, it can be determined by the sum of reciprocals method. Two or more capacitors connected in series increase the value of the working voltage of the capacitors by the sum of the individual values.

In this experiment, you will see how ac and dc sources of energy respond to capacitors connected in series with a lamp. In addition, you will connect capacitors in series and parallel, then calculate total circuit capacitance. This experiment will help familarize you with capacitor operation in an electric circuit.

## EXPERIMENT OBJECTIVES

As a result of this laboratory experience, you should be able to accomplish the following:

1. Construct an ac circuit and observe the charging action of a capacitor in the circuit.
2. Construct a dc circuit and observe the charging action of a capacitor in this circuit.
3. Connect capacitors in series and parallel, then calculate total capacitance in each type of circuit.

## REFERENCE

Gerrish and Dugger, ELECTRICITY AND ELECTRONICS, Chapter 7, pages 103 and 104.

## MATERIALS AND EQUIPMENT

1 — 6.3V, 1A ac source
1 — 6V, 1A dc source
2 — 680 $\mu$ F, 50V dc capacitors
1 — 0.22 $\mu$ F, 100V dc capacitor
2 — No. 47 lamps with sockets
2 — SPST toggle switches

## PROCEDURE

1. Construct circuit shown in Fig. 7-4-1. A 680 $\mu$ F capacitor may be mounted on power supply module board or placed on a single strip.

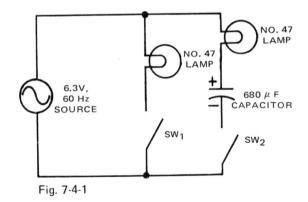

Fig. 7-4-1

2. Turn on switch (SW$_1$) to see normal brilliancy of lamps when 6.3V, 60 Hz ac is applied.
3. Then, turn on other switch (SW$_2$) to see if ac passes through a capacitor. What does this demonstrate about capacitors connected into series ac circuits? _____

_____

4. Capacitance value of C has a great deal to do with amount of opposition it offers to an ac circuit. Large capacitance values offer a minimum of opposition to 60 Hz. Small values of capacitance, by comparison, offer a great deal more opposition to ac.

5. When capacitors are connected in parallel, total capacitance is sum of individual capacitor values. Formula $C_T = C_1 + C_2 \ldots$ expresses their relationship.

6. Next, turn off $SW_2$ and connect a second 680 $\mu$ F capacitor in parallel with the original capacitor. Turn on $SW_2$ and observe operation of circuit. Total capacitance is now _____ $\mu$F.

7. When capacitors are connected in series, total capacitance is smaller than original value.

$$C_T = \frac{C_1 \times C_2}{C_1 + C_2} \quad \text{or} \quad \frac{1}{C_T} = \frac{1}{C_1} + \frac{1}{C_2} \ldots$$

Working voltage rating of series capacitors is sum of individual capacitor working voltage values.

8. Turn off $SW_2$ and connect two 680 $\mu$ F capacitors in series. Turn on $SW_2$ and observe operation of circuit. Total capacitance of circuit is _____ $\mu$F.

9. Turn off $SW_2$ and connect a 0.22 $\mu$ F capacitor in place of the two 680 $\mu$ F capacitors.

10. Turn on $SW_2$ and test circuit. What does this demonstrate about operation of an ac circuit and its capacitance value? _____

_____

_____

11. Turn off both circuit switches. Remove ac source and connect a dc source in its place. See Fig. 7-4-2. Note that $C_1$ is also changed back to original 680 $\mu$ F. Observe correct polarity of capacitor and power source.

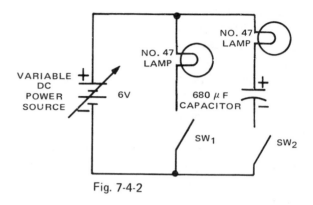

Fig. 7-4-2

12. Turn on $SW_1$ to test operation of first lamp circuit.

13. Then, turn on $SW_2$ to test operation of second lamp. What does this demonstrate about capacitors connected in series dc circuits? _____

_____

14. Turn off both switches and power source. Disconnect circuit and return all components to storage cabinet.

## QUESTIONS

1. If two capacitors of the same value are connected in parallel, what will total capacitance be?

2. If two capacitors are connected in series, what will total capacitance be?

3. Describe the effect of applying ac or dc to a series capacitor circuit.

# Experiment 7-5  CAPACITIVE REACTANCE

## INTRODUCTION

When ac is applied to a capacitor, the initial current flow almost instantaneously reaches a maximum value. As the capacitor begins to build up its charge voltage, the current drops to zero. When the charged capacitor begins to discharge, this action causes the current to rise to a maximum value in the reverse direction. This difference in the phase of I and E are continuous throughout each cycle of ac. In a pure capacitive circuit, I leads E by 90 deg. The amount of current flow passing through the circuit is based upon the value of C and the frequency.

The current flow of a capacitor circuit is very dependent upon the frequency of the applied ac. An increase in frequency will cause a corresponding increase in current flow. This relationship is based upon the capacitive reactance formula:

$$X_c = \frac{1}{2 \pi fC}$$

As frequency increases, $X_c$ decreases because of its location in the denominator of the formula. An increase in capacitance likewise causes a comparable decrease in $X_c$.

In this experiment, you will build a series RC circuit, connect it to an ac source and measure $E_c$ and $E_R$ voltages with a VOM. $E_c$ and $E_R$ values cannot be added directly to equal the source voltage because they are out of phase. Therefore, you will prepare a graph using measured values of $E_c$ and $E_R$ to determine circuit impedance voltage $E_z$. Upon completion, you will be able to see the phase relationship of these voltage values directly on the graph.

Also: you will be able to observe the influence that frequency has upon $E_c$ and $E_R$. You will know how to determine the phase angle of the circuit by calculation or by measurement with a protractor. Capacitor circuits are commonly used to filter out unwanted frequencies and to maintain voltage amplitude at a constant level through filtering circuit applications.

## EXPERIMENT OBJECTIVES

As a result of this laboratory experience, you should be able to accomplish the following:
1. Construct a series RC circuit.
2. Compute the total voltage ($E_L$) and phase angle in the circuit.
3. Observe the effect of frequency on the voltage across the capacitor ($E_c$) and across the resistor ($E_R$).

## REFERENCE

Gerrish and Dugger, ELECTRICITY AND ELECTRONICS, Chapter 7, pages 104 to 107.

## MATERIALS AND EQUIPMENT

1 — Volt-ohm-milliampere (VOM) meter
1 — 6.3V, 60 Hz ac source
1 — Signal generator or function generator
1 — 0.22 $\mu$ F, 100V dc capacitor
1 — 5K, 1/4 watt resistor from a decade module or 1 — 4.7K, 1/4 watt resistor
1 — SPST toggle switch

## PROCEDURE

1. Construct capacitive reactance test circuit shown in Fig. 7-5-1.

Fig. 7-5-1

2. Turn on circuit switch and prepare VOM to measure ac across R and C. Record these measured values on Fig. 7-5-1. Measure 6.3V, 60 Hz source voltage and record its actual value as $E_s$ in circuit diagram.

3. In a series RC circuit of this type, why is it that $E_c$ plus $E_R$ does not equal $E_s$?

4. To add values of $E_c$ and $E_R$, use graph in Fig. 7-5-2. Note that zero reference of this graph starts at top left corner of graph. Compare this with $E_L - E_R$ graph in Fig. 6-7-2.

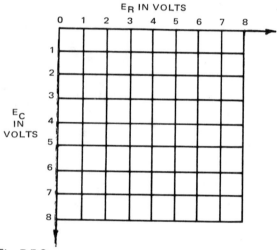

E_R IN VOLTS

E_C IN VOLTS

Fig. 7-5-2

5. Select value of $E_c$ on vertical or Y axes and $E_R$ value on horizontal or X axes of graph.

6. Project value of $E_c$ to right where it intersects with a line projected down from $E_R$ value. Mark the intersection of these two points as $E_z$.

7. With a straightedge, draw a line that will connect $E_z$ and 0 points.

8. Measure length of $E_z$ line, using same scale as $E_c$ or $E_R$. Voltage value of $E_z$ is _____ volts. In this circuit, $E_z$ should equal $E_s$. How close does measured value compare with graphed value of $E_z$?

9. Calculate $X_c$ of capacitor, using $X_c = 1/2 \pi fC$. $X_c$ is _____ ohms.

10. The ac current passing through circuit is based upon $E_R/R$. I is _____ amperes.

11. Using formula $E_c = I \times X_c$, calculate voltage across capacitor. Calculated value of $E_c$ is _____ volts. How close does calculated value of $E_c$ compare with measured value of $E_c$?

12. Turn off circuit switch and remove 6.3V ac source from circuit. In its place, connect a 50K Hz ac source from a signal generator. Using VOM, adjust signal level to 5V ac.

13. Measure and record $E_c$ and $E_R$ voltage values for each signal generator frequency on chart in Fig. 7-5-3. Input voltage $E_s$ must be 5V for each frequency setting.

| FREQUENCY | $E_S$ | $E_C$ | $E_R$ |
|---|---|---|---|
| 50 KHz | 5V | | |
| 5 KHz | 5V | | |
| 500 Hz | 5V | | |
| 50 Hz | 5V | | |

Fig. 7-5-3

14. Turn off circuit switch. How does value of $X_c$ change with frequency? _____

15. If $X_c$ is high, voltage across it will be _____ (small or large). Does chart agree with statement?

16. Turn off signal generator and disconnect circuit. Return all parts to storage cabinet.

## QUESTIONS

1. Explain the relationship of $X_c$ and frequency when applied to a single valued capacitor.

2. Using either a protractor or the formula, Phase angle = cos of $E_R/E_z$, determine the phase angle of the graph in Fig. 7-5-2.

3. What is the phase relationship of I and E when ac is applied to a capacitor in a circuit?

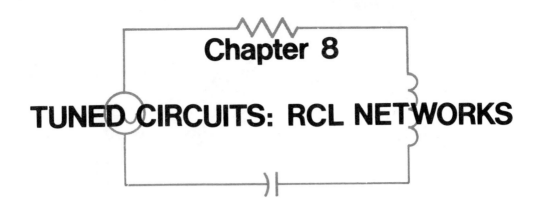

# Chapter 8

# TUNED CIRCUITS: RCL NETWORKS

## Experiment 8-1 SERIES RESONANT PRINCIPLES

### INTRODUCTION

When an inductor, a capacitor and a resistor are connected in series and ac is applied, resonance will occur at a certain frequency. At resonant frequency, $X_L = X_C$, resistance is the only remaining opposition to ac. As a result of this condition, circuit impedance (Z) is at a minimum and current flow is at a maximum value.

The frequency at which resonance occurs can be calculated by using the following formula:

$$f_o = \frac{1}{2\pi\sqrt{LC}} \text{ or } f_o = \frac{.159}{\sqrt{LC}}$$

Resonance may be achieved by changing the values of either L or C independently or combined when a single frequency is applied. With fixed values of L and C, circuit resonance is also fixed. An indication of resonance occurs when the measured voltage across a resistor is at highest value.

In this experiment, you will test a resonant circuit with a single value of ac applied. The inductor part of the circuit is varied by physically changing the laminated core of the coil. You will be able to observe resonance by making various tests. You will plot voltage values of the circuit on a graph to show the effect of the resonant condition. Resonant circuits are commonly used in tuning applications for communication circuits.

### EXPERIMENT OBJECTIVES

As a result of this laboratory experience, you should be able to accomplish the following:
1. Construct a series LC circuit.
2. Observe the point of resonance by changes in lamp intensity, voltage measurements and oscilloscope waveforms.
3. Measure voltage values in the series LC circuit and plot resonance on a graph.

### REFERENCE

Gerrish and Dugger, ELECTRICITY AND ELECTRONICS, Chapter 8, pages 111 to 113.

### MATERIALS AND EQUIPMENT

1 — Volt-ohm-milliampere (VOM) meter
1 — 6.3V, 60 Hz source
1 — Oscilloscope
1 — 25 $\mu$ F, 50V dc capacitor
1 — Coil No. 1 of transformer assembly (Hickok coil - 3320-383)
1 — No. 47 lamp and socket
1 — SPST toggle switch

### PROCEDURE

1. Connect series resonant circuit, Fig. 8-1-1.
2. Turn on circuit switch and slide laminated core of coil No. 1 in and out of coil. There should be a noticeable point where lamp is at its brightest level. This represents point of resonance. What actually occurs in this circuit at point of resonance? _____

_____

3. Prepare a VOM to measure ac voltage and connect it across lamp. Adjust laminated core of coil No. 1 to produce highest voltage reading. Record this measured value as $E_R$ volts on diagram.

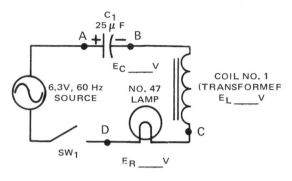

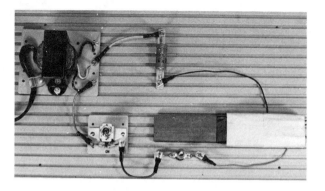

Fig. 8-1-1

4. Measure and record capacitor voltage $E_C$ and inductor voltage $E_L$. Ideally, these voltage values should be equal at resonance.

5. Using measured values of $E_L$, $E_C$ and $E_R$, make a vector diagram of resonant circuit on graph A in Fig. 8-1-2.

6. Since value of $E_L$ and $E_C$ are in opposite directions on graph A, they can be combined by subtracting smallest value from largest value. Add values of $E_R$ and combined $E_L - E_C$ value to graph B. Ideally, graph B should display only $E_R$ if circuit and graph are in a perfect resonant condition. What does this indicate about combined opposition to ac at point of resonance? _____

_____

7. Prepare oscilloscope for operation so that it will display one or two sine waves when connected to 6.3V, 60 Hz source. Switch oscilloscope to line sync or a line trigger source position.

8. Adjust horizontal position control so that it causes trace to move to right somewhat. You should be able to see beginning edge of ac waveform being displayed.

9. Connect common probe of oscilloscope to circuit point D and vertical probe to point C in Fig. 8-1-1. Slide laminated core in and out of coil while observing waveform. At resonance, waveform will produce largest vertical trace. What other change in wave occurs when laminated core is moved?

_____

_____

10. Adjust laminated core to resonance again. With common probe of oscilloscope connected to point A and vertical probe to

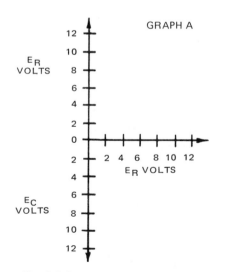

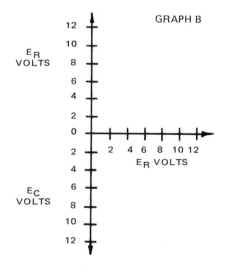

Fig. 8-1-2

test point B, observe waveform. Note starting point of wave at left side of display. Make a sketch of this wave in provided space of Fig. 8-1-3.

13. Turn off circuit switch, oscilloscope and power supply. Detach oscilloscope leads. Disconnect circuit and return all parts to storage cabinet.

$E_C$
WAVEFORM _____

$E_L$
WAVEFORM _____

Fig. 8-1-3

11. Remove oscilloscope probes from capacitor and connect common probe to point B and vertical probe to point C. Observe waveform. Pay particular attention to starting point of wave at left side of display. Make a sketch of this wave in provided space of Fig. 8-1-3.
12. How would you describe phase relationship of two waves of Fig. 8-1-3? _____

_____

**QUESTIONS**
1. Why is the current flow greatest at the point of resonance in a series resonant circuit?
2. What is the resonant frequency of a 10 mH coil and a 5 $\mu$ F capacitor?
3. Draw a vector diagram of a series resonant circuit with an $X_L$ of 120 ohms, an $X_C$ of 100 ohms and an R of 50 ohms. What condition does this indicate about the current?

## INTRODUCTION

In a series resonant circuit at a specific frequency, the value of $X_L$ cancels the value of $X_C$. When this occurs, opposition offered to the resonant frequency is determined only by circuit resistance. Therefore, the total impedance of the circuit drops to a minimum value. As a result, current flow of the circuit rises to a maximum level. These characteristics of the series resonant circuit distinguish it from other resonant circuits.

When a series resonant circuit is not in its resonant condition, $X_L$ and $X_C$ are unequal. At frequencies lower than resonance, capacitive reactance becomes the dominant reactive component. Voltage appearing across this part of the circuit is significantly larger than $X_L$ or R.

At frequencies higher than the resonant frequency, inductive reactance becomes the dominant reactive component. Voltage appearing across $X_L$ is significantly larger than that of $X_C$ or R. The resulting current flow through the circuit is reduced according to the amount of increased reactance.

In this experiment, you will construct a series RCL circuit and measure the voltages across each component at resonance and above or below resonance. Resonant circuits have broad application in the communications area of electronics.

### EXPERIMENT OBJECTIVES

As a result of this laboratory experience, you should be able to accomplish the following:
1. Construct a series RCL circuit.
2. Measure voltages across the inductor, capacitor and resistor in the circuit.
3. Observe characteristics of a functioning resonant circuit.

### REFERENCE

Gerrish and Dugger, ELECTRICITY AND ELECTRONICS, Chapter 8, pages 112 to 114.

### MATERIALS AND EQUIPMENT

1 — Volt-ohm-milliampere (VOM) meter
1 — Signal generator
1 — 0.01 $\mu$F, 100V dc capacitor
1 — 0.22 $\mu$F, 100V dc capacitor
1 — 25 mH inductor
1 — 1K, 1/4 watt resistor
1 — SPST toggle switch

### PROCEDURE

1. Construct series resonant test circuit as in Fig. 8-2-1.

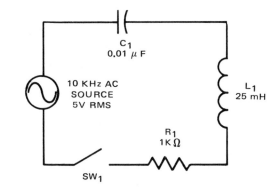

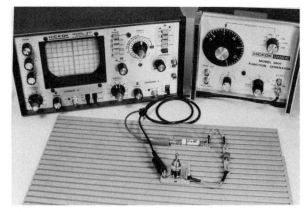

Fig. 8-2-1

2. Turn on signal generator and adjust it to produce a sine wave of approximately 10 KHz. Adjust signal level to an output of 5V as read on an ac scale of VOM.

3. Calculate resonant frequency ($f_o$) of circuit, using the following formula:

$$f_o = \frac{.159}{\sqrt{LC}}$$

$$f_o = \underline{\hspace{2cm}} \text{KHz}$$

4. Connect VOM across R to measure ac circuit output voltage. Adjust frequency of signal generator above and below 10 KHz to find resonant frequency point. A definite peak voltage indication will appear across R at resonance. There should be a noticeable decrease in voltage above and below resonant point.

5. Resonant point indicated on signal generator dial is _____ KHz.

6. With VOM, measure and record ac voltage across capacitor, inductor and resistor at resonance. $E_c$ is _____ volts. $E_L$ is _____ volts. $E_R$ is _____ volts. Ideally, value of $E_c$ should equal or be very close to value of $E_L$ at resonance.

7. Adjust signal generator to a frequency below resonant point by approximately 1 KHz. Measure and record voltage across C, L and R. $E_c$ is _____ volts. $E_L$ is _____ volts. $E_R$ is _____ volts. Largest voltage indicates dominant reactive component of circuit in this condition. Below resonance _____ _____ greatest.

8. Adjust signal generator to a frequency above resonant point by approximately 1 KHz. Measure and record voltage across C, L and R with VOM. $E_c$ is _____ volts. $E_L$ is _____ volts. $E_R$ is _____ volts. Dominant reactive component above resonance is _____ _____.

9. If time permits, remove 0.01 $\mu$F capacitor from circuit and connect a 0.22 $\mu$F capacitor in its place. With a larger capacitor, resonant frequency point of circuit will be _____ (higher or lower) than previous circuit.

10. Using signal generator and VOM, determine resonant frequency of modified circuit. Does your prediction agree with tested frequency?

11. Turn off circuit switch and signal generator. Disconnect circuit and return all components to storage cabinet.

## QUESTIONS

1. If the inductor of the first series resonant circuit is changed to a larger value, the point of resonance would _____

2. If $E_L = E_c$ at resonance, why does $E_R$ increase?

3. Why does the value of $E_R$ drop above and below resonance?

# Experiment 8-3 PARALLEL RESONANT PRINCIPLES

## INTRODUCTION

When an inductor and a capacitor are connected in parallel and ac is applied, resonance will occur at a certain frequency. At this frequency, current flow in the $X_L$ branch lags behind the applied source voltage by approximately 90 deg. Current flow in the $X_C$ branch, on the other hand, leads the source voltage by 90 deg. The combined effect of these conditions cancels the current flow in both branches of the circuit.

The characteristics of a parallel resonant circuit show high impedance and minimum current flow at the point of resonance. Above or below the point of resonance, impedance is at a minimum and current flow rises to a maximum level. Parallel resonant circuits are commonly used in radio transmitter circuits to tune the final amplifier stage to resonance. This condition is achieved by adjusting the tuned circuit to produce a dip in the plate current meter reading.

In this experiment, you will test a parallel resonant circuit that has single frequency ac applied. The inductor part of this circuit is

1. Construct a parallel RCL circuit.
2. Vary the inductance in the circuit and note how this affects resonance.
3. Observe the point of resonance in the circuit by changes in lamp intensity, voltage measurements and oscilloscope waveforms.

## REFERENCE

Gerrish and Dugger, ELECTRICITY AND ELECTRONICS, Chapter 8, pages 114 to 117.

## MATERIALS AND EQUIPMENT

1 — Volt-ohm-milliampere (VOM) meter
1 — 6.3V, 60 Hz source
1 — Oscilloscope
1 — 10 $\mu$ F, 25V dc capacitor
1 — Coil No. 1 of transformer assembly, with laminated core
1 — No. 47 lamp with socket
1 — SPST toggle switch
2 — 20 ohm, 1/4 watt resistors of decade module or separately mounted resistors

## PROCEDURE

1. Connect parallel resonant circuit as in Fig. 8-3-1.

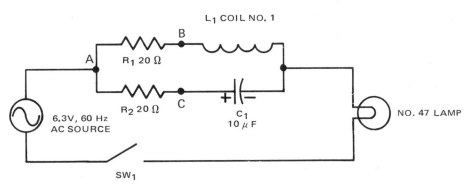

Fig. 8-3-1

varied by physically changing the position of the laminated core of the coil. You will be able to observe resonance by making various tests.

## EXPERIMENT OBJECTIVES

As a result of this laboratory experience, you should be able to accomplish the following:

2. Turn on circuit switch and slide laminated core of coil No. 1 in and out of coil. There should be a noticeable point where lamp is adjusted to its dimmest level. This represents point of resonance. What actually occurs in circuit at resonance to cause the lamp to dim? _____

3. Prepare VOM to measure ac voltage and connect it across lamp. Adjust laminated core of coil No. 1 to produce highest voltage reading. Then, adjust it to resonance. Change or total range of voltage is _____ to _____ volts.

4. Adjust laminated core of coil No. 1 while observing voltmeter. Explain how meter value "dips" at resonance. _____

_____

5. At resonance, current flowing in $X_L$ branch

sync or line trigger should be used.

8. Adjust horizontal position control so that it causes trace to move to right somewhat. You should be able to see beginning edge of ac waveform.

9. Connect common or ground of oscilloscope to point A and vertical probe to point B. Notice polarity of beginning edge of waveform.

10. Make a sketch of observed wave at points A-B in space provided in Fig. 8-3-2.

A-B
WAVEFORM _____

A-C
WAVEFORM _____

Fig. 8-3-2

is lagging applied source voltage while current in $X_C$ branch is leading source voltage. These currents cancel each other which causes a large reduction in output current. This effect can be shown by measuring voltage across $R_1$ and $R_2$ in respective branches of parallel circuit:

$E_{R_1}$ = _____ volts

$E_{R_2}$ = _____ volts

Ideally, at resonance, $E_{R_1}$ should equal $E_{R_2}$.

6. Calculate current flow in inductive branch and capacitive branch of the circuit by using:

$$\frac{E_{R_1}}{R_1} \text{ and } \frac{E_{R_2}}{R_2}$$

$I_{R_1}$ = _____ amps

$I_{R_2}$ = _____ amps

7. Prepare oscilloscope for operation so that it will display one or two sine waves when connected to 6.3V, 60 Hz source. Line

11. Move vertical probe of oscilloscope to point C to observe waveform across $R_2$. Note polarity of beginning edge of wave.

12. Make a sketch of observed wave at points A-C in space provided in Fig. 8-3-2. What is the phase relationship of two waveforms?

_____

_____

13. Since a resistor does not alter phase relationship of a circuit, what is phase of respective current flow through $R_1$ and $R_2$? _____

_____

14. Turn off switch and disconnect circuit. Return all parts to storage cabinet.

## QUESTIONS

1. At resonance, what is the relationship of ac flow in the inductive and capacitive branches of a parallel connected circuit?

2. What is the resonant frequency of a $1 \mu$ F capacitor and a 5 H inductor?

3. What is the relationship of current and impedance of a parallel resonant circuit?

# Experiment 8-4  PARALLEL RESONANT CIRCUITS

## INTRODUCTION

In a parallel resonant circuit, $X_L = X_C$ at resonance. As a result, current flow in the $X_L$ leg or branch lags behind the applied voltage by as much as 90 deg. Current flow in the $X_C$ branch causes a similar reaction but leads the applied source voltage by as much as 90 deg. Therefore, the combined current flow of this type of circuit is held to a minimum level because of this cancelling effect. With current flow at a minimum, total impedance must be at a maximum level when resonance occurs. At frequencies above or below resonance, current flow is high and impedance is low.

In this experiment, you will build a parallel resonant circuit and measure the voltage across components at resonance and above or below resonance. You will see how certain frequency signals can be selected or rejected by tuned

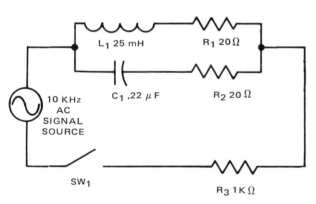

Fig. 8-4-1

circuits. The operating principle of this type of circuit is commonly used to "dip the final power amplifier" of a radio frequency transmitter.

## EXPERIMENT OBJECTIVES

As a result of this laboratory experience, you should be able to accomplish the following:
1. Construct a parallel RCL circuit.
2. Measure voltages in the parallel RCL circuit.
3. Observe how parallel resonant circuit can select certain frequencies and reject others.

## REFERENCE

Gerrish and Dugger, ELECTRICITY AND ELECTRONICS, Chapter 8, pages 114 to 117.

## MATERIALS AND EQUIPMENT

1 — Signal generator
1 — Volt-ohm-milliampere (VOM) meter
1 — 25 mH inductor
1 — 0.22 $\mu$ F, 100V dc capacitor
1 — 0.01 $\mu$ F, 100V dc capacitor
1 — SPST toggle switch
2 — 20 ohm, 1/4 watt resistors of decade module or separately mounted
1 — 1K, 1/4 watt resistor of decade module or separately mounted

## PROCEDURE

1. Construct parallel resonant test circuit as in Fig. 8-4-1.

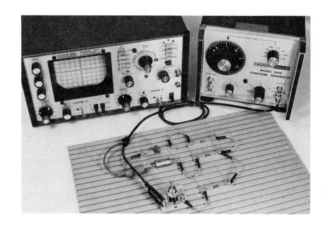

2. Turn on signal generator and adjust it to produce a sine wave of approximately 10 KHz. Adjust signal level to an output of 3V ac as read on VOM.
3. Calculate resonant frequency ($f_o$) of circuit, using the following formula:

$$f_o = \frac{.159}{\sqrt{LC}}$$

Or, use nomograph chart in Fig. 8-24, page 125 of text.

$f_o =$ _____ KHz

4. Connect VOM across $R_3$ to measure circuit output voltage. Adjust signal generator frequency above and below calculated resonant frequency point. Resonance is indicated by lowest reading or a pronounced dip in output voltage. As a general rule, the output voltage will rise above and below resonant point.

5. Resonant frequency point indicated on signal generator dial is _____ KHz.

6. Measure and record ac voltage across $R_1$ and $R_2$:

$E_{R_1} =$ _____ volts

$E_{R_2} =$ _____ volts

Ideally, $E_{R_1}$ should equal $E_{R_2}$ if proper resonant frequency has been selected.

7. Adjust frequency of signal source to approximately 10 KHz above resonant frequency. Predict which leg of circuit _____ (inductive or capacitive) will offer highest reactance to this frequency. Explain why this occurs. _____

8. With VOM, measure and record voltage across $R_1$ and $R_2$:

$E_{R_1} =$ _____ volts

$E_{R_2} =$ _____ volts

9. An increase in frequency causes a parallel resonant circuit to have a larger current flow in _____ (L or C) leg because _____ ($X_L$ or $X_C$) is smaller. This is demonstrated by larger voltage reading across _____ ($R_1$ or $R_2$).

10. Adjust frequency of signal source to approximately 10 KHz below resonant frequency. Predict which leg of circuit _____ (inductive or capacitive) will offer highest reactance to this frequency. Explain why this occurs. _____

11. With VOM, measure and record voltage across $R_1$ and $R_2$:

$E_{R_1} =$ _____ volts

$E_{R_2} =$ _____ volts

12. A decrease in frequency causes a parallel resonant circuit to have a larger current flow in _____ (L or C) leg because _____ ($X_L$ or $X_C$) is smaller. This is demonstrated by a larger voltage reading across _____ ($R_1$ or $R_2$).

13. If time permits, remove 0.22 $\mu$F capacitor from circuit and replace it with a 0.01 $\mu$F capacitor. With a smaller capacitor in circuit, resonant frequency will be _____ (higher or lower) than previous circuit.

14. Using signal generator and VOM, determine resonant frequency of modified circuit. Does your prediction agree with measured frequency?

15. Turn off circuit switch and signal source. Disconnect circuit and return all components to storage cabinet.

## QUESTIONS

1. Explain the relationship of impedance (Z) and current (I) of a parallel resonant circuit.
2. Explain the relationship of $X_L$ and $X_C$, $I_L$ and $I_C$, $E_{R_1}$ and $E_{R_2}$ at a frequency above resonance.
3. Explain the relationship of $X_L$ and $X_C$, $I_L$ and $I_C$, $E_{R_1}$ and $E_{R_2}$ at a frequency below resonance.

# Experiment 8-5  FILTER CIRCUITS

## INTRODUCTION

Resistors and capacitors are in frequent use in filter circuits to pass certain signal components and reject others. If a circuit contained both ac and dc components, the ac component could be selected by connecting a capacitor in series with a resistor. Since dc is blocked by a capacitor, only the ac component will appear across the resistor.

Another form of filtration is achieved by connecting a resistor and capacitor in parallel. In this type of circuit, the ac component is bypassed around the resistor, leaving only dc to pass through the resistor. A common design rule calls for a capacitor with a capacitive reactance ($X_c$) ten times less than the resistor value. Bypass applications are commonly found in audio and radio frequency circuits.

In this experiment, a simple filter circuit is used to separate the ac component from a circuit that contains both ac and dc. In addition, a bypass circuit will be constructed and tested to demonstrate the bypassing principle. You will learn how filtering circuits are used to select specific parts of a combined ac-dc signal and reject others.

## EXPERIMENT OBJECTIVES

As a result of this laboratory experience, you should be able to accomplish the following:
1. Construct a simple filter circuit.
2. Observe how a filter circuit passes certain signals and rejects others.

## REFERENCE

Gerrish and Dugger, ELECTRICITY AND ELECTRONICS, Chapter 8, pages 119 to 122.

## MATERIALS AND EQUIPMENT

1 – Volt-ohm-milliampere (VOM) meter
1 – 6.2V, 60 Hz source
1 – Variable dc power supply
1 – 680 $\mu$F, 50V dc capacitor on power supply module
1 – 25 $\mu$F, 50V dc capacitor
2 – 200 ohm, 1/4 watt resistors of decade module

1 – 5K, 1/4 watt resistor of decade module or a 4.7K, 1/4 watt resistor
1 – SPST toggle switch

## PROCEDURE

1. Connect dc filter circuit as in Fig. 8-5-1.

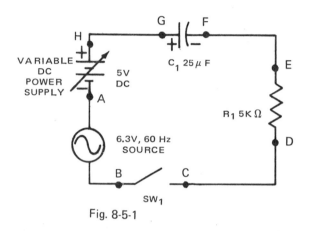

Fig. 8-5-1

2. Prepare VOM to measure dc and connect it across variable dc power source. With circuit switch off, turn on dc power supply and adjust it to produce 5V dc.

3. Change VOM to measure ac and connect it across test points A-B. A-B is _____ volts ac.

4. Measure and record ac voltage at test points C-G. C-G is _____ volts ac. Change VOM to measure dc. Measure and record voltage at points C-G. C-G is _____ volts dc. How would you describe voltage present at test points C-G. _____

_____

5. Measure and record dc voltage at test points G-F. Be certain to observe dc polarity. G-F is _____volts dc. Change VOM to measure ac and connect it across G-F. Voltage at points G-F is _____ volts ac.

6. Measure and record ac voltage and dc voltage at test points E-D. The ac voltage at E-D is _____ volts. The dc voltage at E-D is _____ volts. What does this demonstrate about the circuit? _____

7. Turn off circuit switch and change circuit of Fig. 8-5-1 to conform with Fig. 8-5-2.

8. Turn on circuit switch and measure dc

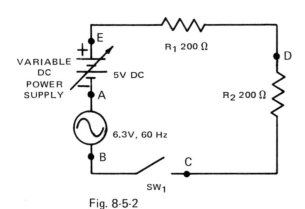

VARIABLE DC POWER SUPPLY

E

$R_1$ 200 Ω

5V DC

A

6.3V, 60 Hz

B

D

$R_2$ 200 Ω

C

$SW_1$

Fig. 8-5-2

voltage at various test points. A-E is _____ volts. E-C is _____ volts. C-D is _____ volts. D-E is _____ volts.

9. Prepare VOM to measure ac voltage. Measure and record ac voltage at various test points. A-B is _____ volts. C-E is _____ volts. C-D is _____ volts. D-E is _____ volts.

10. Since $R_1$ and $R_2$ are equal, amount of ac and dc voltage developed across these resistors should be _____

11. Turn off circuit switch and connect a 680 $\mu$F capacitor across $R_1$. Positive terminal of capacitor must be connected to point E and negative terminal to point D.

12. Turn on circuit switch. Measure and record dc voltage at various test points. A-E is _____ volts. E-C is _____ volts. C-E is _____ volts. D-E is _____ volts.

13. Prepare VOM to measure ac voltage. Measure and record ac voltage at various test points. A-B is _____ volts. C-E is _____ volts. C-D is _____ volts. D-E is _____ volts.

14. Comparing measured dc voltages of steps 8 and 12, what can be said about dc component passing through circuit? _____

_____

15. Comparing measured ac voltages of steps 9 and 13, what can be said about ac component passing through circuit? _____

_____

16. Turn off circuit switch and power supply. Disconnect circuit and return all parts to storage cabinet.

## QUESTIONS

1. Why does only ac appear across resistor in circuit in Fig. 8-5-1 when input contains both ac and dc components?
2. Modification of Fig. 8-5-2 with a capacitor across $R_1$ demonstrates what filtering principles?
3. The capacitive reactance ($X_c$) of the modified Fig. 8-5-2 circuit is _____ ohms.
4. As a general design rule, the $X_c$ of a bypass capacitor should be at least 10 times smaller than the resistor it is bypassing. Does this rule apply to the modified circuit of Fig. 8-5-2?

## INTRODUCTION

In communication applications, specific filters are used to transfer frequencies above or below a certain range into other existing circuits. This type of filter is commonly called a "pass filter." Low-pass filters are designed to pass all frequencies below a certain level and reject frequencies above this level. High-pass filters, by comparison, transfer all frequencies above its lower pass limit and reject those below it. Pass filters are commonly used to reject noise, hum and interfering signals.

A low-pass filter contains a series inductor with a capacitor connected in parallel with the load. Low frequency ac easily passes through the inductor and is applied to the load. Capacitor connected across the load bypasses high frequency ac around the load. Low-pass filters pass all frequencies from dc to the upper pass frequency level.

A high-pass filter contains a series capacitor with an inductor connected in parallel with the load. Capacitive reactance of the series capacitor offers a high level of opposition to all low frequencies. Above the pass frequency, $X_c$ becomes low and permits frequencies to pass with a minimum of opposition. With the parallel inductor connected across the load resistor, any low frequency that passes through the capacitor is bypassed around the load. Through this type of LC circuit, only frequencies above the low frequency pass level are applied to $R_L$.

In this experiment, you will build and test a low-pass filter and apply different frequencies from an ac signal source. Next, you will use an oscilloscope to observe the output of the filter across the load resistor. Then, you will build a high-pass filter, test its output and observe where the output signal is reduced or attenuated to half power. Pass filters are used in numerous communication electronic circuits.

## EXPERIMENT OBJECTIVES

As a result of this laboratory experience, you should be able to accomplish the following:
1. Construct a basic low-pass filter and test its operation.
2. Construct a basic high-pass filter and test its output.
3. Observe application of these filter circuits.

## REFERENCE

Gerrish and Dugger, ELECTRICITY AND ELECTRONICS, Chapter 8, pages 122 and 123.

## MATERIALS AND EQUIPMENT

1 — Variable frequency ac signal generator
1 — Oscilloscope
1 — 0.01 $\mu$F, 100V dc capacitor
1 — 0.22 $\mu$F, 100V dc capacitor
1 — 25 mH inductor
1 — 5K, 1/4 watt resistor of decade module or a 4700 ohm, 1/4 watt mounted resistor
1 — SPST toggle switch

## PROCEDURE

1. Construct low-pass filter circuit shown in Fig. 8-6-1. Use 0.01 $\mu$F capacitor ($C_1$) first.

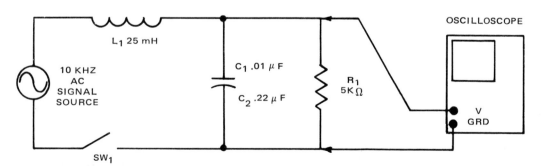

Fig. 8-6-1

2. Turn on ac signal source and oscilloscope. Adjust signal source to produce a sine wave frequency of approximately 10 KHz.

higher pass filter circuit shown in Fig. 8-6-2. Use 0.01 $\mu$ F capacitor ($C_1$) in circuit first.

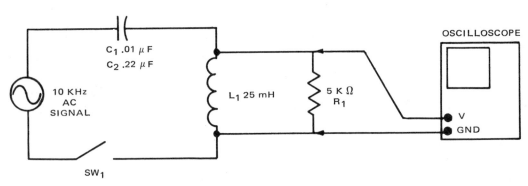

Fig. 8-6-2

3. Adjust oscilloscope to produce a vertical display of 2 cm in 2V/cm range. Only vertical amplitude of display is considered in this measurement. Horizontal time/cm should be set to slow sweep rate of 1 m sec/cm or 1 KHz. A 2 cm vertical display is considered as reference output of test circuit.

4. Increase frequency of signal source while observing oscilloscope display. There should be a point where applied frequency causes oscilloscope to produce a display less than 2 cm. Adjust frequency to a precise point where 2 cm vertical amplitude drops 30 percent (to 1.7 cm). Signals producing an output less than this are considered to be attenuated or reduced to half power. This is also called the high frequency cutoff point of filter circuit. Cutoff point is _____ KHz.

5. Adjust frequency of signal source to frequencies of a lower value. How do they respond?

6. Turn off circuit switch and remove capacitor from circuit. Replace it with 0.22 $\mu$ F capacitor ($C_2$).

7. Turn on circuit switch and determine high frequency cutoff of circuit, using procedure outlined in steps 3 and 4. High frequency cutoff of circuit (with $C_2$) is _____ KHz.

8. Turn off circuit switch and construct

9. Turn on circuit switch and adjust ac signal source to produce a 10 KHz reference frequency for 2 cm of vertical deflection.

10. Adjust frequency of signal source to frequencies in excess of reference frequency. How does output display respond?

11. Reduce frequency of signal source to values lower than reference frequency. There is a specific frequency point where amplitude of signal across $R_L$ drops. When it drops 30 percent (1.7 cm) of vertical deflection, this is considered as low-pass frequency limit. Low-pass frequency limit is _____ KHz.

12. Turn off circuit switch and remove capacitor from circuit. Connect 0.22 $\mu$ F capacitor ($C_2$) in its place. Using same procedure outlined in steps 10 and 11, determine low-pass frequency limit. Low-pass frequency limit is _____ KHz.

13. Turn off circuit switch, signal source and oscilloscope. Disconnect circuit and return all parts to storage cabinet.

## QUESTIONS

1. What causes the low-pass filter circuit of Fig. 8-6-1 to reach a high frequency cutoff point?

2. What causes the high-pass filter circuit of Fig. 8-6-2 to only pass frequencies above the low-pass frequency limit?

3. What is changed in a low-pass filter to increase its pass frequency?

# Chapter 9
# ELECTRIC MOTORS

## Experiment 9-1   PERMANENT MAGNET MOTORS

### INTRODUCTION

A motor is a device that accepts electrical energy from a source and produces rotating mechanical energy. In order to operate, an electric motor must have a stationary magnetic field and a rotating member that has a magnetic field. Interaction between these two magnetic fields causes the rotating member to move or rotate within the structure.

In a permanent magnet motor, the magnets form the stationary field. An electromagnetic field rotates. Normally, the electromagnet is called an "armature." Electrical energy is supplied to the armature through brush contacts that ride on a split ring commutator. As the armature rotates, it causes the polarity of its coil to change when reaching a certain position. Through this action, the armature coil creates a repelling force when it is positioned near the permanent magnets. This force repels the coil, forcing it to move. After the next half revolution, the armature changes polarity again, thus causing continuous rotation.

In this experiment, you will build a permanent magnet motor. While this device has limited application today, the principles demonstrated are very basic to all motor operations.

### EXPERIMENT OBJECTIVES

As a result of this laboratory experience, you should be able to accomplish the following:

1. Construct a permanent magnet motor using a St. Louis motor-generator unit.
2. Experiment with the basic principles of polarity, commutation and direction of rotation of this device.

### REFERENCE

Gerrish and Dugger, ELECTRICITY AND ELECTRONICS, Chapter 9, pages 127 to 130.

### MATERIALS AND EQUIPMENT

1 — Volt-ohm-milliampere (VOM) meter
1 — St. Louis motor unit (Hickok)
1 — Variable dc power source
1 — SPST toggle switch
1 — Compass

### PROCEDURE

1. Remove a St. Louis motor unit from storage and position it at your work station.
2. Momentarily remove two permanent magnets from spring holders and set magnets aside.
3. Place split ring commutator armature in armature holder and adjust knurled nut and top tension screw so that armature turns freely (without wobbling) between two pivot points.
4. Position two brushes so that they ride on commutator with a minimum of pressure.
5. Prepare VOM to measure resistance and connect it to two brush connection bolts. If brushes are properly positioned, there should be an indication of resistance when armature is rotated. Resistance should be constant except when gap between commutator segments is reached.
6. Adjust brushes so that they make contact with a minimum of friction. It is difficult for this motor to overcome large amounts of commutator friction.

7. Connect 5V dc from variable dc power source to two brush holder bolts as shown in Fig. 9-1-1. Turn on circuit switch and slowly rotate armature. Note and describe action of commutator and brush assembly.

_____

_____

_____

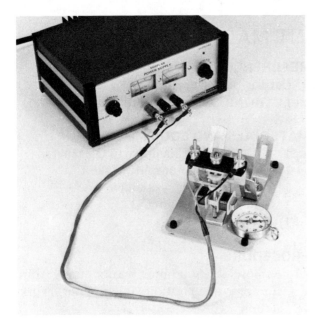

Fig. 9-1-1

8. Place a compass near right hand side of armature. See Fig. 9-1-1. Rotate armature one complete revolution. What is polarity of armature on right side? _____ How does rotation affect polarity? _____

_____

9. Place compass near left side of armature. Rotate armature one complete revolution while observing influence of armature on compass. Describe polarity of armature at left side. _____

10. Turn off circuit switch and slide permanent magnets into spring holder clips. Left magnet should be of south (S) polarity; right magnet should be of north (N) polarity. Position magnets as close to armature without touching it during rotation.

11. Turn on power source and circuit switch.

12. As a general rule, this motor requires a push to get it started. Try pushing it first in one direction, then in other until rotation occurs. If it does not run, disconnect power supply and test armature brush connections for resistance and contact friction. Permanent magnets must be of opposite polarity and positioned near armature. Disconnect ohmmeter and apply 5V dc. Try starting procedure again.

13. Direction of armature rotation is _____ (clockwise or counterclockwise).

14. Turn off circuit switch and reverse polarity of dc power supply. Then turn on switch and test direction of rotation. Rotation is _____ (clockwise or counterclockwise).

15. Turn off circuit switch and reverse polarity of two magnets. Then, turn on switch and test direction of rotation. How does polarity of field influence direction of rotation?

_____

_____.

16. Turn off circuit switch and power supply. Disconnect motor unit and return all parts to storage.

## QUESTIONS

1. What determines the direction of rotation of a PM motor?
2. What determines the rotational speed of a PM motor?
3. What does the split ring commutator actually do in the operation of a PM motor?

## INTRODUCTION

A series dc motor has a field coil and armature coils connected in series. Current flow from dc source finds only one complete path through the entire motor circuit. Total current flow is based on the combined resistance of the field coil and the armature coils. Current flow is the same throughout the entire circuit.

A series dc motor has the ability to start under heavy loads. Generally, when the armature speed is kept slow, counter electromotive force (counter emf) is reduced. The field and armature windings usually are made of large size wire to accomodate the heavy current flow developed by the motor. As the speed of the motor increases, its counter emf builds up. This decreases line current which, in turn, reduces the motor's turning power or torque.

In this experiment, you will build a series connected dc motor. You will become familiar with a wound field coil, test its polarity and see how this polarity influences the operation of the motor. You will also test the current flow of this motor and reverse its direction of rotation. The series motor built in this experiment is used primarily to show basic operating principles. Typical motors of the series type do not resemble this laboratory motor at all. Applications of series wound dc motors are found in automobile starting motors, electric trains and cranes.

## EXPERIMENT OBJECTIVES

As a result of this laboratory experience, you should be able to accomplish the following:
1. Construct a series dc motor from the St. Louis motor-generator unit.
2. Test the polarity of a wound field coil and observe how polarity affects the operation of the motor.
3. Measure the current flow in the series motor.

## REFERENCE

Gerrish and Dugger, ELECTRICITY AND ELECTRONICS, Chapter 9, pages 131 to 133.

## MATERIALS AND EQUIPMENT

1 — Volt-ohm-milliampere (VOM) meter
1 — Variable dc power supply
1 — St. Louis motor unit (Hickok)
1 — SPST toggle switch
1 — Compass

## PROCEDURE

1. Remove St. Louis motor unit from storage and place it on your workbench. Remove two permanent magnets from spring clip holders and set them aside.
2. Before attaching electromagnetic field coil to motor unit, connect a variable power supply set for 2V dc. See Fig. 9-2-1.

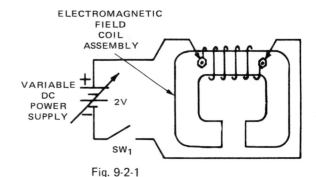

Fig. 9-2-1

3. Look at field coil and note direction that coil is wound on core. With negative side of source connected to right terminal and positive side connected to left terminal, determine polarity of coil using left hand rule of magnetism. (See page 53 of text.)
4. Mark predicted polarity of coil at ends of core.
5. Turn on circuit switch and determine polarity of coil by placing a compass near each end of core. Does your left hand rule prediction compare with compass observation? _____
6. Turn off circuit switch and attach field coil to motor base unit as shown in Fig. 9-2-2. Turn spring clip magnet holders inward to make room for field coil. Bolt field coil into place.
7. Connect power supply to motor and turn on circuit switch. If motor does not start

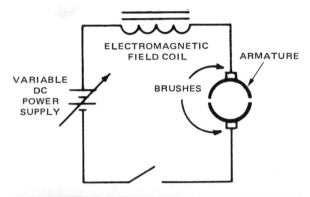

Fig. 9-2-2

by itself, you may need to push armature. If brush friction is too great, motor will not operate properly. Direction of rotation is _____

8. After motor has been running for a minute, momentarily increase voltage to 15V dc. What influence does this have upon motor speed? _____

9. Turn off circuit switch and reverse polarity of dc power supply. Then, turn on circuit switch and test operation of motor. What influence does this have upon operation of motor? _____

10. Turn off circuit switch and reverse two

leads connected to brush assembly. Then, turn on circuit switch and test operation of motor. What influence does this change have upon operation of motor? _____

_____

11. Turn off circuit switch and reverse two leads connected to field coil. Then, turn on circuit switch and test operation of motor. What influence does this change have upon operation of motor? _____

_____

12. Turn off circuit switch. Prepare VOM to measure dc, starting at a high value. Insert meter between brush assembly and field coil on right side of motor. Turn on circuit. Measure and record current flow. Current flow is _____ amps.

13. Turn off circuit switch and remove VOM. Return connecting wire between field coil and brush assembly. Using same procedure, measure current flow between positive side of source and left field coil connection. Current flow is _____ amps.

14. Describe current flow observed at these two test points. _____

_____

15. Turn off circuit switch and power supply. Disconnect motor and return it to storage.

## QUESTIONS

1. How can you change the direction of rotation of a series wound dc motor?
2. What conclusion can be made regarding current flow of the motor tested in this experiment?
3. In the following space, make a symbol drawing of a series wound dc motor. Show the relationship of the field coil and the armature. Label each part.

# Experiment 9-3  SHUNT DC MOTORS

## INTRODUCTION

Shunt motors have the field coil and armature coil connected in parallel with the dc energy source. Current flow from the source divides into two distinct paths. One path is through the field coil; the second is through the armature. Total current flow is the sum of the individual currents in each path. Total or combined resistance of this type of motor is less than the resistance of either the field coil or armature by itself.

Shunt motors generally are classified as constant speed devices. Applications for this type of motor require constant speed under changing loads. When this motor operates without a load, there is a rather small current flow because the counter electromotive force (counter emf) is nearly equal to the source voltage. As the load is increased, armature speed is reduced which, in turn, reduces counter emf. As a result, the torque of the motor increases, which causes a corresponding increase in speed. Through this changing action, shunt motors maintain a rather constant running speed.

In this experiment, you will build a shunt wound dc motor with the St. Louis motor-generator unit. You will become familiar with a simple motor testing procedure, change rotational direction and alter current flow into the field coil to see how added resistance alters motor operation.

The shunt wound motor in this experiment is used to demonstrate primary operating principles of a specific type of dc motor. Typical shunt motors of the commercial type resemble this laboratory unit only in operating theory.

## EXPERIMENT OBJECTIVES

As a result of this laboratory experience, you should be able to accomplish the following:
1. Construct a shunt wound dc motor using the St. Louis motor-generator unit.
2. Observe the basic operating principles of the shunt wound dc motor.
3. Test the shunt wound dc motor and observe how to change the direction of rotation in the motor.

## REFERENCE

Gerrish and Dugger, ELECTRICITY AND ELECTRONICS, Chapter 9, pages 132 to 134.

## MATERIALS AND EQUIPMENT

1 — Volt-ohm-milliampere (VOM) meter
1 — Variable dc power supply
1 — St. Louis motor unit (Hickok)
2 — SPST toggle switches
1 — No. 47 lamp with socket

## PROCEDURE

1. Remove St. Louis motor unit from storage and place it on your workbench. Remove two permanent magnets from spring clip holders and set them aside. Turn spring clip holders inward to make room for field coil. Place field coil mounting bolts in place and attach nuts to bolts on bottom side of motor base.
2. Prepare VOM to measure resistance and connect it across terminals of brush assembly. Rotate split ring commutator armature while observing circuit continuity. Armature resistance is _____ ohms.
3. Rotate armature and adjust brush tension to a minimum level while still making contact. This is a very important adjustment.
4. Measure resistance of field coil with VOM. Field coil resistance is _____ ohms.
5. Connect field coil terminal and brush terminal on right side of motor by means of a connecting wire. Likewise, connect brush terminal and field coil terminal on left side of motor, using a jumper wire. With VOM, measure total resistance of field coil and armature in parallel. Motor resistance is _____ ohms.
6. Connect variable dc power supply and circuit switch to motor as shown in Fig. 9-3-1.
7. Turn on circuit switch and test operation of motor. It may be necessary to push armature to get motor started. Direction of rotation is _____
8. Turn off circuit switch and reverse polarity

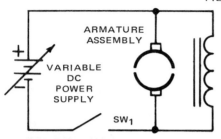

ELECTROMAGNETIC
FIELD COIL

ARMATURE
ASSEMBLY

VARIABLE
DC
POWER
SUPPLY

+

SW₁

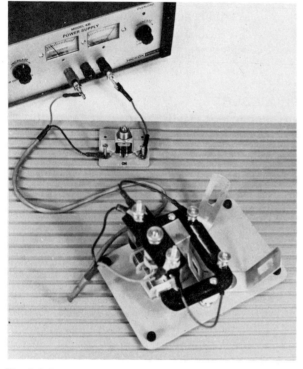

Fig. 9-3-1

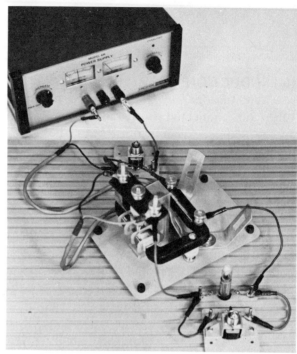

Fig. 9-3-2

of power supply connecting wires. Turn on circuit switch and test operation of motor. How does this alter operation of motor?

_____

_____

9. Turn off circuit switch and reverse the two field coil connection wires. Then, turn on circuit switch and test operation of motor. How does this modification alter operation of motor? _____

_____

10. With motor operating, carefully pivot brush assembly clockwise, then counterclockwise. Is there an ideal position for brushes to produce best operation? Describe best brush location. _____

11. Turn off circuit switch and add No. 47 lamp and switch to motor as indicated in Fig. 9-3-2.

12. Initially, SPST switch should be in ON position. Then, turn on switch to test operation of motor. After motor is in operation, place toggle switch in OFF position. Lamp should light, indicating current through lamp. What influence does added lamp have on operation of motor?

_____

_____

13. Turn off circuit switch and power supply. Disconnect motor circuit and return all parts to storage cabinet.

## QUESTIONS

1. Reversing the polarity of the dc source does not alter the direction of rotation. Why not?
2. Reversing the polarity of the field coil with respect to the armature also reverse the rotational direction of the motor. Why?
3. What accounts for the change in rotational speed when the lamp was added to the field coil circuit of the motor?

# Experiment 9-4 UNIVERSAL MOTORS

## INTRODUCTION

Universal motors run equally as well on either ac or dc energy. The basic design of a universal motor is similar to that of the series wound dc motor. The field coil and the armature are connected in a series arrangement. As a result, ac or dc will produce a usable form of rotation.

A rather significant point in the operation of a universal motor is the direction of current flow. As you will see in this experiment, the direction of current flow does not alter the direction of armature rotation. Therefore, ac applied to this type of motor will cause it to rotate in the same direction as it does when dc is applied. The direction of rotation is changed, however, by reversing the polarity of the field coil with respect to the armature.

The rotational speed of a universal motor is based on the strength of the interacting fields of the armature and field coil. By increasing the applied voltage of the source, there will be a corresponding increase in current flow. Since the strength of the field is dependent upon current flow, its strength increases accordingly. This action ultimately causes a corresponding increase in armature speed.

In this experiment, you will build a universal motor and test its rational direction for each polarity of the dc source. Then, you will reverse its direction by altering the polarity of the field coil with respsect to the armature. Ultimately the same motor will be tested with ac serving as the source. In practice, all universal motors operate on the same basic principles utilized by the St. Louis motor. Commercial universal motors usually employ multi-coil armature and field structures to make their operation more efficient.

## EXPERIMENT OBJECTIVES

As a result of this laboratory experience, you should be able to accomplish the following:
1. Construct a universal motor, using the St. Louis motor-generator unit.
2. Change direction of rotation of motor and check for polarity of the dc source.

3. Connect the universal motor to an ac source and observe its operation.

## REFERENCE

Gerrish and Dugger, ELECTRICITY AND ELECTRONICS, Chapter 9, pages 136 and 137.

## MATERIALS AND EQUIPMENT

1 — St. Louis motor unit (Hickok)
1 — Variable dc power supply
1 — 6.3V, 60 Hz ac power source
1 — SPST toggle switch

## PROCEDURE

1. Remove St. Louis motor unit from storage and place it on your workbench. Remove two permanent magnets from spring clip holders and set them aside. Turn two spring clip holders inward to make room for field coil. Place field coil mounting bolts in place and attach nuts to bolts from bottom side of motor base.
2. Connect field coil and armature brush terminals as indicated in Fig. 9-4-1.
3. Turn on circuit switch and test operation of motor. Adjust dc power supply to 6V dc. Direction of rotation is _____
4. Turn off circuit switch and reverse polarity of power supply connection wires. Then, turn on circuit switch. How does direction of rotation compare with step 3? _____
   What conclusion can be drawn from this test _____

   _____
5. With motor operating, increase source voltage to 10V dc. What influence does this have upon operation of motor? _____

   _____
6. Turn off circuit switch and disconnect dc power supply. In its place, connect a 6.3V, 60 Hz ac source. Turn on circuit switch and test operation of motor.
7. Direction of rotation is _____ How does this operation compare with that of dc motor? _____

   _____

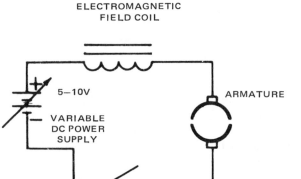

ELECTROMAGNETIC
FIELD COIL

5—10V

VARIABLE
DC POWER
SUPPLY

ARMATURE

SW₁

Fig. 9-4-1

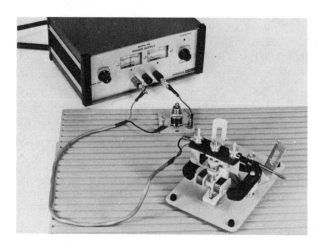

8. Explain how direction of rotation of this motor can be changed. _____

_____

9. Turn off circuit switch and connect motor as described in step 7.

10. Turn on circuit switch and test operation of motor. Direction of rotation is _____
Did your theory of direction changing work? _____

_____

11. Turn off circuit switch and power supply.

Disconnect motor unit and return all parts to storage cabinet.

## QUESTIONS

1. Since ac energy flows first in one direction, then in another, how can it produce rotation in one direction?
2. In a dc motor, the total opposition to current flow is _____
3. In an ac motor, the total opposition to current flow is _____

# Experiment 9-5 INDUCTION MOTORS

## INTRODUCTION

The induction motor contains a stationary field coil or stator and a rotating member. When ac is applied to the stator, it causes the field to change polarity in step with the applied frequency. The stator winding responds as the primary winding of a transformer. Changes in ac applied to the stator causes the resulting magnetic field to be in a constant state of motion. This field cuts across the rotor and produces a voltage and resulting magnetic field by the induction process. The rotor then tracks (follows) the field changes of the stator, thus producing rotation.

Induction motors are energized by either three phase or single phase ac. Three phase ac produces a natural form of rotation across each coil of the stator, which causes the rotor to start automatically. Single phase induction motors require some form of auxiliary starting mechanism in order to start automatically. Phase splitting, repulsion and pole shading are typical auxiliary starting techniques associated with induction motors.

In this experiment, you will build a single phase induction motor. This type of motor is not self-starting, so you will be able to observe its operation through manual starting techniques. The physical appearance of a practical induction motor differs a great deal from the demonstration unit. However, principles of operation demonstrated by this experimental motor are basic to all induction motors.

### EXPERIMENT OBJECTIVES

As a result of this laboratory experience, you should be able to accomplish the following:
1. Construct a single phase induction motor, using the St. Louis motor-generator unit.
2. Identify parts of the induction motor.
3. Observe the operation of this motor, using manual starting methods.

### REFERENCE

Gerrish and Dugger, ELECTRICITY AND ELECTRONICS, Chapter 9, pages 138 to 142.

## MATERIALS AND EQUIPMENT

1 — St. Louis motor unit (Hickok)
1 — 6.3V, 60 Hz ac source
1 — SPST toggle switch

## PROCEDURE

1. Remove St. Louis motor from storage and place it on your workbench. If bar magnets are connected to motor, remove them from spring clip holders and set them aside. Turn spring clips inward and attach field coil to motor base. Loosen armature setscrew and knurled nut. Carefully remove brush holder and split ring commutator armature. Avoid bending brush holder if at all possible.

2. Place ac rotor into armature holder assembly. Rotor does not have a wound coil or commutator. Adjust setscrew so that rotor turns freely (without wobbling) between pivot points.

3. Connect field coil or stator winding of this motor to ac source as indicated in Fig. 9-5-1.

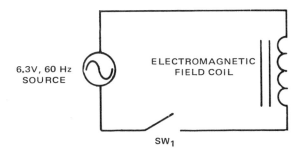

Fig. 9-5-1

4. Turn on circuit switch. This motor is not self-starting because field polarity changes

3600 times per minute.

5. To produce rotation, rotor must be turned to a speed that equals polarity change of stator winding. At top side, rotor shaft is knurled. Roll shaft between your thumb and finger to turn rotor. It may take several practice rolls to cause rotor to reach correct speed.

6. Rotor may turn for a few seconds, then stop if it does not reach correct speed. By using thumb finger of right hand, rotor will turn in clockwise direction. Rotor turns at a speed of 3600 rpm when it has been properly started.

7. After motor has been started and runs satisfactorily, turn off circuit switch. If stator coil is connected to ac source for several minutes, it usually begins to get warm. Wait a minute or so for coil to cool before doing next step.

8. Turn on circuit switch and start motor again. This time, rotate it in counterclockwise direction. It must reach a speed of 3600 rpm in this direction (as in step 6) in order to rotate continuously. It may take several trials to get rotor to reach this speed.

9. Turn off circuit switch. Explain why polarity of stator winding changes at 3600 rpm when 60 Hz of ac is applied. _____

_____

_____

10. Disconnect 60 Hz ac source from motor. Remove rotor and replace it with armature and brush assembly. Remove stator winding assembly and twist magnet clip springs into place. Return magnets to spring clips. Place St. Louis motor in storage. Return all other parts to storage cabinet.

## QUESTIONS

1. How does the rotor receive energy to turn?
2. How could an induction motor be made to start automatically?
3. What determines the rotational speed of an ac induction motor?

# Chapter 10

# INSTRUMENTS AND MEASUREMENTS

## Experiment 10-1  METER RESISTANCE

### INTRODUCTION

The basic D'Arsonval meter movement is installed in a large number of hand deflection meters in use today. This type of meter employs a permanent magnet (PM) and a moving coil assembly attached to an indicating hand. When current flows through the meter coil, it produces a magnetic field that is proportionate to the current flow. An interaction between the PM field and the coil causes meter deflection.

The moving coil of a meter movement offers a certain amount of internal resistance to current passing through it. The value of this resistance is an important consideration when preparing a meter to measure specific values. Knowing the internal resistance of a meter movement permits one to select precise resistance values to extend the measuring range of the meter. Shunt resistors and series resistors are connected to a basic meter for ammeter and voltmeter applications.

In this experiment, you will connect a basic D'Arsonval meter movement into a circuit that will produce a full scale deflection. Then, a resistor is placed in parallel with the meter to divert some of the current flow through an alternate path. By changing the value of the resistance until only half of the full scale deflection current occurs, the internal resistance of the meter can be determined. With half of the current flowing through the meter and half through the external resistance, the two paths are of equal resistance. Therefore, removing the resistance and measuring its value is a simple method of determining the internal resistance

of the meter movement. Then, this measured value is used to determine shunt resistors to extend the ammeter range. Similarly, series resistors are used in voltmeter circuits to extend the voltmeter range.

### EXPERIMENT OBJECTIVES

As a result of this laboratory experience, you should be able to accomplish the following:
1. Connect a D'Arsonval meter into an operating dc circuit.
2. Observe how a shunt is used in a meter circuit.
3. Determine the resistance of the meter.

### REFERENCE

Gerrish and Dugger, ELECTRICITY AND ELECTRONICS, Chapter 10, pages 143 and 144.

### MATERIALS AND EQUIPMENT

1 — 0-1 mA meter
1 — Volt-ohm-milliampere (VOM) meter
1 — 5K, 2 watt potentiometer
1 — Resistance decade unit

### PROCEDURE

1. Connect meter resistance test circuit shown in Fig. 10-1-1. Do not turn on circuit switch at this time.
2. Adjust dc power to 0V as indicated by a VOM. Turn on circuit switch and slowly increase power supply voltage until a full scale deflection of 1 mA occurs.
3. Turn off circuit switch and do not alter voltage control of dc power supply.

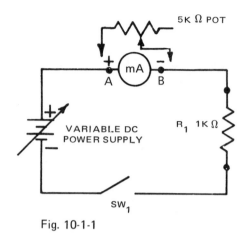

Fig. 10-1-1

4. Connect a 5K potentiometer across meter at points A-B.
5. Turn on circuit switch and adjust potentiometer to produce exactly 0.5 mA or one half of full scale deflection.
6. Turn off circuit switch and disconnect potentiometer from meter. Do not change resistance setting of potentiometer.
7. Prepare VOM to measure resistance of potentiometer. Resistance is _____ ohms.
8. As a check of measured resistance of step 7, prepare resistor decade to produce a resistance equal to measured value. This may necessitate connecting some resistors in series to produce correct value.
9. Connect prepared resistor decade in parallel with mA meter at points A-B. Turn on

circuit switch and test meter deflection. If a half scale deflection does not occur, total resistance of decade must be altered. Amount of resistance change required depends upon how far meter is above or below half scale mark. With resistor decade, precise changes of one ohm can be achieved by adding or reducing certain resistor values.
10. When a half scale deflection is satisfactorily achieved, record total resistance of resistor decade unit. Resistance is _____ ohms. As a general rule, resistor decade should give a more precise indication of meter resistance than potentiometer method because it does not require a secondary measuring source.
11. Resistance of meter will be used in some experiments that follow to determine shunts and multiplier resistors for extending range of ammeters and voltmeters.
12. Turn off circuit switch and power supply. Disconnect circuit and return all parts to storage cabinet.

**QUESTIONS**
1. How does the half scale resistance technique of this experiment determine meter resistance?
2. What causes the D'Arsonval meter movement to have resistance?
3. What is included in the physical makeup of a D'Arsonval meter?

# Experiment 10-2  AMMETER SHUNTS

## INTRODUCTION

In a VOM, a single meter movement is used to measure current flow in several ranges. In order to extend the range of the ammeter to measure larger current values, resistors are connected in parallel or shunt with the primary meter of the VOM. The shunt resistor provides an alternate path for current to flow around the meter. To achieve this function, the resistance of the shunt must be proportionately smaller than the internal resistance of the meter.

The correct shunt resistor can be selected by first calculating the voltage appearing across the primary meter. Full scale meter current ($I_M$) times internal meter resistance ($R_{int}$) equals meter voltage ($E_M$). With the shunt in parallel with the meter, both receive the same voltage. Therefore, shunt resistance ($R_S$) equals $E_M$ divided by shunt current ($I_S$). The $I_S$ is based on the extended range of the meter. A 1 mA meter extended to measure 100 mA would have 99 mA of $I_S$ and 1.0 mA of $I_M$. To extend the same meter to 10 mA would only necessitate an $I_S$ of 9 mA and an $I_M$ of 1 mA. The resistance of the shunt is always smaller than the internal resistance of the meter. To extend a meter to measure large current values requires very low resistant shunts.

In this experiment, you will build and test a circuit, then extend the range of the meter to measure larger current values by selecting and installing a shunt resistor. The basic principles of shunt selection can be applied to any meter, providing you know its internal resistance.

## EXPERIMENT OBJECTIVES

As a result of this laboratory experience, you should be able to accomplish the following:
1. Construct a simple dc circuit and measure the current in it.
2. Determine how to compute values of shunts.

## REFERENCE

Gerrish and Dugger, ELECTRICITY AND ELECTRONICS, Chapter 10, pages 144 to 146.

## MATERIALS AND EQUIPMENT

1 — Volt-ohm-milliampere (VOM) meter
1 — Variable dc power supply
1 — 0-1 mA meter
1 — Resistor decade unit or suitable discrete resistor values
1 — SPST toggle switch

## PROCEDURE

1. Construct meter test circuit shown in Fig. 10-2-1. Do not turn on circuit switch at this time.

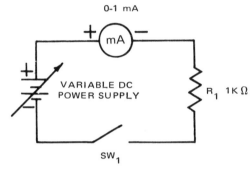

Fig. 10-2-1

2. Prepare VOM to measure voltage and connect it across dc power supply. Adjust power supply to 0V dc.
3. Turn on circuit switch and carefully adjust power supply to produce a full scale deflection of 1.0 mA on milliampere meter.
4. Measure and record dc power supply voltage. Supply voltage is _____ volts.
5. According to Ohm's Law, E = IR. Using 1.0 mA current reading and value of $R_1$ calculate source voltage of circuit. How close does calculated voltage value compare with measured value? _____

6. Record internal resistance ($R_{int}$) of 0-1 mA meter determined in previous experiment. $R_{int}$ is _____ ohms.
7. Assume that 1.0 mA meter is to be extended to measure 10 mA with a full scale deflection. To determine appropriate

shunt resistor, first calculate voltage needed to make meter deflect 1.0 mA with its internal resistance. Meter voltage ($E_M$) equals full scale current flow of meter ($I_M$) times internal meter resistance ($R_{int}$) or $E_M = I_M$ x R. Calculated meter voltage is _____ volts.

8. To extend this meter to measure 10 mA, 9/10 of current or 9 mA must flow through shunt resistor when 1.0 mA flows through meter. Since a shunt resistor is connected in parallel with meter, same voltage applied to meter ($E_M$) will be applied to shunt. Therefore, resistance of shunt ($R_s$) equals $E_M$ divided by shunt current flow $I_s$. The calculated value of $R_s$ is_____ ohms.

9. Check your calculated $R_s$ value. It should be approximately 1/9 of value of $R_{int}$. How close does your calculated value compare with this approximation?_____

_____

10. Turn off circuit switch and connect decade module to produce appropriate shunt resistance. Connect decade shunt in parallel with 1.0 mA meter.

11. Turn on circuit switch and test current flow. Meter, in this case, has been extended to produce a full scale deflection of 10 mA. What current value is displayed on shunted meter?_____

_____

12. Turn off circuit switch and disconnect 1K resistor. In its place, connect a 500 ohm resistor. Turn on circuit switch and measure current flow. Measured I is_____ mA.

13. If time permits, measure current flow produced by 400 ohm, 200 ohm and 100 ohm resistors with shunted meter.

14. Turn off circuit switch and power supply. Disconnect circuit and return all parts to storage cabinet.

## QUESTIONS

1. A 10 mA meter with an $R_{int}$ of 50 ohms is to be extended to 100 mA. What value of shunt resistor is needed?

2. How does the resistance of a shunt and the $R_{int}$ of a meter compare?

3. If four shunts were used with a multirange switching circuit, which shunt resistor would be the smallest value?

## INTRODUCTION

Voltage can be measured by connecting a high valued resistance in series with a milliampere meter. The series resistor usually is called a "multiplier," because it extends the meter to indicate voltage instead of current. Essentially, a voltmeter is a series circuit with a large voltage drop across the series resistor and a small voltage drop across the internal resistance of the meter. Meters that measure high voltage values require extremely large multiplier resistors.

When the internal resistance and current rating of a milliampere meter are known, the voltage required to produce full scale deflection can be calculated. The meter voltage ($V_M$) of a typical milliampere meter generally is quite small. To extend this voltage, a large multiplier resistor ($R_m$) is placed in series with the meter. The voltage drop across $R_m$ plus $V_M$ equals the total voltage measuring capability of the voltmeter. To extend the meter to measure larger voltages would require different multiplier resistors. Typically, multirange voltmeters may employ four or five multipliers with a range selector switch.

In this experiment, you will study a typical meter circuit that is the basis of practically all voltmeters today. You will convert a milliampere meter into a voltmeter, and learn how to calculate multiplier resistor values. You will see how the accuracy of a selected resistor influences voltage indications, and learn how to determine the ohms-per-volt rating of the meter.

### EXPERIMENT OBJECTIVES

As a result of this laboratory experience, you should be able to accomplish the following:
1. Use a milliampere meter as a voltmeter.
2. Calculate the value of a multiplier resistor.
3. Learn about meter sensitivity (ohms-per-volt rating).

### REFERENCE

Gerrish and Dugger, ELECTRICITY AND ELECTRONICS, Chapter 10, pages 146 to 148.

## MATERIALS AND EQUIPMENT

1 — Volt-ohm-milliampere (VOM) meter
1 — 0-1 mA meter
1 — Variable dc power supply
1 — Resistor decade module or a 10K potentiometer

## PROCEDURE

1. Record internal resistance of meter being used in this experiment. $R_{int}$ is _____ ohms. (This value was measured in experiment 10-1.) Meter current ($I_M$) needed to produce a full scale deflection is _____ mA.

2. Assume now that milliampere meter being used in this experiment is to be changed to a dc voltmeter with a full scale deflection of 10V dc. First, calculate meter voltage ($V_M$) needed to produce a full scale deflection with $R_{int}$ x $I_M$. $V_M$ is _____ volts.

3. Secondly, select desired voltmeter range (10V) and subtract $V_M$ from this value. This represents multiplier resistor voltage ($V_{R_m}$). $V_{R_m}$ is _____ volts.

4. Final calculation deals with multiplier resistor, ($R_m$).

$$R_m = \frac{V_{R_m}}{I_M}$$

$R_m$ = _____ ohms
Ask instructor to approve your $R_m$ calculation before constructing voltmeter circuit. Instructor's approval_____

5. Construct 10V meter as in Fig. 10-3-1. Value of $R_m$ is achieved with resistance decade module or a 10K potentiometer. Measure value of $R_m$ with VOM before assuming that it is correct.

6. Turn on variable dc power supply and adjust it to 1V dc as read on VOM.

7. Connect constructed voltmeter to power supply and measure dc power supply voltage. How does accuracy of constructed meter compare with measured VOM value?

_____

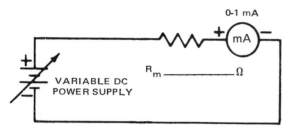

0-1 mA

$R_m$ _____ $\Omega$

VARIABLE DC
POWER SUPPLY

Fig. 10-3-1

8. Increase power supply voltage to 5V as read on VOM. Constructed voltmeter shows_____ volts.

9. Adjust power supply to 9V dc as read on VOM. Constructed voltmeter shows power supply voltage to be_____ volts.

10. Total resistance of constructed meter is $R_m + R_{int}$. $R_T$ is _____ ohms.

11. Sensitivity of a voltmeter normally is based on its ohms-per-volt rating (ohms/V). Ohms-per-volt rating of a meter is determined by its total resistance ($R_T$) divided by its full scale voltage ($V_{fs}$). Sensitivity of constructed meter is_____ ohms/V.

12. If time permits, design a 100V dc meter using same meter. Show all of your calculations and have instructor approve your circuit before testing its operation.

13. Turn off power supply and disconnect circuit. Return all components to storage cabinet.

**QUESTIONS**

1. If the same meter used in this experiment was extended to 1000V, the multiplier resistor ($R_m$) would need to be _____ (larger or smaller) than the one used for the 10V range? Why?

2. When using the milliampere meter as a 10V meter, what must be done to the meter scale to indicate 10V?

3. What is the ohms/volt rating of the VOM used in this experiment? Is it more sensitive than your constructed meter?

# Experiment 10-4  OHMMETERS

## INTRODUCTION

An ohmmeter is an instrument used to measure the value of an unknown resistance. Essentially, an ohmmeter contains a sensitive milliampere or microampere meter, a dc voltage source, a current limiting resistor and an ohms adjust control. When the two meter probes are touched together, the circuit is made complete and current is indicated on the meter. With zero resistance between the probes, the meter should indicate zero resistance. The scale of the ohmmeter is designed to display this value. When resistance is placed between the probes, circuit current flow is reduced accordingly. The ohmmeter scale is marked to reflect different resistance values.

The graduations of an ohmmeter scale generally are unequal. Near the infinite end of the scale, tiny graduations represent thousands of ohms of resistance. Near the zero end of the scale, graduations are quite large. Only a few ohms of resistance are needed to make the meter deflect half of its scale near the zero end. Resistance readings are obviously more accurate near the low resistant end of the scale because of this factor.

In this experiment, you will become more familiar with the ohmmeter and its working parts. The ohmmeter is a very valuable measuring instrument used in the study of electricity and electronics. It is commonly used as a test instrument to determine circuit continuity and component condition.

## EXPERIMENT OBJECTIVES

As a result of this laboratory experience, you should be able to accomplish the following:
1. Construct a basic ohmmeter circuit.
2. Test the operation of the ohmmeter.
3. Calibrate a simple ohmmeter scale.

## REFERENCE

Gerrish and Dugger, ELECTRICITY AND ELECTRONICS, Chapter 10, page 148.

## MATERIALS AND EQUIPMENT

1 — 0-1 mA meter
1 — 1.5V "C" type cell with holder
1 — Resistor decade module
1 — 5K, 2 watt potentiometer
1 — SPST toggle switch
3 — Strips of masking tape

## PROCEDURE

1. Construct ohmmeter test circuit as in Fig. 10-4-1.

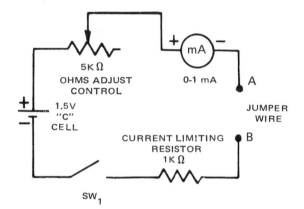

Fig. 10-4-1

2. Place a jumper wire between probe connection terminals at points A-B. Turn on circuit switch. Turn ohms adjust control to set meter hand at full scale deflection end of scale.
3. When ohmmeter is energized, full scale deflection equals _____ mA, which corresponds to "zero" resistance between points A-B.
4. Disconnect jumper wire connected between points A-B. Ohmmeter is now in ready state with nothing connected to its probes.
5. Place three or four pieces of masking tape on top of plastic cover of meter scale, as indicated in Fig. 10-4-2.
6. On tape, mark "0" at full scale end and infinite ( ∞ ) at other end of scale.
7. Further calibration of ohmmeter scale is achieved by adding resistance between terminals A and B, Fig. 10-4-1. With a 1.5V dc source and 1.0 mA of current flow, total resistance of circuit is _____ ohms.

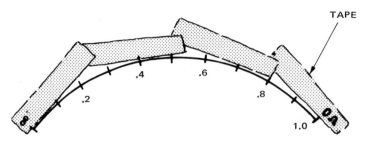

Fig. 10-4-2

8. To produce a half scale deflection, add resistance at points A-B that will equal value of calculated total resistance of step 7. Use a resistor decade, a mounted resistor or a potentiometer to achieve this value. Mark position of deflected hand on masking tape. Indicate resistance needed to produce this amount of deflection on tape.

9. Remove resistor added for step 8, then connect a 500 ohm resistor between circuit points A-B. Mark location of hand on tape and label it 500 ohms.

10. Remove 500 ohm resistor and add a 400 ohm, a 200 ohm then a 100 ohm resistor, marking each deflection value of meter on tape and labeling it accordingly.

11. Using same procedure, connect a 1K, 2K, 5K and a 10K resistor across A-B. Mark and label each value on the tape.

12. Is there any noticeable difference between graduations on calibrated ohmmeter scale?

13. Test some resistor values with experimental ohmmeter. What are some limitations of experimental ohmmeter?_____

_____

14. Turn off circuit switch and disconnect experimental ohmmeter. Remove tape strips from meter and return all parts to storage cabinet.

## QUESTIONS

1. The ohmmeter used in this experiment is _____ (series or shunt) connected.

2. If an ohmmeter has its zero located at the left and infinite at the right of the scale, it is a_____ connected meter.

3. Why is it harmful to connect an ohmmeter to a circuit with voltage applied to it?

## INTRODUCTION

In order to measure ac voltage on a D'Arsonval or permanent magnet meter, the voltage must be changed to an equivalent dc value. The process of changing ac to dc is called "rectification." A basic dc voltmeter will not effectively respond when ac is applied. During one alternation, the meter will deflect upscale, then deflect downscale during the other alternation. With 60 Hz of ac applied to a dc meter, the indicating hand is essentially at rest for both alternations.

Multifunction meters that use D'Arsonval meter movements must employ diode rectifying devices to change ac to dc. Half-wave rectifiers will only produce dc output for one alternation of the ac cycle. The resulting dc equivalent meter deflection is only 0.45 of the applied rms voltage. A special ac meter scale is needed to make a meaningful ac reading on the meter for this value. The 0.45 factor is the equivalent dc output of a half-wave rectified ac voltage. This value represents the applied rms value x 1.414. This is used to determine the peak value of the ac input voltage. Its rectified output is then determined by multiplying the peak value by 0.637 and dividing by 2. Therefore, 1.414 x 0.637 ÷ 2 = 0.45 or the dc equivalent of the applied ac.

Normally, bridge rectifier units are used to change ac to an equivalent dc voltage for meter circuits. Bridge rectifiers employ four diodes and produce full-wave rectification. Both alternations of the ac sinewave are transposed into dc output through this rectifying process. The equivalent dc developed by a full-wave rectifier is 0.90 of the rms value. This value is represented by rms x 1.414 to produce a peak value. The average value or 0.637 x peak value is representative of the 0.9 x rms conversion factor. Full-wave rectification is commonly used in meters because it necessitates only a slight modification of the dc scale into an equivalent ac scale.

In this experiment, you will be able to observe the internal workings of an ac voltmeter and see how both half-wave and full-wave

rectification are used to produce an equivalent ac output. Multifunction meters employ special ac scales that indicate values from equivalent dc voltage produced by rectification.

## EXPERIMENT OBJECTIVES

As a result of this laboratory experience, you should be able to accomplish the following:
1. Build an ac voltmeter.
2. Test this ac voltmeter in an operating circuit.
3. Observe how half-wave rectification and full-wave rectification affects an ac voltmeter.

## REFERENCE

Gerrish and Dugger, ELECTRICITY AND ELECTRONICS, Chapter 10, pages 152 and 153.

## MATERIALS AND EQUIPMENT

1 — Volt-ohm-milliampere (VOM) meter
1 — 12.6V CT, 60 Hz ac source
1 — 0-1 mA meter
1 — Resistor decade module or a 9.9K, 1/4 watt resistor
1 — Power supply module or 4 — 1N4004 diodes
1 — SPST toggle switch

## PROCEDURE

1. Connect 10V dc voltmeter circuit shown in Fig. 10-5-1. Turn on circuit switch. What causes meter to respond as it does?
2. Turn off circuit switch and add a diode to

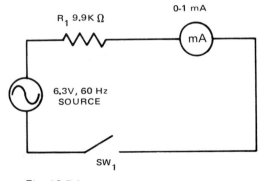

Fig. 10-5-1

circuit as shown in Fig. 10-5-2. $D_1$ can be obtained from the power supply module or from a separately mounted 1N4004 diode. The diode changes the applied ac into a half-wave rectified voltage.

ac input. Calculated meter voltage is _____ volts. How closely does this value compare with measured value of step 3?

_____

_____

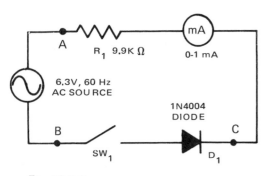

Fig. 10-5-2

3. Turn on circuit switch and record value of voltage observed on meter. Measured meter voltage is _____ volts.

4. With a VOM, measure applied ac. The ac voltage input is _____ volts. Constructed voltmeter reading actually is 0.45 of applied

5. In practice, multifunction meters would have separate ac and dc voltage scales to indicate specific voltage values. The ac value in this case is the applied rms x 1.414, which indicates peak value of ac input. Since ac input is half-wave rectified, average value

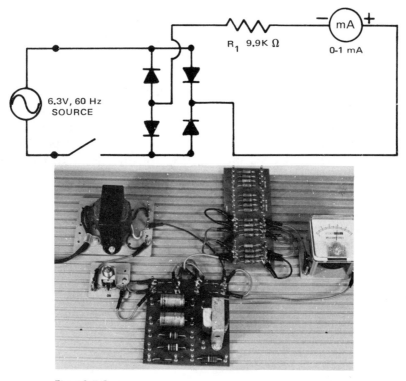

Fig. 10-5-3

of this wave is 0.637 ÷ 2 or 0.318 of peak value. Therefore, 1.414 x 0.318 = 0.45 x rms input value. On a dc scale, this voltage indication would not be very meaningful. On a separate ac scale, this value would read approximately 12.6 rms of ac.

6. Many ac voltmeters use four diodes in a bridge rectifier circuit (instead of a single diode) that achieves half-wave rectification. A bridge rectifier will transpose both alternations of ac wave into single direction current flow. Then, on a dc meter scale, output of a bridge rectifier would produce a deflection that is 0.9 of rms input. This value represents rms input x 1.414, which indicates peak value of input. Therefore, average value or 0.637 x peak value equals ac equivalent or 0.90 of rms input value.

7. Turn off circuit switch. Disconnect diode from circuit and replace it with bridge circuit of Fig. 10-5-3. Diodes $D_1$, $D_2$, $D_3$ and $D_4$ are mounted on power supply module. If power supply module is not available, use separately mounted 1N4004 diodes.

8. Turn on circuit switch and record ac indicated on meter scale. Observed as meter voltage is _____ volts. This value actually represents 0.9 x rms value. On a multifunction meter with ac measuring capabilities, this would indicate actual voltage value on a separate ac scale. With VOM, measure and record this ac value. The ac voltage is _____ volts.

9. Turn off circuit switch and ac power source. Disconnect circuit and return all components to storage cabinet.

## QUESTIONS

1. Why does a permanent magnet meter need rectification to produce a meter deflection?
2. What is the difference between half-wave rectification and full-wave rectification?
3. Why are bridge rectifiers more commonly used in meters than single diode rectifiers?

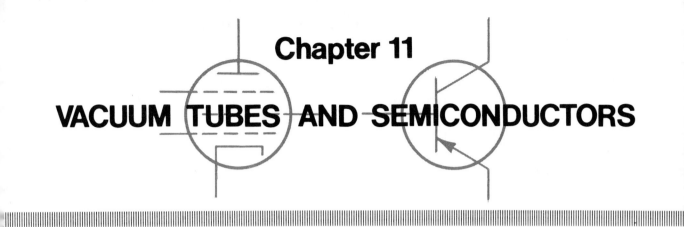

# Chapter 11

# VACUUM TUBES AND SEMICONDUCTORS

## Experiment 11-1  SEMICONDUCTOR DIODE TESTING

### INTRODUCTION

Semiconductor diodes contain an "N" type of material connected to a "P" type of material. The P material is developed by mixing a trivalent impurity with either silicon or germanium. The N material is developed in a similar manner by mixing a pentavalent impurity with either silicon or germanium. A PN diode (made of both materials) has uniconduction capabilities. It conducts well in one direction and is nonconductive in the reverse direction.

An ohmmeter is an effective means of testing a semiconductor diode. When the positive side of the ohmmeter dc source is connected to the P material and the negative side is connected to the N material, conduction will occur and indicate low resistance. Reversing the ohmmeter leads to the diode should indicate a high or infinite resistance. A good diode will show low resistance in the forward biased direction and high resistance in the reverse biased direction. A shorted diode will show low resistance in both directions. An open diode will show high or infinite resistance in both directions.

In this experiment, you will see how a good diode responds to an ohmmeter test procedure. The unidirectional conductivity of a diode is also demonstrated. This capability is used to light a lamp in the forward biased direction and to be nonconductive in reverse bias direction. Later, these capabilities of a diode will be used to demonstrate various electronic functions.

### EXPERIMENT OBJECTIVES

As a result of this laboratory experience, you should be able to accomplish the following:

1. Use an ohmmeter to test some semiconductor diodes.
2. Observe how a diode will block current in one direction and pass it in the other direction.

### REFERENCE

Gerrish and Dugger, ELECTRICITY AND ELECTRONICS, Chapter 11, pages 159 to 162.

### MATERIALS AND EQUIPMENT

1 — Volt-ohm-milliampere (VOM) meter
1 — Variable dc power source
1 — 1N4004 diode or a diode from power supply module
1 — SPST toggle switch
1 — No. 47 lamp

### PROCEDURE

1. Select a 1N4004 diode from storage cabinet. This experiment calls for a single mounted diode or one of four diodes of a power supply module.
2. Prepare VOM to measure a low resistance value. The R x 1 range generally is perferred for this test.
3. Typically, negative side of VOM is connected to dc source of ohmmeter; positive side is connected to VOA terminal. Some VOMs make an exception to this rule and are connected with a reverse ohmmeter polarity. This will be noted in next step if your VOM has reverse polarity.
4. Connect positive probe to VOM to anode of diode and common or negative terminal to cathode, as indicated in Fig. 11-1-1.

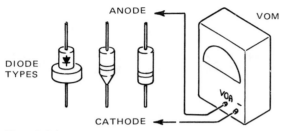

Fig. 11-1-1

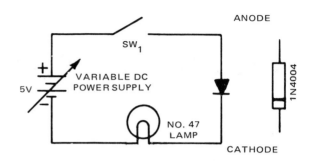

Fig. 11-1-2

5. If diode is good and ohmmeter has straight polarity, there should be a low resistance indication on VOM. This normally represents forward bias test of a diode. Forward bias resistance equals _____ ohms.

6. Reverse ohmmeter test probes so that VOM positive probe is connected to cathode, and negative probe to anode. If diode is good and ohmmeter has straight polarity, a high resistance will be indicated. This normally represents a reverse bias condition. Reverse bias equals _____ ohms.

7. Switch ohmmeter to its highest range and make test again. Is there any change in reverse indication? _____

8. Test other diodes on power supply module or ask your instructor for three or four additional diodes to test. A shorted diode will show a low resistance in both directions. An open diode usually tests with an infinite amount of resistance in both directions.

9. A more graphic demonstration of diode conduction can be made with circuit shown in Fig. 11-1-2.

10. Turn on dc power supply, adjust it to 5V dc then turn on circuit switch. How does lamp respond? _____ Diode is connected in a _____ (forward or reverse) biased direction.

11. Turn off circuit switch and reverse polarity of diode. Turn on circuit switch and describe reaction of lamp. _____ Diode is connected in a _____ (forward or reverse) biased direction.

12. Turn off circuit switch and power supply. Disconnect circuit and return all parts to storage cabinet.

## QUESTIONS

1. Explain how an ohmmeter is used to indicate the condition of a shorted, open or good diode.

2. The anode of a diode corresponds to the _____ material while the cathode is _____ material.

3. What is meant by the statement that a diode has "unidirectional conductivity?"

# SEMICONDUCTOR DIODE CHARACTERISTICS

## INTRODUCTION

The operating characteristics of a semiconductor diode are primarily the same as those of a vacuum tube diode. A diode is conductive when connected in the forward bias direction and nonconductive when reverse biased. The uniqueness of this device is shown by the current-voltage relationship of its anode-cathode junction.

Maximum anode-cathode current ($I_{AK}$) of a diode occurs when a very small value of anode-cathode voltage ($V_{AK}$) is applied in the forward bias direction. In the reverse bias direction, current flow is very minute. In practice, reverse bias current usually is considered negligible. The maximum reverse bias voltage that can be applied before damage to the diode occurs is called the peak reverse voltage (PRV).

In this experiment, you will build a semiconductor test circuit and plot $V_{AK} - I_{AK}$ curve that shows the relationship of these two characteristics. Semiconductor diodes will be used in numerous applications throughout the remainder of this manual. An understanding of characteristics and conduction operation is extremely important in the study of electronics.

## EXPERIMENT OBJECTIVES

As a result of this laboratory experience, you should be able to accomplish the following:

1. Construct a circuit to test semiconductor diode $V_{AK} - I_{AK}$ characteristics.
2. Collect data in this test circuit and plot a $V_{AK} - I_{AK}$ curve.
3. Become familiar with operating characteristics of a semiconductor diode.

## REFERENCE

Gerrish and Dugger, ELECTRICITY AND ELECTRONICS, Chapter 11, Pages 162 to 164.

## MATERIALS AND EQUIPMENT

1 — Volt-ohm-milliampere (VOM) meter
1 — 1N4004 diode
1 — Variable dc power supply
1 — 0-1 mA meter
1 — 2 ohm, 1/4 watt resistor or a resistor decade unit
1 — 100 ohm, 1/4 watt resistor or a decade module
1 — SPST toggle switch

## PROCEDURE

1. Construct semiconductor diode test circuit as in Fig. 11-2-1. Note that 0-1 mA meter has a shunt resistor which extends its range to 50 mA.
2. Adjust variable dc power supply to "0" position and turn it on. Prepare VOM to

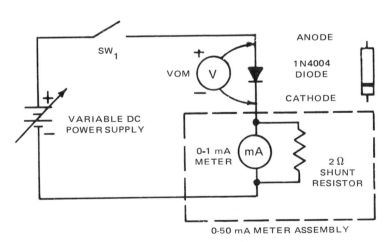

Fig. 11-2-1

read anode-cathode voltage ($V_{AK}$) developed across diode. Shunted milliampere meter is used to measure anode-cathode current ($I_{AK}$) passing through diode.

3. Turn on circuit switch and adjust variable dc power supply to produce a 0 mA value on shunted $I_{AK}$ meter. Note that any current value indicated by meter is multiplied by a factor of 50.

4. Record $V_{AK}$ value indicated by VOM for 0 mA of $I_{AK}$ in chart of Fig. 11-2-2.

7. Turn off circuit switch and return variable dc power supply to 0 volts.

8. Using measured $I_{AK}$ and $V_{AK}$ values, Fig. 11-2-2, plot a graph showing relationship of these values in Fig. 11-2-3.

9. Reverse polarity of diode in Fig. 11-2-1.

10. Turn on circuit switch and adjust dc voltage source to 0V as indicated by $V_{AK}$ meter. Record resulting $I_{AK}$ in graph of Fig. 11-2-4.

11. Using same procedure, adjust $V_{AK}$ to 1V,

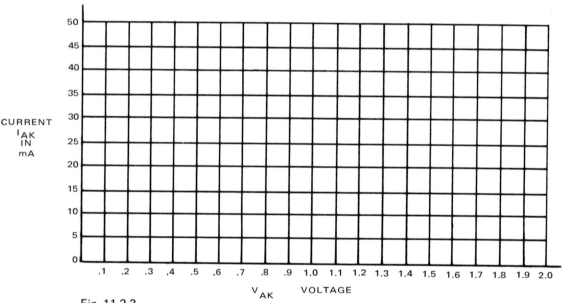

FORWARD $V_{AK} - I_{AK}$ CHART

| ANODE-CATHODE VOLTAGE ($V_{AK}$) | | | | | | | | | | | |
|---|---|---|---|---|---|---|---|---|---|---|---|
| ANODE-CATHODE CURRENT ($I_{AK}$) IN mA | 0 | 5 | 10 | 15 | 20 | 25 | 30 | 35 | 40 | 45 | 50 |

Fig. 11-2-2

Fig. 11-2-3

REVERSE $V_{AK} - I_{AK}$ CHART

| $V_{AK}$ IN VOLTS | 0 | 1 | 2 | 3 | 4 | 5 | 6 | 7 | 8 | 9 | 10 | |
|---|---|---|---|---|---|---|---|---|---|---|---|---|
| $I_{AK}$ IN mA | | | | | | | | | | | | |

Fig. 11-2-4

5. Increase $I_{AK}$ to 5 mA and record resulting $V_{AK}$ value in chart.

6. Using same procedure, increase $I_{AK}$ to 10 mA and record resulting $V_{AK}$ value. Use same procedure for remaining $I_{AK}$ values.

2V, 3V, etc., and record indicated $I_{AK}$ in chart. What does this show about conduction in reverse direction?

12. Turn off power supply. Disconnect circuit. Return all components to storage cabinet.

## QUESTIONS

1. Consider the $V_{AK} - I_{AK}$ characteristic curve of the semiconductor diode shown in Fig. 11-2-3. What does the curve reveal about the operation of the device?

2. Use the following formula to calculate the forward resistance of the diode:

$$R_{AK} = \frac{V_{AK}}{I_{AK}}$$

Calculate forward resistance at 5 mA, 15 mA, 25 mA, 30 mA and 50 mA.

3. Why does a diode conduct when forward biased?

# Chapter 12

# POWER SUPPLIES

## Experiment 12-1
## SEMICONDUCTOR HALF-WAVE RECTIFIERS

### INTRODUCTION

Direct current power supplies usually derive their primary source of energy from the ac power line. The ac may be either stepped-up or stepped-down, according to the design of the supply. Then, rectification is used to change ac to dc. Half-wave rectification changes only one alternation or half of sine wave into dc output.

Rectification is achieved by a unidirectional conductivity (one-way flow) device such as a diode. With ac applied to this device, only half of the sine wave will produce a resulting dc output. Either vacuum tube or semiconductor diodes can be used to achieve rectification. In this experiment, a semiconductor diode will be used to rectify the applied ac.

When a semiconductor diode is forward biased, it produces a resulting output. With ac applied, forward biasing only occurs during one alternation. This takes place when the "P" material is positive and the "N" material is negative. During this alternation, the sine wave input produces conduction and causes an output to appear across the load resistor of the circuit.

When the negative alternation of a sine wave occurs, it reverse biases the diode. The "N" material (cathode) becomes positive and the "P" material (anode) becomes negative. Therefore, the resulting output of this conduction is zero. This means that current only flows through the circuit during the positive alternation. With ac applied, only single directional current or dc appears across the output of a half-wave rectifier circuit.

In this experiment, you will build and test a half-wave rectifier circuit using a semiconductor diode. Then, using an oscilloscope, you will see the effect of half-wave rectification. This circuit represents an important operating principle of a power supply.

### EXPERIMENT OBJECTIVES

As a result of this laboratory experience, you should be able to accomplish the following:
1. Construct a half-wave rectifier circuit using a semiconductor diode.
2. Calculate and measure the dc output from the circuit.
3. Observe the dc output on an oscilloscope.

### REFERENCE

Gerrish and Dugger, ELECTRICITY AND ELECTRONICS, Chapter 12, pages 165 to 167.

### MATERIALS AND EQUIPMENT

1 — Volt-ohm-milliampere (VOM) meter
1 — 6.3V - 0 - 6.3V, 60 Hz ac source
1 — Oscilloscope
1 — 1N4004 diode or a power supply module
1 — 270 ohm, 1 watt resistor
1 — SPST toggle switch

### PROCEDURE

1. Construct half-wave rectifier circuit as in Fig. 12-1-1. Diode and load resistor of circuit are either mounted on power supply module or mounted separately on individual component strips. If a power supply

module is not available, use separately mounted components having values indicated.

For half-wave rectification, this value is divided by two. Therefore, 0.318 times peak value of applied ac equals dc output

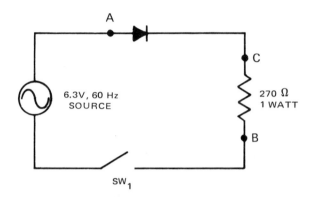

Fig. 12-1-1

2. Prepare VOM to measure value of applied ac. Applied rms ac voltage is _____ volts.

3. Peak or maximum value of an alternation or half of sine wave is 0.637 x peak value.

of a half-wave rectifier. Calculated dc output is _____ volts.

4. Prepare VOM to measure dc voltage. Turn on circuit switch and measure voltage at points C-B. The dc voltage is _____

```
AC
INPUT
WAVEFORM _____
AT POINTS
  A-B

OUTPUT
WAVEFORM _____
AT POINTS
  C-B
```

Fig. 12-1-2

volts. Point C is _____ (+ or −). Point B is _____ (+ or −).

5. Prepare oscilloscope for operation with a sweep rate of 5m sec or for 10 to 100 Hz sweep.

6. Connect common or ground probe to B and vertical probe to A. Adjust oscilloscope to produce a display of two or three complete sine waves. This represents ac input to circuit.

7. Make a sketch of observed input waveform at points A-B in provided space in Fig. 12-1-2.

8. Connect vertical probe of oscilloscope to test point C and common or ground probe to point B. Make a sketch of observed waveform in Fig. 12-1-2.

9. Turn off circuit switch and reverse polarity of diode.

10. Turn on circuit switch and measure polarity of dc voltage across points C-B. Point C is _____ (+ or −). Point B is _____ (+ or −).

11. Turn off circuit switch and disconnect 6.3V, 60 Hz input source. In its place, connect 12.6V, 60 Hz ac source.

12. Turn on circuit switch. Measure value of ac input. Peak value is _____

13. Calculated average half-wave dc output across $R_L$ is:

Peak value x $\dfrac{.637}{2}$ or _____ volts

14. With VOM, measure and record dc voltage appearing across $R_L$. The dc output voltage equals _____ volts. How close do calculated and measured values compare?

_____

15. Turn off switch and disconnect circuit. Return all components to storage cabinet.

## QUESTIONS

1. If the efficiency of a half-wave rectifier is based upon dc output over rms input x 100, what is the percentage of efficiency?

2. Explain how a diode circuit achieves half-wave rectification?

3. If 120V rms is applied to a half-wave rectifier, what is the dc output across $R_L$?

## INTRODUCTION

Full-wave rectification is a very important power supply function. In this rectification process, both alternations of ac input are changed into dc output. The resulting dc output is 0.9 of the applied rms ac. Due to this high level of efficiency, full-wave rectification circuitry is used in a large number of electronic power supplies today.

In this experiment, a center tapped transformer and two diodes are used to produce full-wave rectification. With ac applied to the primary winding of the transformer, the secondary winding produces an equal voltage on each side of the center tap. Because of the construction of the transformer, these voltages are of equal value but of opposite polarity with respect to the center point. For one alternation, the top winding is positive while the bottom winding is negative. For the next alternation, the polarity of the two windings reverses. As a result, one diode conducts for the positive alternation and the other conducts during the negative alternation. The cathodes or output of the two diodes are connected together and serve as the positive dc output terminal. The center connection of the transformer serves as the negative output terminal.

In this experiment, you will build and test a semiconductor full-wave rectifier with a tapped transformer. You will see the effect of a full-wave rectifier in an actual operating circuit. Semiconductor rectifiers of this type have numerous applications in electronics equipment.

## EXPERIMENT OBJECTIVES

As a result of this laboratory experience, you should be able to accomplish the following:
1. Construct a full-wave rectifier circuit using a semiconductor diode.
2. Calculate and measure the dc output.
3. Observe the dc output on an oscilloscope.

## REFERENCE

Gerrish and Dugger, ELECTRICITY AND ELECTRONICS, Chapter 12, pages 167 and 168.

## MATERIALS AND EQUIPMENT

1 — Volt-ohm-milliampere (VOM) meter
1 — 6.3V - 0 - 6.3V, 60 Hz ac source
1 — Oscilloscope
1 — 270 ohm, 1 watt resistor or power supply module
2 — 1N4004 diodes or a power supply module

## PROCEDURE

1. Connect a full-wave semiconductor circuit as in Fig. 12-2-1. The ac source voltage for this circuit comes from a center tapped transformer.

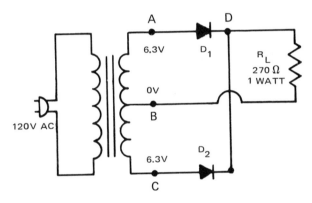

Fig. 12-2-1

2. Prepare VOM to measure ac voltage at test points A-B and B-C. A-B is _____ volts. B-C is _____ volts.
3. Maximum value of ac applied to diode $D_1$ (points A-B) is _____ volts. Maximum value of ac applied to diode $D_2$ (points

B-C) is _____ volts.

4. Average value of conduction voltage of $D_1$ is 0.637 x maximum value which equals _____ dc volts. Conduction voltage of $D_2$ is _____ dc volts.

5. Prepare VOM to measure dc voltage appearing across $R_L$. Measured dc output voltage is _____

6. Prepare oscilloscope for operation with a sweep rate of 5m sec or for 10 to 100 Hz sweep. Trigger or sync selector should be set to line position.

7. Connect common or ground probe to point B and vertical probe to test point A. Adjust horizontal position control so that left side or beginning part of wave may be observed. Make a sketch of observed waveform in provided space in Fig. 12-2-2.

8. With common probe remaining at point B, first connect vertical probe to test point C. Observe waveform. Then, connect vertical probe to test point D and observe waveform. Make sketches of observed waveforms in provided space in Fig. 12-2-2. How would you describe relationship of these wave-forms? _____

_____

9. Disconnect ac source transformer from power source. Disconnect circuit and return all parts to storage cabinet.

## QUESTIONS

1. What is the major advantage of full-wave rectification over half-wave rectification?
2. Explain how a two-diode circuit achieves full-wave rectification.
3. Trace the conduction path in Fig. 12-2-1 when point A is positive and point C is negative. Start at point B. Also trace the circuit when point A is negative and point C is positive.

```
AC
INPUT
AT POINTS    _____
  A-B
```

```
AC
INPUT
AT POINTS    _____
  B-C
```

```
OUTPUT
WAVEFORM
AT POINTS    _____
  D-B
```

Fig. 12-2-2

## INTRODUCTION

Bridge rectifiers are commonly used in power supply applications that require full-wave rectification without center tapped transformers. In this type of circuit, the full secondary voltage serves as the ac input. Conduction takes place through two diodes and the load during one alternation and through the other two diodes and $R_L$ during the second alternation. Both alternations of the input produce current flow through the load resistor in the same direction.

The dc output of a full-wave rectifier is primarily based on the value of the applied ac input. In practice, the dc output of a bridge rectifier is 0.9 times the rms input voltage minus 1.4V. The 0.9 figure is based on the rms to maximum value factor times the average value factor or 1.414 x 0.637. The 1.4 volt factor of the expression is based on the conduction of current through two diodes. A silicon diode, in this case, has a 0.7V drop across it when conduction occurs. Therefore, two times 0.7V equals 1.4V drop. This voltage is deducted from the total dc output voltage of the rectifier circuit.

In this experiment, you will build and test a bridge rectifier circuit. Then, using an oscilloscope, you will see the input, positive and negative alternation conduction times and the resulting dc output. The bridge rectifier is commonly used in low voltage, semiconductor power supplies.

## EXPERIMENT OBJECTIVES

As a result of this laboratory experience, you should be able to accomplish the following:
1. Construct a bridge rectifier circuit using semiconductor diodes.
2. Calculate and measure the dc output.
3. Observe output waveforms on an oscilloscope.

## REFERENCE

Gerrish and Dugger, ELECTRICITY AND ELECTRONICS, Chapter 12, pages 168 and 169.

## MATERIALS AND EQUIPMENT

1 — Volt-ohm-milliampere (VOM) meter
1 — Oscilloscope
1 — 6.3V - 0 - 6.3V, 60 Hz ac source
1 — Power supply module or following mounted components:
    4 — 1N4004 diodes
    1 — 270 ohm, 1 watt resistor

## PROCEDURE

1. Connect bridge rectifier as in Fig. 12-3-1. Transformer supplying ac input for this circuit does not need a center connection as in previous full-wave rectifier circuit.

2. Plug in ac source transformer primary to 120V ac. Prepare VOM to measure ac voltage to test points A-C. A-C voltage is _____ volts.

3. Calculated dc output of this circuit is 0.9

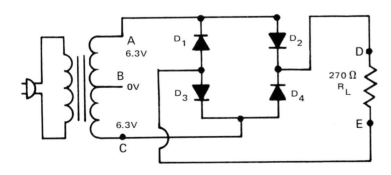

Fig. 12-3-1

of applied rms voltage minus 1.4V. Calculated dc voltage is _____ volts.

4. Prepare VOM to measure dc voltage across $R_L$ at test points D-E. Measured dc output voltage is _____ volts.

5. How do measured dc and calculated dc values compare?

6. Prepare oscilloscope for operation with 5m sec horizontal sweep time or for 10 to 100 Hz horizontal sweep frequency. Set trigger source or sync selector to line sync position.

7. Connect ground or common probe to test point C and vertical probe to point A. Adjust variable sweep control to produce two or three sine waves. Adjust horizontal position control to move display to right so that left or beginning of wave can be observed.

8. Make a sketch of observed waveform in provided space in Fig. 12-3-2.

9. Move common or ground probe of oscilloscope to test point E and vertical probe to test point A. Make a sketch of observed waveform in provided space in Fig. 12-3-2. What does this test show about circuit?

_____

_____

10. With common probe remaining at point E, move vertical probe to point C. Make a sketch of observed waveform in provided space in Fig. 12-3-2. What does this test show about circuit? _____

_____

11. With common probe remaining at point E, move vertical probe to point D. Make a sketch of observed waveform in provided space in Fig. 12-3-2.

12. Describe relationship of waveforms E-A and E-C with respect to D-E. _____

_____

13. Unplug ac supply from power source. Disconnect circuit and return all parts to storage cabinet.

## QUESTIONS

1. Explain the conduction path in Fig. 12-3-1 when point A is positive and C is negative. Start at point C.

2. Explain the conduction path in Fig. 12-4-1 when point A is negative and C is positive. Start at point A.

3. If 120V rms ac input is applied to a bridge rectifier, what is dc output?

INPUT
AT POINTS
A-C _____

OUTPUT
AT POINTS
D-E _____

INPUT
AT POINTS
E-C _____

INPUT
AT POINTS
E-A _____

Fig. 12-3-2

# Experiment 12-4  FILTER CIRCUITS

## INTRODUCTION

In order for the output of a rectifier power supply to be usable in an electronic circuit, it must be a relatively pure form of dc. Typically, rectifier outputs of either the half-wave or full-wave type are applied to a filter circuit. The primary function of the filter is to smooth out the ripple of the rectified output so that it is a relatively pure form of dc.

The filtering capability of a circuit is determined by the percent of ripple at its output. This is determined by measuring the rms value and dividing it by the dc output voltage and multiplying by 100. The lower the percent of ripple, the purer the dc output.

There are many different types of filters in operation today. A "C" type of filter is achieved by simply connecting a capacitor across the load resistor ($R_L$). A "CL" filter has a capacitor across the load, but an inductor is connected in series between the capacitor input and $R_L$. The dc voltage is reduced somewhat when a series inductor is used in a filter circuit. An "L" type of filter has a series inductor first, followed by a capacitor across $R_L$. A pi filter is "CLC" type. It has capacitor input, a series inductor and an output capacitor across $R_L$.

In this experiment, you will build and test a number of filter circuits for a rectifier power supply. First, the percentage of ripple is calculated. Then, input and output waveforms are observed on the oscilloscope to see the effect of typical filtering action. The filter performs a very important function in the power supply.

## EXPERIMENT OBJECTIVES

As a result of this laboratory experience, you should be able to accomplish the following:
1. Build some basic filter circuits.
2. Test these filter circuits.
3. Use an oscilloscope to observe the amount of ripple from the filter circuits.

## REFERENCE

Gerrish and Dugger, ELECTRICITY AND ELECTRONICS, Chapter 12, pages 169 to 171.

## MATERIALS AND EQUIPMENT

1 — Volt-ohm-milliampere (VOM) meter
1 — Oscilloscope
1 — 6.3V - 0 - 6.3V ac source
1 — Power supply module or following mounted components:
    4 — IN4004 diodes
    2 — 680 $\mu$ F, 50 V capacitors
    1 — 4.5H, 50 mA inductor
    1 — 270 ohm, 1 watt resistor
1 — SPST toggle switch

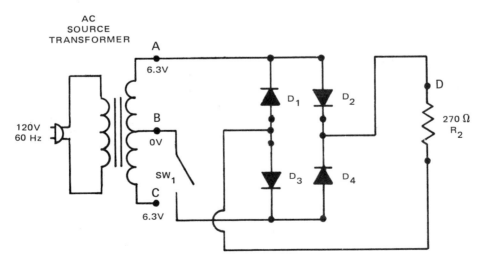

Fig. 12-4-1

## PROCEDURE

1. Construct bridge rectifier as in Fig. 12-4-1.
2. Plug in ac source transformer primary winding to 120V ac to energize circuit. Turn on circuit switch.
3. Prepare oscilloscope for operation with 5m sec horizontal sweep time or for 10 to 100 Hz horizontal sweep frequency. Set trigger source or sync selector to line sync.
4. Connect ground or common probe to test point C and vertical probe to point D. Adjust sweep control to produce approximately six pulses of full-wave output waveform. Total change in waveform amplitude is representative of output ripple. This voltage is typically measured as an rms value. Percentage of ripple is rms value divided by average dc value times 100. To determine percent of ripple, use VOM to measure rms value, then measure dc value and calculate percent of ripple. Indicate observed waveform before filtering in Fig. 12-4-2.

7. Make a sketch of observed D-C output across $R_L$ with $C_2$ connected in provided space in Fig. 12-4-2.
8. Turn off circuit switch and connect filter circuit to bridge rectifier output as indicated in Fig. 12-4-3.
9. With oscilloscope, observe waveform at E-C, then D-C to see influence of filter circuit. Increase vertical sensitivity of oscilloscope to determine ripple at points D-C. The rms measured at D-C with VOM is _____ volts. The dc is _____ volts. Percent of ripple is _____
10. Turn off circuit switch and connect a second 680 $\mu$ F capacitor ($C_1$) to circuit with positive terminal to E and negative to C. Then disconnect $C_2$ from the circuit.
11. Turn on circuit switch and observe waveform at E-C, then at D-C with oscilloscope. Measure and record rms voltage and dc voltage at points D-C with VOM. The rms is _____ volts. The dc is _____ volts. Percent of ripple is _____

DC WAVEFORM BEFORE FILTERING (STEP 4) _____

DC WAVEFORM WITH $C_2$ (STEP 7) _____

Fig. 12-4-2

5. Prepare VOM to measure ac voltage. Connect it across points C-D and record rms ripple. The rms is _____ volts. Disconnect VOM and prepare it to measure dc voltage across C-D. The dc voltage is _____ volts. Percent of ripple is _____
6. Connect a 680 $\mu$ F capacitor ($C_2$) across $R_L$ with positive lead to D and negative lead to C. With VOM, measure rms ripple voltage across $R_L$ and dc voltage. The rms is _____ volts. The dc is _____ volts. Percent of ripple is _____

12. Turn off circuit switch and connect $C_2$ to test point D-C as in Fig. 12-4-3. $C_1$ should remain connected to points E-C. With oscilloscope, observe waveforms at points E-C and D-C to see influence of filter circuit. With VOM, measure and record rms and dc voltage at points D-C. The rms is _____ The dc is _____ volts. Percent of ripple is _____
13. Turn off circuit switch and unplug ac source transformer. Disconnect circuit and return all parts to storage cabinet.

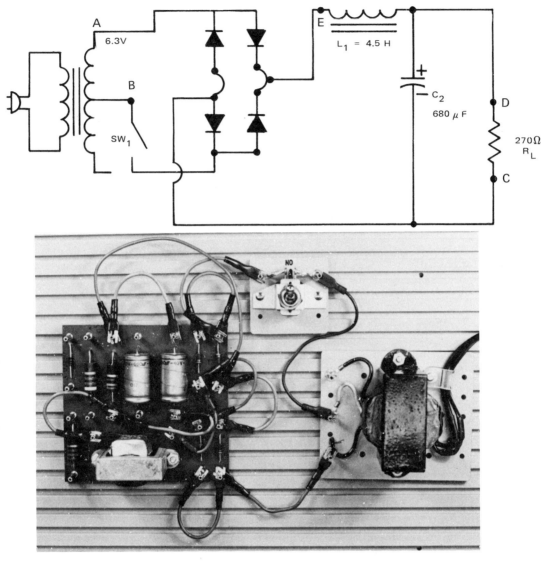

Fig. 12-4-3

## QUESTIONS

1. What determines the filtering capability of a filter circuit?
2. Make sketches of the four types of filter circuits in the space provided below and on page 164.

   a. C type filter circuit

3. Which test filter circuit produces the purest dc output: C type? LC type? CL type? CLC type?
4. What types of filter circuits are constructed in steps 6, 8, 10 and 12?

b. LC type filter circuit

c. CL type filter circuit

d. CLC type or pi filter circuit

# Experiment 12-5  VOLTAGE REGULATION

## INTRODUCTION

Voltage regulator circuits are attached to a dc power supply to reduce changes in the output voltage. Power supply output voltage without regulation varies considerably due to changes in load resistance and fluctuations in ac input supply voltage. Regulated power supplies minimize these changes so that a constant output voltage can be developed.

A zener diode is used as a regulating device in this experiment. This diode is connected in parallel or shunt with the dc output. The regulator circuit also contains a series resistor. The zener diode is connected in the reverse bias direction and goes into conduction at a specific voltage. As a result, voltage across the diode is maintained at a constant value over a large range of current values.

In this experiment, you will build a zener diode shunt regulator. Then, with the diode connected to the power supply, various tests are made using measured no-load and full-load values. When a regulator has a low percentage of regulation, the dc output is maintained at a rather constant value. This is a very desirable feature in many critical electronic circuits.

## EXPERIMENT OBJECTIVES

As a result of this laboratory experience, you should be able to accomplish the following:
1. Construct a zener diode shunt regulator circuit and connect it to the output of a dc power supply.
2. Observe how changes in the input supply voltage and load affects the output voltage.
3. Calculate percentage of voltage change in the circuit.

## REFERENCE

Gerrish and Dugger, ELECTRICITY AND ELECTRONICS, Chapter 12, pages 171 to 174.

## MATERIALS AND EQUIPMENT

1 — Volt-ohm-milliampere (VOM) meter
1 — 6.3V - 0 - 6.3V ac source
1 — Power supply module or following components:

4 — 1N4004 diodes
1 — 4.5H, 50 mA inductor
2 — 680 $\mu$F, 50V capacitors
1 — 470 ohm, 1 watt resistor
1 — 270 ohm, 1 watt resistor
1 — 2.2K, 1 watt resistor
1 — 2.9V zener diode
1 — Resistor decade module or a 1K, 1/4 watt resistor
1 — SPST toggle switch

## PROCEDURE

1. Connect bridge circuit power supply as in Fig. 12-5-1. This circuit is considered to be an unregulated dc source.
2. Plug in ac source and turn on circuit switch.
3. Prepare VOM to measure dc voltage at test points A-B, B-C and A-C. A-B is _____ volts. B-C is _____ volts. A-C is _____ volts.
4. Turn off circuit switch and apply 6.3V ac to circuit. Turn on circuit switch and measure voltages at A-B, B-C and A-C. A-B is _____ volts. B-C is _____ volts. A-C is _____ volts.
5. How does a change in input voltage affect voltage at points B-C? _____
   _____
6. Turn off circuit switch and remove 270 ohm resistor ($R_2$). In its place, connect a zener diode. Banded end of diode must be connected to point B with plain end to point C.
7. Turn on circuit switch and measure voltage across zener diode at points B-C. B-C is _____ volts. Turn off circuit switch and apply 12.6V ac to input.
8. Turn on circuit switch and measure voltage at points B-C. B-C voltage is _____ How does B-C voltage of regulated circuit (steps 7 and 8) compare with unregulated B-C voltage (steps 3 and 4)? _____
   _____
9. Turn off circuit switch and connect a 2.2K resistor across points B-C with zener diode

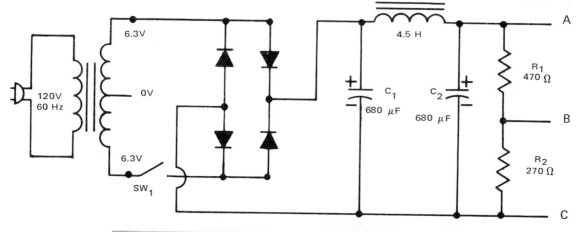

Fig. 12-5-1

remaining in circuit.

10. Turn on circuit switch and measure dc voltage at points B-C with 2.2K load. Full-load B-C voltage ($E_{fl}$) is _____ volts.

11. Disconnect 2.2K load resistor and measure dc voltage at points B-C. No-load B-C voltage ($E_{nl}$) is _____ volts.

12. Calculate percent of regulation using following formula:

$$\% \text{ Regulation} = \frac{E_{nl} - E_{fl}}{E_{fl}} \times 100$$

Percent of regulation for a 2.2K load is

_____

13. Using same procedure, connect a 270 ohm load across zener diode. Measure and record no-load and full-load voltages and calculate percent of regulation. $E_{nl}$ is _____ volts. $E_{fl}$ is _____ volts. Percent of regulation is _____

14. Using same procedure, connect a 1K load across zener diode. Measure and record necessary voltages to calculate percentage of regulation. Percent of regulation is

_____

15. Unplug ac source and disconnect circuit. Return all parts to storage cabinet.

## QUESTIONS

1. What two improvements can be noted when a zener diode regulator power supply replaces an unregulated power supply?
2. Why is it more desirable to have a regulator with a small percentage of regulation?
3. Why does a zener diode connected in the reverse direction achieve regulation?

166

## INTRODUCTION

Voltage doubler power supplies are used in circuits that require dc voltage greater than values that can be derived from the ac power source. Typically, voltage doublers do not employ transformers to raise voltage to a higher level. Portable television receivers with vacuum tubes use double power supplies to produce dc for tube element voltages.

There are two rather common voltage doubler circuits in operation today. In the first circuit, a half-wave voltage doubler charges a capacitor to the peak of the line voltage through a diode during one alternation of ac input. During the next alternation, a second diode conducts to the peak of the line voltage plus the charged peak of the first alternation. The dc output of this circuit is calculated as follows: 2 x rms input x .45 = dc output.

The second major type of voltage doubler is a full-wave type. In this circuit, the first alternation of the rms input charges a capacitor to the peak value through a diode. During the next alternation, an additional capacitor is charged to the peak value of the rms input through a second diode. The dc output is then based on the total charge accumulation across the two series connected capacitors. This value is calculated as follows: rms voltage x 1.414 x 2 = dc output. The dc output of a full-wave doubler is nearly twice the output of the half-wave doubler.

In this experiment, you will build and test half-wave and full-wave voltage doubler circuits. You will note that in both voltage doubler circuits, the output voltage is developed by capacitor charging action. When large valued capacitors are used, the voltage output can be increased somewhat.

The current output of a voltage doubler type of power supply is limited. As with voltage output, current output is dependent upon capacitor charging. Therefore, voltage doubler circuits are especially useful in producing high voltages for circuits that require low current values. However, doubler power supplies have rather poor dc voltage regulation characteristics.

## REFERENCE

Gerrish and Dugger, ELECTRICITY AND ELECTRONICS, Chapter 12, pages 174 and 175.

## MATERIALS AND EQUIPMENT

1 – Volt-ohm-milliampere (VOM) meter
1 – 6.3V - 0 - 6.3V, 60 Hz ac source
1 – Power supply module or following components:
   2 – 1N4004 diodes
   2 – 680 $\mu$F, 50V capacitors
   1 – 25 $\mu$F, 50V capacitor
   1 – 470 ohm, 2 watt resistor
   1 – 2.2K, 1 watt resistor
1 – SPST toggle switch

## PROCEDURE

1. Construct half-wave voltage doubler as in Fig. 12-6-1.

Fig. 12-6-1

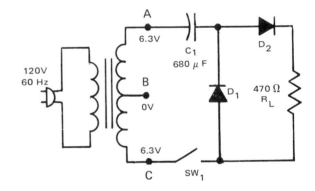

2. Plug ac source transformer into 120V, 60 Hz power line and turn on circuit switch.

3. Prepare VOM to measure dc voltage across 470 ohm load resistor ($R_L$). The dc output voltage is _____ volts.

4. Prepare VOM to measure ac input at test points A-C. The rms input voltage is _____ volts.

5. Calculated dc output voltage of a half-wave doubler is 2 x rms input x .45. Using measured rms voltage of step 4, calculated dc output is _____ volts. How does calculated dc value compare with measured dc value? _____

_____

6. Turn off circuit switch and connect ac input to points A-B on transformer. Measure and record ac input voltage. Measured ac input is _____ $V_{rms}$.

7. Calculated dc output voltage of half-wave doubler circuit is _____ Measured dc output is _____

8. Turn off circuit switch and disconnect half-wave voltage doubler circuit.

9. Connect full-wave doubler as in Fig. 12-6-2.

10. Turn on circuit switch and measure ac input voltage at test points A-B. Measured ac input voltage is _____ $V_{rms}$.

11. Calculated dc output voltage of a full-wave doubler is rms x 1.414 x 2. Using measured rms value of step 10, calculated dc output voltage is _____ volts.

12. Prepare VOM to measure dc output voltage across test points D-E. Measured dc output voltage is _____ volts.

13. Turn off circuit switch and unplug ac source transformer from power line. Disconnect circuit and return all parts to storage cabinet.

## QUESTIONS

1. If 120V rms is applied to a full-wave doubler, what is the calculated dc output?

2. If 120V rms is applied to a half-wave doubler, what is the calculated dc output?

3. Why is the dc output of a half-wave doubler less than dc output of a full-wave doubler?

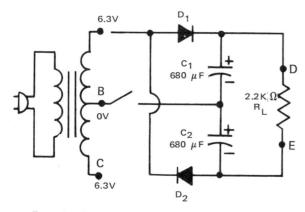

Fig. 12-6-2

# Chapter 13

# ELECTRON AMPLIFIERS

## Experiment 13-1  TRANSISTOR FAMILIARIZATION

### INTRODUCTION

There are two general types of junction transistors in operation today. The terms "NPN" and "PNP" are commonly used to describe these devices. Their theory of operation is primarily the same. The only real difference is in the current carriers and the direction of current flow. In order to make a junction transistor operate, the polarity of the source voltage applied to the transistor must be reversed.

In a conventional transistor circuit, the emitter-base junction must be forward biased with the base collector junction reverse biased. Forward biasing is achieved when the polarity of the crystal material matches the polarity of the dc voltage source. In an NPN transistor, the emitter is made of an "N" material and the base is a "P" material. Forward biasing is achieved when the emitter is connected to the positive side. A forward biased PNP transistor, by comparison, would have its emitter positive and its base negative. The polarity of the source voltage still matches the polarity of the crystal material. The collector of an NPN transistor must have the positive side of a dc source connected to its N material. The P type of base material must be negative in order to be reverse biased. A PNP transistor, in the same regard, has its collector connected to the negative side of the source, while the base is attached to the positive side. A reverse biased base-collector junction normally produces high resistance and a very minute amount of current flow.

When the emitter-base (E-B) junction of a transistor is forward biased, current will flow from the E-B junction into the base-collector (B-C) junction. As a result, the normally reverse biased collector now has a rather significant amount of current passing through its junction. This causes a corresponding current gain over the normal reverse biased collector current.

In this experiment, you will utilize the internal battery of an ohmmeter to bias the NPN and PNP transistor junctions. Through these steps, you will learn about biasing principles and transistor characteristics. The transistors used represent one of a wide variety of distinct packaging arrangements or housing types available today.

### EXPERIMENT OBJECTIVES

As a result of this laboratory experience, you should be able to accomplish the following:

1. First connect an NPN, then a PNP transistor, to an ohmmeter to observe the forward and reverse bias concept.
2. Become familiar with transistor lead names, base diagrams and element layout work.

### REFERENCE

Gerrish and Dugger, ELECTRICITY AND ELECTRONICS, Chapter 13, pages 196 and 197.

### MATERIALS AND EQUIPMENT

1 — Volt-ohm-milliampere (VOM) meter
1 — 2N3397 transistor
1 — 2N3702 transistor

### PROCEDURE

1. Remove 2N3397 transistor from storage

cabinet and place it on circuit construction board. The 2N3397 is an NPN silicon transistor housed in a TO-92 case. See base diagram, lead assignments, element names and crystal structure in Fig. 13-1-1.

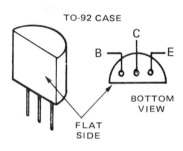

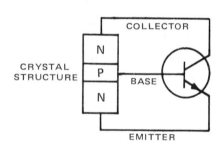

Fig. 13-1-1

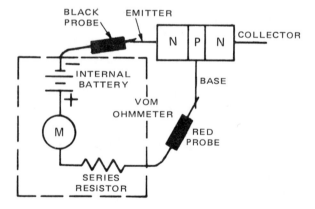

Fig. 13-1-2

2. Prepare VOM for measuring resistance by switching it to R x 100 or R x 1000 range.
3. Connect common or negative lead of ohm-meter to emitter. Connect positive probe to base of transistor. If ohmmeter has straight polarity and lead selection is correct, a low resistance should be indicated on ohm-

meter. Forward biased E-B resistance is _____ ohms.
4. When an ohmmeter is connected in this manner, it forward biases transistor. See Fig. 13-1-2.
5. Reverse probes of ohmmeter as indicated in Fig. 13-1-3. This action reverse biases emitter-base junction. Reverse bias resistance of transistor is _____ ohms.

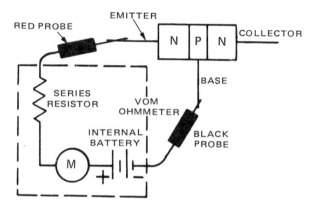

Fig. 13-1-3

6. Connect ohmmeter as indicated in part A and part B in Fig. 13-1-4.

Fig. 13-1-4

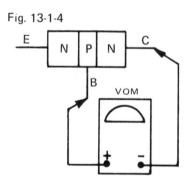

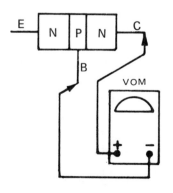

7. Complete drawing of Fig. 13-1-5 by indicating resistance values across transistor elements. E-B resistance values were measured in steps 3 and 5.

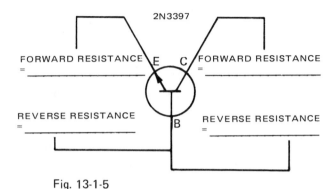

Fig. 13-1-5

8. Remove 2N3702 transistor from storage cabinet and place it on circuit construction board. This transistor is a silicon PNP transistor in a TO-92 case. Refer to the base diagram, lead assignments, element names and crystal structure in Fig. 13-1-6.

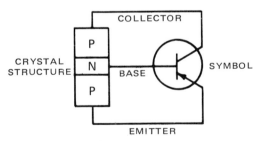

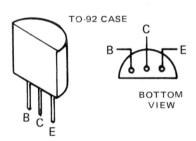

Fig. 13-1-6

9. Connect ohmmeter between emitter-base elements and measure forward and reverse resistance. Forward bias resistance is _____ ohms. Reverse bias resistance is

_____ ohms.

10. Connect ohmmeter leads to base-collector elements and measure forward and reverse resistance. Forward bias resistance is _____ ohms. Reverse bias resistance is _____ ohms.

11. Complete drawing of Fig. 13-1-7 by supplying measured resistance values.

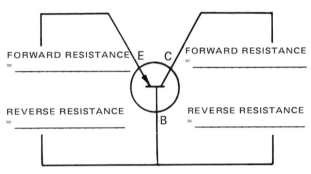

Fig. 13-1-7

12. Complete diagrams in Fig. 13-1-8 by sketching in battery symbol that would forward bias E-B junction of two transistor circuits.

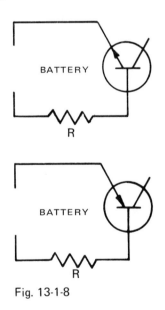

Fig. 13-1-8

13. Complete diagrams in Fig. 13-1-9 by sketching in battery symbol that would reverse bias B-C junction of two transistor circuits.

14. Return all parts to storage cabinet.

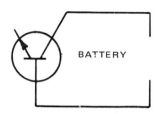

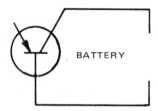

Fig. 13-1-9

## QUESTIONS

1. Forward biasing of a conventional junction transistor circuit is achieved when the polarity of the crystal material matches the polarity of the dc voltage source. Therefore, the emitter-base junction is _____ biased while the base-collector junction is _____ biased.

2. Forward biasing of a conventional junction transistor circuit causes the _____ to become low resistant which, in turn, causes _____ (an increase or a decrease) in current flow.

3. A reverse bias junction, on the other hand, is _____ resistant.

## INTRODUCTION

Transistor testing is a common procedure that must be performed periodically when working with semiconductor devices. An ohmmeter is often used to test for leakage or gain and to indicate transistor type as either NPN or PNP. These tests usually are quite indicative of a transistor's general condition.

A good transistor must show low resistance when the emitter-base and base-collector are forward biased with an ohmmeter. When reversing the polarity of the ohmmeter, the same two crystal junctions must indicate an extremely high resistance. Likewise, the emitter-collector junctions must show high resistance to either ohmmeter polarity if the transistor is good. If not, transistor leakage is indicated. The term $I_{CEO}$ or "emitter-collector current with the base open" is often used to describe this condition to the transistor.

In this experiment, you will use an ohmmeter to perform basic transistor test procedures. This is a very common service practice and represents a quick and easy method of testing without specialized equipment.

### EXPERIMENT OBJECTIVES

As a result of this laboratory experience, you should be able to accomplish the following:
1. Use an ohmmeter to test the polarity of a transistor.
2. Test the general condition of the transistor.

### REFERENCE

Gerrish and Dugger, ELECTRICITY AND ELECTRONICS, Chapter 13, pages 196 and 197.

### MATERIALS AND EQUIPMENT

1 — Volt-ohm-milliampere (VOM) meter
1 — 2N3397 transistor
1 — Assortment of used transistors

### PROCEDURE

1. Remove 2N3397 transistor from storage cabinet and place it on circuit construction board for testing.

2. Prepare VOM for measuring resistance on R x 100 or R x 1000 range.
3. The 2N3397 is a silicon transistor in a TO-92 plastic case. See base diagram, lead assignments, element names and crystal structure in Fig. 13-2-1.

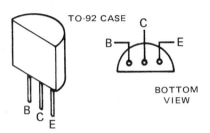

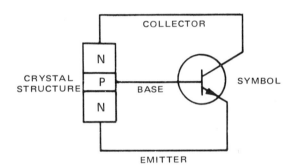

Fig. 13-2-1

4. First test is used to determine transistor type and forward bias condition of emitter-base junction. Connect positive probe of VOM to base lead of transistor and connect common or negative lead to emitter. If ohmmeter has straight meter polarity and lead selection is correct, meter should indicate a low resistance.
5. With positive probe remaining on base, switch negative ohmmeter lead to collector. If everything is correct, this condition should also produce a low resistance base-collector reading.
6. Since a transistor has two crystal junctions in its structure, this ohmmeter test can be used to identify polarity of these junctions. When negative lead of ohmmeter is connected to "N" material element and posi-

tive lead is connected to "P" material element, forward biasing occurs because of internal battery of ohmmeter. Resistance of a forward biased junction usually is quite low. Emitter-base and base-collector elements will both show low resistance when connected in this manner. Base element of any bipolar transistor can be determined by this process.

7. Connect negative lead of ohmmeter to base and positive lead to emitter. Internal battery of ohmmeter reverse biases transistor elements when connected in this manner. A good transistor should indicate an extremely high resistance in this test.

8. Using same procedure, test B-C resistance with reverse meter polarity.

9. Next test is a measure of resistance between emitter-collector elements of transistor. Polarity of ohmmeter does not matter. In either direction, E-C junction must indicate high resistance if transistor is good. This test measures E-C leakage current or $I_{CEO}$.

10. Another test is used to indicate current gain capability of a transistor. Connect positive ohmmeter lead to collector and connect negative lead to emitter. Then, touch your finger to collector and base leads at same time. Ohmmeter should show a decrease in resistance.

11. Remove 2N3702 PNP transistor from storage cabinet and place it on circuit board for testing.

12. First, connect negative ohmmeter probe of VOM to base of transistor and connect positive lead to emitter. This test should indicate a _____ (low or high) resistance value if transistor is good.

13. With negative probe remaining on base, switch positive probe to collector. A _____ (low or high) resistance should be indicated.

14. Next test measures reverse bias resistance of E-B and B-C junctions. Connect positive probe of ohmmeter to base and switch negative lead between emitter and collector. Both E-B and B-C junctions should indicate _____ (low or high) resistance.

15. Finally, measure $I_{CEO}$ of emitter-collector junctions with base open. $I_{CEO}$ resistance should read _____ (low or high) in either ohmmeter polarity direction if transistor is good.

16. Final test is to measure transistor current gain capability. Connect positive ohmmeter probe to emitter and connect negative probe to collector. Touch your finger to base and collector leads at same time. Ohmmeter should indicate _____ (low or high) resistance.

17. If time permits, ask your instructor for some additional transistors to be tested with ohmmeter. Apply following tests:
    a. Determine base element and transistor type (NPN or PNP).
    b. Test reverse bias resistance of E-B and B-C junction.
    c. Test $I_{CEBO}$ of E-C junctions.
    d. Test current gain capability.

**QUESTIONS**

1. What does $I_{CEO}$ demonstrate about a transistor?
2. Why should a good transistor show low resistance between the E-B and the B-C with the same ohmmeter polarity?
3. Why does an ohmmeter cause a transistor to be forward or reverse biased?

## INTRODUCTION

One of the more important accomplishments of a transistor is its ability to achieve current gain. Current gain of a transistor amplifier can be determined by dividing its output current by its input current. Collector current is a common measure of output. Emitter current is representative of input of a common base amplifier.

When the input of an amplifier is applied to the emitter-base junction and output is developed across the base-collector junction, the transistor is called a "common base amplifier." Since emitter current is always larger than collector current, this type of current gain is less than one. Current gain is called "alpha" ( $\propto$ ).

$$\text{Alpha} = \frac{I_c}{I_E}$$

This formula is used to determine the current gain of a common base transistor amplifier.

In a common base amplifier, the base element usually is connected to both input and output leads. The other input lead is connected to the emitter while the output is connected to the collector. In this type of circuit, the emitter-base junction is normally forward biased and the collector-base is reverse biased. A forward biased emitter-base junction is low resistant and produces a rather large input current flow. The reverse biased collector-base junction is extremely high resistant and normally produces a minute current flow.

When both the emitter-base and collector-base junctions are energized, a large amount of emitter current flows into the collector circuit. A rather small amount of base current also flows. Therefore, the resulting output ($I_c$) represents a substantial increase in current flow through the reverse biased B-C junction.

The resistance ratio between the output and input of a common base transistor amplifier accounts for voltage gain or amplification. Voltage amplification ($A_v$) is equal to output resistance divided by input resistance times alpha (current gain). For example, if the output resistance of a transistor is 100 kilohms and its input resistance is 1 kilohm:

$$A_v = \frac{R_{output}}{R_{input}} \text{ x alpha}$$

$$A_v = \frac{100,000}{1000} \text{ x } 0.98 = 98$$

In this experiment, you will construct and test a common base amplifier. These transistors are used in a very small percentage of amplifier applications today. This type of amplifier is used here to demonstrate operating principles related to all amplifier types.

## EXPERIMENT OBJECTIVES

As a result of this laboratory experience, you should be able to accomplish the following:
1. Construct a common base transistor amplifier.
2. Measure $I_E$, $I_B$ and $I_C$ in the amplifier circuit.
3. Calculate alpha and determine the voltage gain of the circuit.

## REFERENCE

Gerrish and Dugger, ELECTRICITY AND ELECTRONICS, Chapter 13, pages 196 to 198.

## MATERIALS AND EQUIPMENT

1 — Volt-ohm-milliampere (VOM) meter
1 — 0-1 mA meter
1 — 2N3397 transistor
2 — "C" type dry cells with holders
1 — 500K, 2 watt potentiometer
1 — 1.5K, 1/4 watt resistor
2 — SPST toggle switches

## PROCEDURE

1. Connect transistor circuit as in Fig. 13-3-1. Test points A, B and C are milliampere meter connection points. To insert this meter at any point, the circuit must be broken. Then, meter is placed in series with the two connections. Polarity of meter is also important to get an upscale deflection.
2. Insert a 0-1 mA meter at test point A. Install VOM as a mA meter at point B.
3. Turn on $SW_1$ with $SW_2$ remaining in OFF position while observing meter for proper

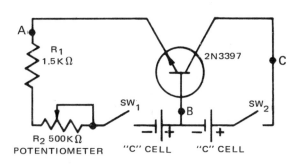

Fig. 13-3-1

deflection. Adjust $R_2$ for a maximum current reading. If a current indication does not occur, check circuit connections, battery voltage and transistor. Emitter current ($I_E$) reading at test point A is _____ mA. Base current ($I_B$) at test point B is _____ mA.

4. If circuit is working properly, $I_E$ should equal $I_B$. Why does $I_E$ equal $I_B$ in this circuit? _____

_____

5. With $SW_1$ remaining on, turn on $SW_2$. Record indicated values of $I_E$ and $I_B$. $I_E$ is _____ mA, while $I_B$ is _____ mA. The value of $I_B$ usually is quite small and must be read on a range less than 1 mA if possible.

6. Turn off both $SW_1$ and $SW_2$. Disconnect 0-1 mA meter from point A and complete circuit path at this test point. Insert 0-1 mA meter at point C.

7. Turn on $SW_1$ and $SW_2$. Collector current ($I_C$) at point C is _____ mA.

8. A check of meter readings should indicate that $I_C + I_B = I_E$.

9. Calculate current gain or alpha of this circuit:

$$\text{Alpha} = \frac{I_C}{I_E}$$

10. Turn off $SW_1$ and $SW_2$. Remove meter from test point B and insert it at test point A.

11. Turn on $SW_1$ and $SW_2$. Both $I_E$ and $I_C$ are observed in this circuit. Adjust value of $R_2$ while observing change in $I_E$ and $I_C$. Describe your observations. _____

_____

12. Turn off switches $SW_1$ and $SW_2$. Disconnect transistor and return all parts to storage cabinet.

13. Assume now that resistance of reverse biased base-collector junction of transistor circuit is a high resistance value of 100 kilohms or more. Resistance of forward biased emitter-base junction is quite low as measured in previous experiment. In this case, assume a typical E-B resistance of 1 kilohm. Voltage gain capability of this transistor can be found by calculating voltage amplification:

$$A_V = \frac{\text{alpha} \times \text{output resistance}}{\text{input resistance}}$$

$$A_V = \text{_____}$$

## QUESTIONS

1. Why is the alpha of this circuit less than one?
2. If the value of $R_1$ in Fig. 13-3-1 were doubled, how would this effect $I_C$?
3. Why does the value of $I_B$ in step 5 decrease when $SW_1$ and $SW_2$ are both ON, compared with step 3 where $I_B = I_E$?

# ▌▌▌▌▌▌▌▌▌ Experiment 13-4  COMMON EMITTER AMPLIFIERS ▌▌▌▌▌▌▌▌

## INTRODUCTION

When a transistor is connected in a common emitter configuration, the current gain is much larger than one. In this type of circuit, collector current is the output and base current is the input. A very small change in $I_B$ produces a very significant change in $I_C$. The term "beta" ($\beta$) is used to describe this current gain relationship.

In a common emitter amplifier, the input signal is applied across the base-emitter junction with its output removed across the emitter-collector junction. Therefore, the emitter element is commonly connected to both input and output. This type of transistor circuit configuration has both high current gain and high voltage gain possibilities.

In this experiment, you will construct and test a common emitter amplifier. You will become familiar with a very important transistor amplifier circuit and some of the terms used to describe its operation. Common emitter amplifiers are used in a high percentage of transistor amplifier circuit applications.

## EXPERIMENT OBJECTIVES

As a result of this laboratory experience, you should be able to accomplish the following:
1. Construct a common emitter amplifier.
2. Measure $I_E$, $I_B$ and $I_C$ in the circuit.
3. Calculate beta in the circuit.

## REFERENCE

Gerrish and Dugger, ELECTRICITY AND ELECTRONICS, Chapter 13, pages 197 to 199.

## MATERIALS AND EQUIPMENT

1 — Volt-ohm-milliampere (VOM) meter
1 — 0-1 mA meter
1 — 2N3397 transistor
1 — 1.5V "C" cell and holder
1 — 500K, 2 watt potentiometer
1 — 1.5K, 1/4 watt resistor
2 — SPST toggle switches

## PROCEDURE

1. Connect transistor circuit as in Fig. 13-4-1.

Test points A, B and C are milliampere meter connection points. To insert this meter at any point, break circuit and connect meter in series with the two connections. When the meter is removed from a test point, the circuit path must be made complete. Meter polarity also must be observed to get an up-scale deflection.

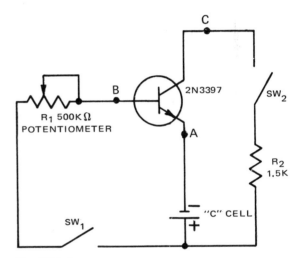

Fig. 13-4-1

2. Connect VOM at test point B and connect 0-1 mA meter at test point A. Turn on $SW_1$ with $SW_2$ remaining in OFF position.
3. Adjust potentiometer $R_1$ through its range while observing meters at test points A and B. Part of circuit is connected in series. Starting at negative terminal of "C" cell, trace current path by marking arrows on diagram.
4. Record base current ($I_B$) and emitter current ($I_E$) shown on meters. $I_B$ is _____ mA. $I_E$ is _____ mA. If circuit is working properly, these current values should be equal.
5. Turn on switch $SW_2$. How does this condition alter values of $I_B$ and $I_E$?
6. Adjust $R_1$ to produce an $I_B$ of 0.005 mA or 5 $\mu$A. Record value of $I_B$ and $I_E$. $I_B$ is _____ mA. $I_E$ is _____ mA.
7. Turn off $SW_1$ and $SW_2$. Remove 0-1 mA meter from test point A and complete

circuit at this point. Insert 0-1 mA meter at test point C.

8. Turn on $SW_1$ and $SW_2$. Record value of $I_c$. $I_c$ is _____ mA. Value of $I_B$ should still be the same as in step 6.

9. Current gain or beta of this circuit is determined by dividing output ($I_c$) by input $I_B$. Beta ( $\beta$ ) is _____

10. Adjust base current to produce a value change of from 5 to 4 $\mu$A or .005 to .004 mA. This change in $I_B$ causes a change in $I_c$ from _____ to _____ mA.

11. A changing value of $I_B$ causes a corresponding value change in $I_c$. A small change in $I_B$ could be caused by an ac signal from a microphone. Output or $I_c$ of circuit would then reflect ac beta of amplifier circuit.

12. Turn off $SW_1$ and $SW_2$. Disconnect circuit and return all components to storage cabinet.

## QUESTIONS

1. Why is beta higher than alpha of the previous experiment?
2. What are the input and output in this type of circuit?
3. What is meant by the term common emitter amplifier?

## INTRODUCTION

A large number of today's transistor amplifer circuits are called upon to increase the level of ac signals. Therefore, this type of amplifier must have an appropriate dc source voltage applied and be able to process an ac signal. The dc source voltage then changes at an ac rate according to the applied signal. The ac signal of this type of amplifier is actually riding upon the dc voltage level of the source.

In this experiment, you will construct a common emitter amplifier that employs emitter biasing. Current passing through the emitter resistor causes it to become slightly positive with respect to ground. The value of the emitter resistor determines the transistor operating point, and capacitor connected in parallel with this resistor reduces signal degeneration.

When an ac signal is applied to the input of the transistor amplifier, it sees a dc voltage level at the base element. This voltage is developed by two resistors forming a voltage divider across source voltage. The incoming ac signal causes a small change in the base voltage which, in turn, causes a change in base current. This change immediately alters the collector current, which produces a voltage drop across the collector resistor. The output signal (amplified version of input signal) appears across the collector resistor as a change in voltage.

In this experiment, you will have an opportunity to apply a signal tracing method with the oscilloscope and observe representative waveforms. The common emitter amplifier used in this experiment has numerous applications in semiconductor circuits today.

### EXPERIMENT OBJECTIVES

As a result of this laboratory experience, you should be able to accomplish the following:
1. Trace the signal path through a transistor amplifier.
2. Calculate signal voltage amplification in the circuit.
3. Using an oscilloscope, observe waveforms of key test points in the amplifier.

## REFERENCE

Gerrish and Dugger, ELECTRICITY AND ELECTRONICS, Chapter 13, Pages 197 to 199.

## MATERIALS AND EQUIPMENT

1 — Volt-ohm-milliampere (VOM) meter
1 — Variable dc power source
1 — Oscilloscope
1 — Variable frequency ac signal source
1 — 2N3397 transistor
1 — 10 $\mu$ F, 50V dc capacitor
1 — 25 $\mu$ F, 50V dc capacitor
1 — .22$\mu$ F, 100V dc capacitor
1 — 15K, 1/4 watt resistor
1 — 2.7K, 1/4 watt resistor
1 — 1.5K, 1/4 watt resistor
1 — 100 ohm, 1/4 watt resistor
1 — SPST toggle switch
1 — Crystal microphone

## PROCEDURE

1. Build transistor amplifier circuit, Fig. 13-5-1.
2. With SW$_1$ off, turn on power supply and adjust it to 9V dc.
3. Prepare oscilloscope for operation. Connect vertical probe to test point A and connect common probe to ground. Set horizontal time to 0.5m sec or horizontal frequency range to 1 KHz. Adjust display to produce 4 or 5 complete sine waves.
4. Turn on SW$_1$ and move vertical probe of oscilloscope to test point E. Adjust ac signal source to produce maximum output signal with a minimum of distortion. Peak-to-peak output is _____ volts.
5. If no signal appears at output, go to signal tracing procedure of step 7.
6. Connect vertical probe to test point B. Measure and observe peak-to-peak input signal level. Input signal is _____ volts. Calculate ac signal voltage gain. A$_v$ is

_____

7. Using vertical probe of oscilloscope, start at test point A, then observe signal path at points B, D and E. Gain of transistor will take place between points B and D. A small

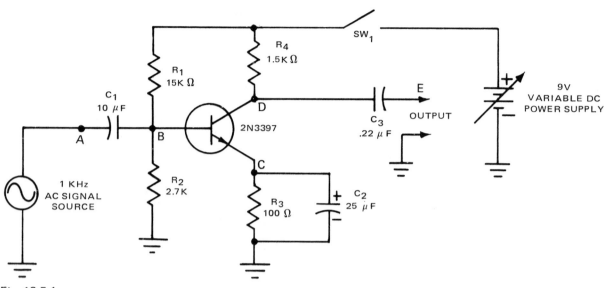

Fig. 13-5-1

emitter signal will also appear at point C.

8. With VOM, measure and record dc base, collector and emitter voltage at test points B, C and D with respect to ground. Note polarity of voltage. Base voltage is _____ volts. Collector voltage is _____ volts. Emitter voltage is _____ volts.

9. Prepare oscilloscope for external trigger or external sync operation. Connect external trigger or sync input probe to test point D.

10. Connect vertical probe to test points B, C and D, and observe phase of waveform. Make a sketch of observed waveforms in provided space in Fig. 13-5-2.

11. Move vertical probe of oscilloscope to test point D. Disconnect capacitor $C_2$ from emitter while observing output waveform. With $C_2$ removed, output level _____ Why? _____

_____

12. Disconnect ac signal source from test point A and connect a crystal microphone to input. Speak into microphone and observe output signal at test point B. How does this signal compare with 1 KHz ac signal?

_____

_____

TEST POINT B _____

TEST POINT C _____

TEST POINT D _____

Fig. 13-5-2

13. Turn off power supply and oscilloscope. Disconnect circuit and return all parts to storage cabinet.

## QUESTIONS

1. The transistor amplifier of this experiment is connected in a common _____ circuit configuration.

2. What is the phase relationship of signals appearing at the base, emitter and collector of this amplifier?

3. Briefly explain how a signal applied to the base of this amplifier achieves gain.

## INTRODUCTION

When two or more transistor amplifiers are connected or "cascaded," the ac signal must be coupled from one amplifier to the next. The dc voltage values of the first amplifier also must be blocked from passing into the second amplifier. A transformer is commonly used to couple the amplifier stages.

The transformer used in this application has two primary functions. Its coupling function is designed to permit ac signals to pass to the next amplifier and to block dc signals. The second function is impedance matching. By changing the turns ratio of the primary and secondary windings, a transformer can be designed with a high impedance input and a low impedance output. This kind of device conveniently matches the high impedance output of the first amplifier to the low impedance input of the next amplifier. An output transformer is used to step-down the signal level by matching output impedance of the transistor to the low impedance of the speaker.

Transformer coupling tends to limit the frequency of signals being transferred through an amplifier. At high frequencies, the inductive reactance of the coils increases and reduces signal gain. Transformer coupling also is more expensive than other methods of coupling, so the advantages of impedance matching must be compared with the disadvantages of cost and poor frequency response.

In this experiment, you will build and test a two-stage transistor amplifier with transformer coupling. Signal tracing techniques are used. Waveforms are observed at key test points. Phase relationships are studied throughout the signal path. Both amplifiers of this circuit are connected in a common emitter configuration. Transformer coupled amplifiers are frequently used in the audio amplifier section of inexpensive transistor radios and communications equipment.

## EXPERIMENT OBJECTIVES

As a result of this laboratory experience, you should be able to accomplish the following:

1. Construct a two-stage transistor amplifier, using transformer coupling.
2. Trace the signal path through the amplifier.
3. Observe waveforms and phase relationships in the amplifier circuit.

## REFERENCE

Gerrish and Dugger, ELECTRICITY AND ELECTRONICS, Chapter 13, Pages 199 and 200.

## MATERIALS AND EQUIPMENT

1 — Volt-ohm-milliampere (VOM) meter
1 — 1 KHz ac signal source
1 — Oscilloscope
1 — Variable dc power supply
1 — SPST toggle switch
1 — Speaker, 3.2 ohm
1 — Phono cartridge
1 — Crystal microphone
1 — Audio frequency amplifier module AF-2 (Hickok Teaching Systems) or the following components:
   3 — 2N3397 transistors
   1 — Input transformer, AR-109
   1 — Output transformer, AR-119
   1 — 10 $\mu$ F, 50V capacitor
   1 — 100 $\mu$ F, 25V capacitor
   1 — 500K, 2 watt potentiometer
   1 — 470K, 1/4 watt resistor
   1 — 6.8K, 1/4 watt resistor
   1 — 1K, 1/4 watt resistor
   1 — 68 ohm, 1/4 watt resistor
   2 — 0.47 ohm, 1/4 watt resistors

## PROCEDURE

1. Connect transformer coupled amplifier circuit shown in Fig. 13-6-1. If audio frequency amplifier module AF-2 is used, test points $TP_1$, $TP_2$, $TP_4$, $TP_5$ and $TP_7$ must have a connecting wire. If the circuit is built with individually mounted parts, these connection points are used as test points.

2. Before turning on $SW_1$, turn on variable dc power source and adjust it to produce 9V. Turn on $SW_1$.

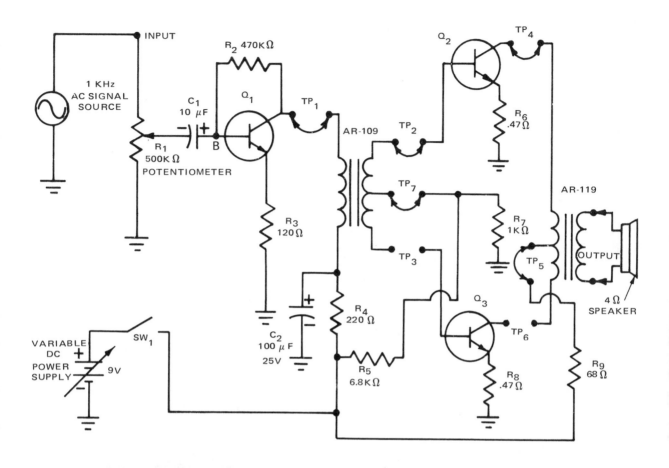

Fig. 13-6-1

3. With a VOM, measure dc voltage at E, B and C of transistors $Q_1$ and $Q_2$. Record measured values in chart in Fig. 13-6-2.

| ELEMENT | TRANSISTORS | |
|---|---|---|
| | $Q_1$ | $Q_2$ |
| BASE VOLTAGE | | |
| EMITTER VOLTAGE | | |
| COLLECTOR VOLTAGE | | |

Fig. 13-6-2

4. Connect high or positive side of signal source to amplifier input and common lead to ground. Turn on signal source and adjust it to 1 KHz. If circuit is properly connected, a 1 KHz tone should appear at speaker. Volume control or potentiometer $R_1$ may need to be adjusted to produce an output signal. If amplifier does not work, move to procedure in step 9 and trace signal to find problem. Then, return to this point and proceed to step 5. If amplifier works properly, proceed to next step.

5. Prepare oscilloscope for operation and connect ground and vertical probe to speaker terminals. Adjust horizontal time base to 0.5m sec sweep or set horizontal frequency to 1000 Hz. A display of 5 or 6 complete waves should appear on scope.

6. Adjust volume control ($R_1$) and ac signal source amplitude control for a maximum output signal with a minimum of distortion. Peak-to-peak output signal level is _____ volts.

7. Connect ground probe of oscilloscope to common ground or negative terminal of amplifier. Connect vertical probe to base or B terminal of $Q_1$. Measured peak-to-peak input signal level is _____ volts.

8. Total signal voltage amplification ($A_V$) between input and output is determined by formula: $A_V$ = output divided by input. $A_V$ is _____

9. With oscilloscope, trace signal path through amplifier. Start at input point, then test point B, $TP_1$, $TP_2$, $TP_4$ and the speaker. Gain achieved by $Q_1$ is based upon input signal at test point B and output at $TP_1$. Gain of $Q_1$ is _____

10. Gain of $Q_2$ is based on output signal at $TP_4$ divided by input signal at $TP_2$. $A_V$ of $Q_2$ is _____

11. Prepare oscilloscope for external trigger input or for external sync. Connect external trigger or sync input lead to $TP_1$. Starting at test point B, observe phase of input signal applied to $Q_1$. Make a sketch of signal, showing its phase relationship in provided space of Fig. 13-6-3. Using same procedure, connect oscilloscope to $TP_1$, $TP_2$ and $TP_4$ and make sketches of the observed waveforms.

$Q_1$ INPUT (B) _____

$Q_1$ OUTPUT ($TP_1$) _____

$Q_2$ INPUT ($TP_2$) _____

$Q_2$ OUTPUT ($TP_4$) _____

Fig. 13-6-3

12. Disconnect ac signal source from input of amplifier and connect a crystal microphone in its place. Speak into microphone. Adjust volume control ($R_1$) to produce a suitable output signal from speaker. Generally, it is better to have one person speak into microphone with a second person listening to output.
13. If time permits, test circuit with a phonograph cartridge input or, if possible, play a record on a phonograph and test its output with amplifier.
14. Disconnect amplifier circuit and return all components to storage cabinet.

## QUESTIONS
1. How do you account for the change in output signal level between $TP_4$ and the speaker?
2. What is the function of transformer AR-109?
3. What are some major disadvantages of transformer coupled amplifiers?

# INTRODUCTION

A push-pull amplifier is a rather common type of circuit found in the output of an audio amplifier. Through this type of circuit, it is possible to increase power output over that developed by a single output transistor.

In order to achieve push-pull amplification, two transistors are connected so that a divided input signal drives each amplifier. The input signals are of equal amplitude but 180 deg. out of phase. The output signal of each transistor is combined to produce a relatively pure signal of a higher power level.

With a push-pull amplifier, an audio frequency signal is first amplified by a single transistor. Next, a coupling transformer with a center tapped secondary winding is used to develop two signals of equal amplitude but 180 deg. out of phase. These signals are processed independently by a transistor amplifier. During the positive alternation, one transistor has increased output while the second transistor has reduced output. During the negative alternation, the process is reversed. Finally, the output from each transistor combines in the center-tapped primary winding of the output transformer.

In this experiment, you will build and test a push-pull amplifier and trace the signal path with an oscilloscope. Transformer coupled push-pull amplifiers are commonly used in expensive audio amplifier circuits.

## EXPERIMENT OBJECTIVES

As a result of this laboratory experience, you should be able to accomplish the following:
1. Construct a push-pull amplifier.
2. Trace the signal through the amplifier circuit.
3. Measure signal level values, calculate gain and observe phase relationships in the push-pull amplifier.

## REFERENCE

Gerrish and Dugger, ELECTRICITY AND ELECTRONICS, Chapter 13, pages 194 to 196 and 206 to 208.

# MATERIALS AND EQUIPMENT

1 — Volt-ohm-milliampere (VOM) meter
1 — Oscilloscope
1 — Variable dc power supply
1 — 1 KHz ac signal source
1 — Crystal microphone
1 — Speaker, 3.2 ohm
1 — 4 ohm, 1/4 watt resistor or resistor decade module
1 — Audio frequency amplifier module AF-2 (Hickok Teaching Systems) or the following components:
  3 — 2N3397 transistors
  1 — Input transformer, AR-109
  1 — Output transformer, AR-119
  1 — 10 $\mu$F, 50V capacitor
  1 — 100 $\mu$F, 25V capacitor
  1 — 500K, 2 watt potentiometer
  1 — 470K, 1/4 watt resistor
  1 — 6.8K, 1/4 watt resistor
  1 — 1K, 1/4 watt resistor
  1 — 68 ohm, 1/4 watt resistor
  2 — 0.47 ohm, 1/4 watt resistor

# PROCEDURE

1. Connect a push-pull audio frequency amplifier circuit as in Fig. 13-7-1. If audio amplifier module AF-2 is used, all test points 1 through 7 must be connected by wire. If this circuit is built with individually mounted components, these connection points will serve as test points.

2. Turn on variable dc power supply and adjust it to produce 9V before turning on $SW_1$.

3. With a VOM, measure voltage at E, B and C of transistors $Q_1$, $Q_2$ and $Q_3$. Record measured values in chart in Fig. 13-7-2.

4. Connect high side of signal source to amplifier input and common lead to ground. Turn on signal source and adjust to 1 KHz. If circuit is properly connected, a 1 KHz tone should be produced by speaker. Volume control or $R_1$ may need to be adjusted to produce an output signal. If amplifier works properly, proceed to next step. If it does not work, move to step 10

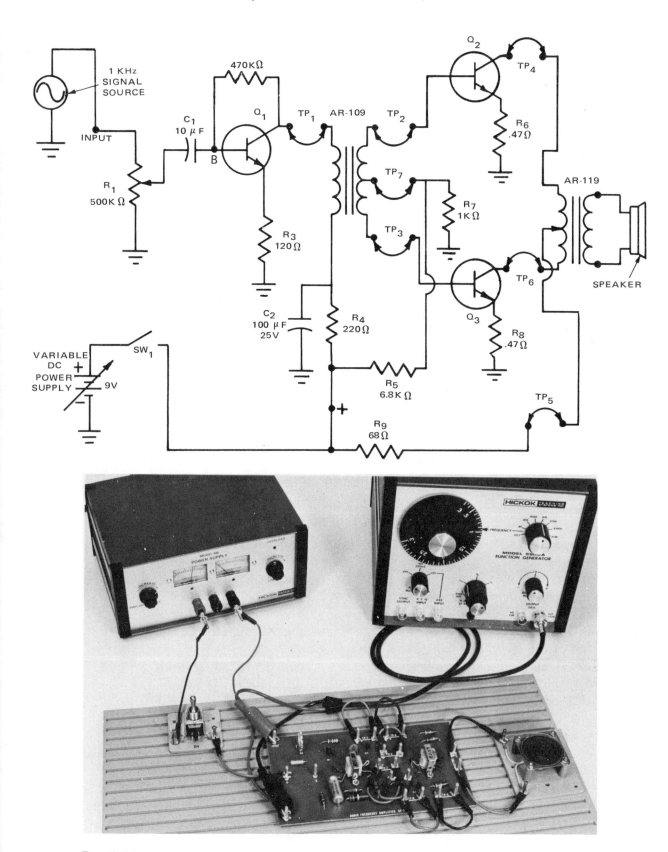

Fig. 13-7-1

| ELEMENT | TRANSISTORS | | |
|---|---|---|---|
| | $Q_1$ | $Q_2$ | $Q_3$ |
| BASE VOLTAGE | | | |
| EMITTER VOLTAGE | | | |
| COLLECTOR VOLTAGE | | | |

Fig. 13-7-2

and trace signal path to find faulty part of circuit. Then, proceed to step 5.

5. Prepare oscilloscope to observe 1 KHz signal appearing across speaker terminals. Adjust so that a display of 4 or 5 complete sine waves appears on CRT.

6. Disconnect speaker from output terminals and connect a 3.2 ohm resistor in its place.

7. Adjust volume control and ac signal source amplitude control for a signal with maximum output and a minimum of distortion. Peak-to-peak output signal has a level of _____ volts.

8. Connect common probe of oscilloscope to negative or ground terminal of amplifier. Connect vertical probe to base or B terminal post of transistor $Q_1$. Peak-to-peak input signal level is _____ volts.

9. Calculate total signal voltage amplification that occurs between input and output. $A_V$ is _____

10. With oscilloscope, trace signal path through amplifier, starting at input, then test point B and $TP_1$. This first part is considered as a single path signal. Then, two signal paths are developed at output winding of AR-109. The $Q_2$ path is $TP_2$, $TP_4$ and speaker. The $Q_3$ path includes $TP_3$, $TP_6$ and speaker. Record peak-to-peak signal values at indicated test points in Fig. 13-7-3.

11. Calculate $A_V$ gain of $Q_1$ using values of test point B and $TP_1$. $A_V$ of $Q_1$ is

_____

12. Calculate $A_V$ gain of $Q_2$ using $TP_2$ and $TP_4$. Calculate gain of $Q_3$ using $TP_3$ and $TP_6$. $A_V$ of $Q_2$ is _____ $A_V$ of $Q_3$ is

_____

13. Prepare oscilloscope for external sync input or external trigger operation. Connect external trigger or sync input lead to $TP_1$. Starting at test point B, observe and record

PEAK-TO-PEAK
SIGNAL VALUES

B = _____ VOLTS    $TP_1$ = _____ VOLTS

$TP_2$ = _____ VOLTS    $TP_4$ = _____ VOLTS

$TP_3$ = _____ VOLTS    $TP_6$ = _____ VOLTS

PHASE RELATIONSHIP

B _____

$TP_1$ _____

$TP_2$ _____

$TP_4$ _____

$TP_3$ _____

$TP_6$ _____

Fig. 13-7-3

phase of signals at each test point in Fig. 13-7-3.

14. Disconnect ac signal source from input of amplifier and connect a crystal microphone in its place. Speak into microphone and test amplifier output. If weak, volume control may need to be adjusted to produce best output.

15. Disconnect circuit and return all parts to storage cabinet.

## QUESTIONS

1. Using the speaker output voltage of step 7 and the 10 ohm resistor, calculate power output of the amplifier with this formula:

$$P = \frac{E^2}{R}$$

2. What is the phase relationship of the input signals to $Q_2$ and $Q_3$?

3. What class of amplification is achieved by $Q_1$, $Q_2$ and $Q_3$ of Fig. 13-7-1?

# Chapter 14

# ELECTRONIC OSCILLATORS

## Experiment 14-1 OSCILLATOR PRINCIPLES

### INTRODUCTION

An electronic oscillator is a circuit designed to change dc into a usable form of ac. The ac from an oscillator is commonly used as the radio frequency source for transmitters and in signal generators. This type of ac generator has no moving parts and can be designed to produce a wide range of frequencies.

To function, an oscillator must have some form of energy feedback from output to input. The feedback from the output must be regenerative or in phase with the input to produce a sustained oscillation. The amplitude of the feedback signal also must be great enough to overcome energy losses dissipated by circuit resistance. An amplifying device such as a transistor or vacuum tube is employed in the circuit to produce signal gain. This device often responds as a switching device and only turns on for a portion of the generated wave.

The generated frequency of an oscillator is primarily determined by the inductive and capacitive components of a tuned circuit. When a capacitor is charged with dc, it produces a damped oscillatory waveform when it discharges through an inductor. The number of cycles of ac that occur within a given time determines the generated frequency. The tuned LC frequency components of an oscillator usually are described as a tank circuit. Feedback energy applied to this circuit restores energy losses dissipated by circuit resistance.

In this experiment, you will build a low frequency Hartley oscillator, which features a tapped inductor. Feedback takes place between the collector and base through the coupling of a

magnetic field between the windings of a center tapped transformer. The Hartley oscillator usually is quite distorted and not very useful in other applications.

### EXPERIMENT OBJECTIVES

As a result of this laboratory experience, you should be able to accomplish the following:
1. Construct a low frequency Hartley oscillator.
2. Change the frequency of the Hartley oscillator.
3. Test voltages in the oscillator as frequencies are varied.

### REFERENCE

Gerrish and Dugger, ELECTRICITY AND ELECTRONICS, Chapter 14, pages 209 to 211.

### MATERIALS AND EQUIPMENT

1 — Volt-ohm-milliampere (VOM) meter
1 — Variable dc power supply
1 — 2N3702 transistor
1 — AR-119 ac output transformer with audio frequency module AF-2 or an equivalent 500 ohm, CT, 3.2 ohm transformer (Hickok)
1 — 15K, 1/4 watt resistor
1 — 500K, 2 watt potentiometer
1 — 5K, 2 watt potentiometer
1 — 25 $\mu$ F, 50V dc capacitor
1 — SPST toggle switch
1 — 3.2 ohm speaker

### PROCEDURE

1. Connect a Hartley oscillator circuit as in Fig. 14-1-1. Transformer $T_1$ is found on

---

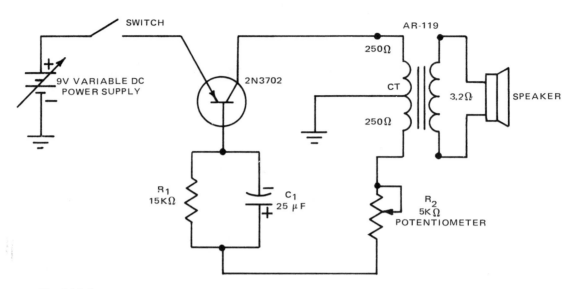

Fig. 14-1-1

audio frequency module AF-2. A separately mounted transformer, AR-119, may be used in place of AF-2 module transformer if it is not available.

2. With $SW_1$ in OFF position, turn on power supply and adjust it to 9V dc.

3. Turn on $SW_1$. If oscillator is working properly, sound should be heard from speaker.

4. Adjust potentiometer $R_2$ through its range. What influence does this have upon oscillator? _____

_____

5. Prepare VOM to measure dc voltage on a suitable range. Measure and record voltage at emitter, base and collector with respect to ground, with $R_2$ set to highest frequency tone. E is _____ volts. B is _____ volts. C is _____ volts.

6. Adjust resistor $R_2$ to its lowest frequency range, then measure and record E, B and C voltage of transistor. E is _____ volts. B is _____ volts. C is _____ volts.

7. Turn off $SW_1$ and remove 5K, $R_2$ potentiometer from circuit. In its place, connect a 500K potentiometer.

8. Turn on $SW_1$ and adjust 500K potentiometer through its range. How does this resistor change alter frequency of oscillator?

9. Connect VOM to base and ground of circuit to measure base voltage.

10. While observing VOM, momentarily touch a jumper wire across $C_1$. How does this change $V_B$? _____

_____

11. What influence does this have on frequency of oscillator? _____

_____

12. Turn off $SW_1$ and power supply. Disconnect circuit and return all parts to storage cabinet.

## QUESTIONS

1. When looking at the circuit shown in Fig. 14-1-1, what component indentifies it as a Hartley oscillator?

2. Starting at the collector of the transistor, what is the feedback path?

3. What is the function of the transistor in the Hartley oscillator of this experiment?

## INTRODUCTION

Hartley oscillators are commonly used in radio receivers and transmitter circuits. This oscillator has unusual stability and can produce a wide range of frequencies. The basic oscillator includes an LC tank circuit, a feedback path and an amplifying device. A transistor is used to achieve amplification. Both variable frequency and fixed frequency oscillators can be built with the Hartley circuit.

When the circuit switch in Fig. 14-2-1 is turned on, current flows from negative side of source through $R_1$ to emitter. With the collector and base both connected to the positive side of the source, the E-B junction is forward biased and C is reverse biased. $I_E$, $I_B$ and $I_C$ flows as a result of this biasing. A feedback path from the collector, through $C_3$ to point $C_B$, and lower coil of $T_1$ produces a magnetic field around the coil. This changing field cuts across the top coil of $T_1$ and induces voltage into it. The induced voltage charges C, which begins to discharge through $T_1$ and produce an ac signal. Part of this ac wave also is applied to the base through $C_1$ which drives it into momentary cutoff. Then, the operational cycle repeats itself. The feedback signal from collector to base must be in-phase or regenerative in order for the circuit to produce a sustained ac signal generation by the tank circuit.

In this experiment, you will build and test an RF Hartley oscillator. The basic principle of this oscillator is a very important circuit operation in the study of communication electronics.

## EXPERIMENT OBJECTIVES

As a result of this laboratory experience, you should be able to accomplish the following:
1. Construct an RF Hartley oscillator.
2. Test the operation of this oscillator.
3. Use an oscilloscope to observe waveforms at key test points.

## REFERENCE

Gerrish and Dugger, ELECTRICITY AND ELECTRONICS, Chapter 14, pages 211 and 212.

## MATERIALS AND EQUIPMENT

1 — Volt-ohm-milliampere (VOM) meter
1 — Oscilloscope
1 — Variable dc power supply
1 — 365 pF variable capacitor
1 — SPST toggle switch
1 — 100 pF capacitor
1 — RF oscillator module RF-1 (Hickok Teaching Systems) or following components:
   1 — 2N3397 transistor
   1 — Hartley oscillator coil
   1 — 47K, 1/4 watt resistor
   1 — 390 ohm, 1/4 watt resistor
   1 — 47 pF, 100V capacitor
   2 — 0.01 $\mu$ F, 100V capacitors
   1 — 25 mH inductor

## PROCEDURE

1. Connect RF Hartley oscillator circuit as in Fig. 14-2-1. RF oscillator module No. RF-1 is a complete Hartley oscillator. Simply connect a capacitor to middle two connection posts to make circuit operational when power is applied. If RF-1 module is not available, use individually mounted components.

2. Connect a 100 pF capacitor across middle two terminal connection posts marked $C_A$ and $C_B$ in circuit diagram.

3. Before turning on switch $SW_1$, adjust variable dc power supply to 9V dc.

4. Prepare VOM to measure dc voltage with reversed polarity. Connect it across output at terminal $C_A$ and ground or negative terminal of RF-1. If oscillator is working, there should be a negative voltage at output. RF-1 output is _____ volts.

5. Prepare oscilloscope for operation with horizontal time base in 1 $\mu$ sec range or sweep frequency in 100 KHz or 1 MHz range. Connect vertical probe to output terminal ($C_A$) and common probe to ground or negative terminal.

6. Make a sketch of observed output waveform in provided space in Fig. 14-2-2.

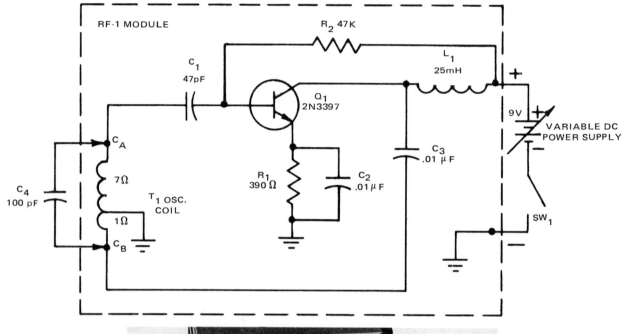

Fig. 14-2-1

7. First, move vertical probe of oscilloscope to base, then to collector and record observed waveforms at each test point in provided space of Fig. 14-2-2.

8. Turn off $SW_1$ and disconnect 100 pF capacitor from points $C_A$ and $C_B$. In its place, connect a 365 pF variable capacitor.

9. Turn on $SW_1$ and connect vertical probe of oscilloscope to terminal $C_A$ with common probe to ground.

10. Adjust variable capacitor to where plates are fully meshed. Capacitor is at its _____ (smallest or largest) capacitance value at this position. Then, adjust capacitor to where plates are completely extended-out stationary plates. Capacitor is at its _____ (smallest or largest) capacitance value at this position.

11. Observing oscilloscope pattern, frequency is _____ (high or low) when capacitor plates are meshed and _____ (high or low) when plates are extended.

OUTPUT
WAVEFORM _____

BASE
WAVEFORM _____

COLLECTOR
WAVEFORM _____

Fig. 14-2-2

12. If an AM radio receiver is available, turn it on and place it near oscillator circuit. Tune receiver to a location near center of dial that is not occupied by a station.

13. Adjust variable capacitor of oscillator through its range while listening for a whistling sound on receiver. When approximate frequency has been located, try tuning receiver to precise spot where whistling occurs. Frequency of receiver is _____ KHz.

14. Turn off power supply and oscilloscope. Disconnect circuit and return all parts to storage cabinet.

## QUESTIONS

1. What components determine the frequency of the oscillator in this experiment?
2. How does feedback from the output occur?
3. What does feedback actually achieve in the operation of an oscillator?

## INTRODUCTION

A Colpitts oscillator is similar in operation to the Hartley oscillator of Experiment 14-2. The Colpitts oscillator, however, develops feedback by means of an electrostatic field across two capacitors. In a strict sense, a Colpitts oscillator has split capacitors and a Hartley oscillator has a tapped inductor.

In a Colpitts oscillator, two capacitors of the tank circuit form a voltage divider circuit for the ac feedback signal. Each capacitor causes the 90 deg. phase shift with a 180 deg. total across both capacitors. The phase of the ac voltage from the collector shifts a full 180 deg. to produce an in-phase or regenerative feedback signal that is returned to the base. The amount of feedback developed by this oscillator is based upon the value ratio of the split capacitors. Feedback must be great enough to overcome tank circuit losses caused by resistance.

The frequency output of a Colpitts oscillator is primarily based upon the LC values of the tank circuit components. In this case:

$$\text{Frequency} = \frac{159}{\sqrt{LC}}$$

Since the two capacitors of the tank circuit are connected in series, their total value must first be calculated by the following formula:

$$\frac{1}{C_T} = \frac{1}{C_1} + \frac{1}{C_2} \cdots$$

A decrease in tank circuit capacitance will cause a corresponding increase in frequency.

In the Colpitts oscillator built for this experiment, a PNP transistor is used in a common base circuit configuration. Because of this configuration, feedback from collector to emitter is in phase. An oscillator of this type is typically 10 times more stable than its common emitter counterpart. Colpitts oscillators are primarily used to generate radio frequency signals in communication circuits.

## EXPERIMENT OBJECTIVES

As a result of this laboratory experience, you should be able to accomplish the following:

1. Construct a Colpitts oscillator.
2. Trace the feedback path in the oscillator.
3. Use an oscilloscope to observe the phase relationships of the circuit waveforms.

## REFERENCE

Gerrish and Dugger, ELECTRICITY AND ELECTRONICS, Chapter 14, pages 212 and 213.

## MATERIALS AND EQUIPMENT

1 — Volt-ohm-milliampere (VOM) meter
1 — Oscilloscope
1 — Variable dc power supply
1 — 2N3702 transistor
1 — 365 pF/125 pF two-ganged variable capacitor
1 — 0.22 $\mu$ F, 100V dc capacitor
1 — 0.1 $\mu$ F, 100V dc capacitor
1 — 0.01 $\mu$ F, 100V dc capacitor
1 — 25 mH inductor
1 — 15K, 1/4 watt resistor
1 — 10K, 1/4 watt resistor
1 — 5K, 2 watt potentiometer
1 — 1.5K, 1/4 watt resistor
1 — SPST toggle switch

## PROCEDURE

1. Connect Colpitts oscillator as in Fig. 14-3-1.
2. Before turning on SW$_1$, turn on variable dc power supply and adjust it to 9V dc.
3. Prepare oscilloscope for operation. Connect it to circuit output of oscillator. Adjust output level or amplitude control R$_4$ for maximum, undistorted signal output. If circuit is connected properly, and SW$_1$ is turned on, a sine wave should appear at output.
4. Using VOM, measure specific operating voltages at emitter, base and collector. Measured values should fall within voltage range indicated at E, B and C in diagram. Note that positive lead of power source is connected to common or ground of circuit. With meter ground connected to circuit

**197**

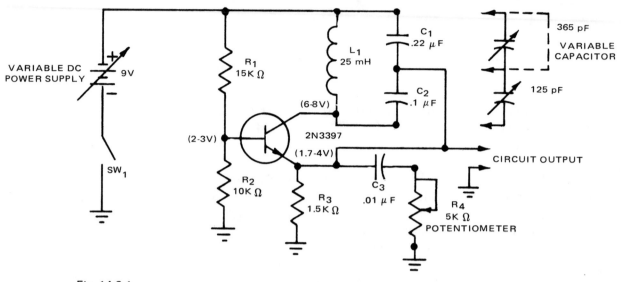

Fig. 14-3-1

ground, all voltage readings will be negative values.

5. Prepare oscilloscope for external sync or trigger input. Connect external input to collector of transistor. With common probe

**BASE WAVEFORM** _____

**EMITTER WAVEFORM** _____

**COLLECTOR WAVEFORM** _____

Fig. 14-3-2

of oscilloscope connected to ground, connect vertical probe to each element of transistor and observe waveforms. Sketch waveforms in provided space in Fig. 14-3-2.

6. Phase relationship of feedback signal from collector to emitter indicates that signals are _____

7. Turn off circuit switch and disconnect capacitors $C_1$ and $C_2$ from circuit. Connect a two-ganged 365 pF/125 pF capacitor in place of $C_1$ and $C_2$. See Fig. 14-3-1.

8. Turn on circuit switch and test output signal. Adjust potentiometer $R_4$ for maximum, undistorted output. What is most obvious difference in modified circuit output and original circuit output? _____

_____

9. Adjust variable capacitor through its range while observing oscilloscope. Highest frequency output occurs when variable capacitor is _____

10. Turn off circuit switch, power supply and oscilloscope. Disconnect circuit and return all parts to storage cabinet.

## QUESTIONS

1. What is the major difference between a Hartley and a Colpitts oscillator?
2. How does the Colpitts oscillator of this experiment achieve feedback?
3. What are the frequency-determining components of the Colpitts oscillator?

# Experiment 14-4  CRYSTAL OSCILLATORS

## INTRODUCTION

A crystal oscillator is an important oscillator classification. Oscillators of this type are designed to generate very stable frequencies for communication circuits. Broadcasting stations, amateur radio transmitters, citizen band transmitters and public service radio transmitters usually are controlled by crystal oscillators.

A crystal oscillator utilizes the piezoelectric effect to produce a stabilized output frequency. When voltage is applied, the crystal responds by vibrating at a natural frequency. These vibrations depend on the crystal size, thickness and kind of crystal material used. Crystals can be purchased at a variety of natural frequencies depending upon application. You can improve the frequency of a crystal oscillator by housing it in an oven to maintain the temperature at an even level.

In this experiment, you will build and test a variation of the Pierce crystal oscillator. This oscillator has variable output capabilities and produces a very stable frequency. Frequently, 100 KHz oscillators of this type are used to calibrate radio receivers. The output of Pierce crystal oscillators produces multiples or harmonics of the fundamental frequency. When tuning across a radio receiver, you should be able to hear a harmonic at each 100 KHz of frequency. A number of basic oscillator types use crystals to produce stabilized output.

## EXPERIMENT OBJECTIVES

As a result of this laboratory experience, you should be able to accomplish the following:
1. Construct a Pierce crystal oscillator.
2. Observe waveforms at key points in circuit.
3. Measure voltage in the circuit.

## REFERENCE

Gerrish and Dugger, ELECTRICITY AND ELECTRONICS, Chapter 14, pages 212 to 215.

## MATERIALS AND EQUIPMENT
    1  —  Volt-ohm-milliampere (VOM) meter
    1  —  Variable dc power supply
    1  —  Oscilloscope
    1  —  100 KHz crystal
    1  —  2N3397 transistor
    1  —  0.22 $\mu$F, 100V capacitor
    1  —  0.01 $\mu$F, 100V capacitor
    1  —  0.001 $\mu$F, 100V capacitor
    1  —  500K, 2 watt potentiometer
    1  —  470K, 1/4 watt resistor
    1  —  25 mH inductor
    1  —  SPST toggle switch

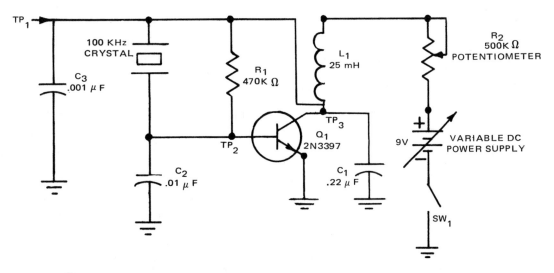

Fig. 14-4-1

**PROCEDURE**

1. Connect crystal oscillator as in Fig. 14-4-1.
2. Before turning on circuit switch $SW_1$, turn on variable dc power supply and adjust it to 9V.
3. Prepare oscilloscope for operation with sweep frequency in 100 KHz range or horizontal time in the $5\,\mu$ sec range.
4. Connect ground lead of oscilloscope to common ground or negative circuit lead. Connect vertical probe to $TP_1$.
5. Adjust potentiometer $R_2$ for a maximum signal with a minimum of distortion.
6. Make a sketch of observed waveform at $TP_1$, $TP_2$ and $TP_3$ in provided space in Fig. 14-4-2. Indicate peak-to-peak amplitude level for each signal.

WAVEFORM

$TP_1$ _____

$TP_2$ _____

$TP_3$ _____

PEAK-TO-PEAK
SIGNAL VALUES

$TP_1$ _____ VOLTS
$TP_2$ _____ VOLTS
$TP_3$ _____ VOLTS

Fig. 14-4-2

7. Prepare VOM to measure dc voltage. Measure dc at base and collector of transistor with respect to common ground. $V_B$ is _____ volts. $V_C$ is _____ volts.
8. Return vertical probe of oscilloscope to $TP_3$ and adjust potentiometer $R_2$ for maximum signal output. This wave will be distorted somewhat. Make a sketch of observed wave in provided space in Fig. 14-4-3. Also record peak-to-peak voltage measured at each test point.

WAVEFORM

$TP_1$ _____

$TP_2$ _____

$TP_3$ _____

PEAK-TO-PEAK
SIGNAL VALUES

$TP_1$ _____ VOLTS
$TP_2$ _____ VOLTS
$TP_3$ _____ VOLTS

Fig. 14-4-3

9. With VOM, measure and record dc voltage at base and collector. $V_B$ is _____ volts. $V_C$ is _____ volts.
10. If an AM radio receiver is available, turn it on and place it near oscillator circuit. Tune receiver through its entire range. How many spots on receiver do you hear oscillator? _____
11. Turn off circuit switch, power supply and oscilloscope. Disconnect circuit and return all components to storage cabinet.

**QUESTIONS**

1. How is the piezoelectric effect used in a crystal oscillator?
2. Why are crystals used in oscillators?
3. Why does the frequency of this oscillator produce a number of different oscillations on a radio receiver?

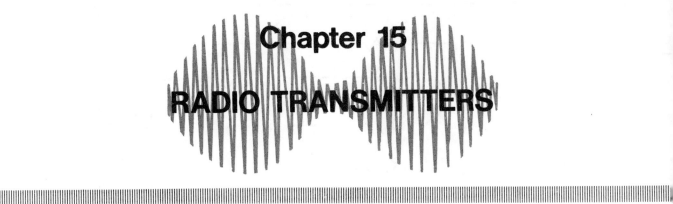

# Chapter 15
# RADIO TRANSMITTERS

## Experiment 15-1  CW TRANSMITTERS

### INTRODUCTION

Today's simplest radio frequency (rf) transmitter is a single stage unit designed to radiate a continuous wave (CW) signal. Essential parts include an rf oscillator, a code key to turn it on and off, an antenna and a power supply.

The oscillator of a CW transmitter is used to generate radio frequency energy. In a single stage transmitter, all rf energy comes directly from the oscillator. Most any oscillator discussed in Chapter 14 could be used to produce the rf wave for this transmitter. These oscillators may be fixed at one specific frequency or may be made variable to adjust to a range of different frequencies.

The oscillator of a CW transmitter is designed to produce an ac sine wave at some desired radio frequency. The signal produced is called "the rf carrier wave." When more powerful signals are desired, the carrier wave is amplified to increase its amplitude. The rf power amplifier is driven by the oscillator and usually represents the final stage of amplification of a CW transmitter.

Ultimately, the rf carrier wave is fed into the antenna, since its primary function is to radiate energy into space. The radiated signal is transformed into electromagnetic waves that are driven away from the antenna. The distance that an rf signal travels after leaving the antenna is based on its power rating and frequency.

To introduce information into a continuous wave transmitter, a code key is used to interrupt the rf signal from the oscillator. When the key is depressed, it turns on the oscillator so that a signal is radiated from the antenna.

Releasing the key causes it to become open by spring action. By opening and closing the key, International Morse coded signals can be produced and radiated from the antenna.

In this experiment, you will build a single stage continuous wave transmitter. You will become familiar with CW transmitter principles, representative signals and terminology. CW transmitters are commonly used in radio telegraph communication systems and amateur radio.

### EXPERIMENT OBJECTIVES

As a result of this laboratory experience, you should be able to accomplish the following:

1. Construct a single stage continuous wave transmitter with a Hartley oscillator.
2. Key the transmitter, using a code key.
3. Observe the signals in the CW transmitter.

### REFERENCE

Gerrish and Dugger, ELECTRICITY AND ELECTRONICS, Chapter 15, pages 218 to 221.

### MATERIALS AND EQUIPMENT

1 — Variable dc power supply
1 — Oscilloscope
1 — Two-gang variable capacitor, 365 pF/ 125 pF
1 — 100 pF, 100V capacitor
1 — Code key
1 — Radio frequency oscillator module RF-1 (Hickok Teaching Systems) or the following components:
1 — 2N3397 transistor
1 — Hartley oscillator coil

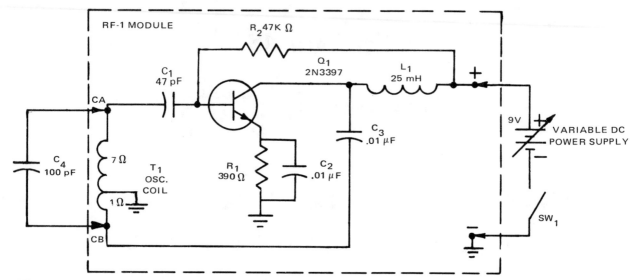

Fig. 15-1-1

1 — 47K, 1/4 watt resistor
1 — 390 ohm, 1/4 watt resistor
1 — 47 pF, 100V capacitor
2 — .01 $\mu$ F, 100V capacitors
1 — 25 mH inductor

## PROCEDURE:

1. Connect Hartley oscillator circuit as in Fig. 15-1-1. If oscillator module is used, connect a 100 pF capacitor ($C_4$) to terminals CA and CB.
2. Before turning on $SW_1$, turn on variable dc power supply and adjust it to 9V.
3. Prepare oscilloscope for operation. Connect ground lead to common ground or negative terminal of power supply. Connect vertical probe to output lead. If circuit is working properly, a continuous sine wave of approximately 1000 KHz should be displayed on oscilloscope.
4. Turn off circuit switch $SW_1$. Connect a code key in place of $SW_1$.
5. Depress code key and observe operation of oscillator on oscilloscope. When code key or toggle switch is closed or turned on, oscillator _____

6. When switch or code key is open or in OFF position, oscillator _____

7. Using International Morse code, send several letters of code with key or switch while observing signal on oscilloscope.
8. With code key open or off, remove 100 pF capacitor from circuit. In its place, connect small, plated side or 125 pF section of two-ganged variable capacitor.
9. Close code key again and adjust variable capacitor to produce highest oscillator frequency. This occurs when rotary plates are fully extended.
10. Test output of circuit again, while observing oscilloscope. How does oscilloscope show this higher frequency? _____

11. If a communications receiver with CW reception capabilities is available, place it near oscillator. Remove oscilloscope from output terminal and connect a 24 in. length of wire to output terminal for an antenna.
12. Key a coded signal into oscillator and tune in signal on receiver. Receiver must be in CW position to receive this signal.
13. Turn off power supply, oscilloscope and receiver. Disconnect circuit and return all components to storage cabinet.

## QUESTIONS

1. How is coded information transmitted by a continuous wave transmitter?
2. What are the fundamental stages or parts of a CW transmitter?
3. What type of signal is radiated from a CW transmitter?

## INTRODUCTION

Amplitude modulation (AM) occurs when the radio frequency carrier of a transmitter changes in amplitude in step with a low frequency or audio signal. Through this modulation process, it is possible to transmit voice and music signals through space. The sound signal or audio frequency (af) information is commonly called the "modulation component of the transmitted signal." When modulation takes place, the rf signal changes in amplitude with the modulating signal. Only rf signals are radiated from the antenna of the transmitter.

Assume that an AM transmitter is assigned a station frequency of 1000 KHz. A musical tone of 1 KHz is applied to the rf frequency signal for amplitude modulation. The amplitude of the rf component of the transmitter signal is made to vary at a 1 KHz rate when modulation takes place. These two signals mix and two sideband frequencies are developed. The upper sideband is representative of the rf component plus the af component. In this case: 1000 KHz plus 1 KHz = 1001 KHz. The lower sideband is the result of the rf component minus the af component: 1000 KHz − 1 KHz = 999 KHz. The combined output signal of an AM transmitter is the algebraic sum of the carrier wave, the upper sideband and the lower sideband. In a strict sense, the sidebands contain the modulated rf signal information and the carrier is unchanged.

In this experiment, you will build a simple diode modulator circuit. When the diode is operated in the nonlinear part of its characteristic curve, it causes the two applied signals to be mixed or modulated. A tank circuit connected to the output of the diode is used to restore part of the waveform lost by rectification. The capacitor charges during diode conduction and discharges when the diode is nonconductive.

Amplitude modulation is an important communication principle that applies to radio reception, television, CB radio and public service communication systems.

## EXPERIMENT OBJECTIVES

As a result of this laboratory experience, you should be able to accomplish the following:
1. Construct a simple diode modulator circuit.
2. Observe amplitude modulation (AM) on an oscilloscope.
3. Vary the percentage of modulation in the circuit.

## REFERENCE

Gerrish and Dugger, ELECTRICITY AND ELECTRONICS, Chapter 15, pages 222 to 225.

## MATERIALS AND EQUIPMENT

1 — Variable dc power supply
1 — Oscilloscope
1 — AF signal generator
1 — 1N34 diode
1 — 500K, 2 watt potentiometer
1 — 1.5K, 1/4 watt resistor
1 — 100 pF, 100V capacitor
1 — 47 pF, 100V capacitor
1 — Two-gang variable capacitor, 365 pF/ 125 pF
1 — 25 mH inductor
1 — RF oscillator module RF-1 (Hickok Teaching Systems) or equivalent discrete components
2 — SPST toggle switches

## PROCEDURE

1. Construct an amplitude modulation circuit as shown in Fig. 15-2-1. RF-1 is the Hartley oscillator module. If this module is not available, it may be built with discrete components as in experiment 15-1.
2. Before turning on $SW_1$ of oscillator, turn on variable dc power supply and adjust it to 9V. Adjust 365 pF variable capacitor of oscillator to middle of its tuning range.
3. Prepare oscilloscope for operation. Test output of oscillator module or circuit at $TP_1$. The rf oscillator peak-to-peak output signal is _____ volts.
4. Turn off $SW_1$ and turn on $SW_2$. Connect oscilloscope to $TP_2$. With af signal source

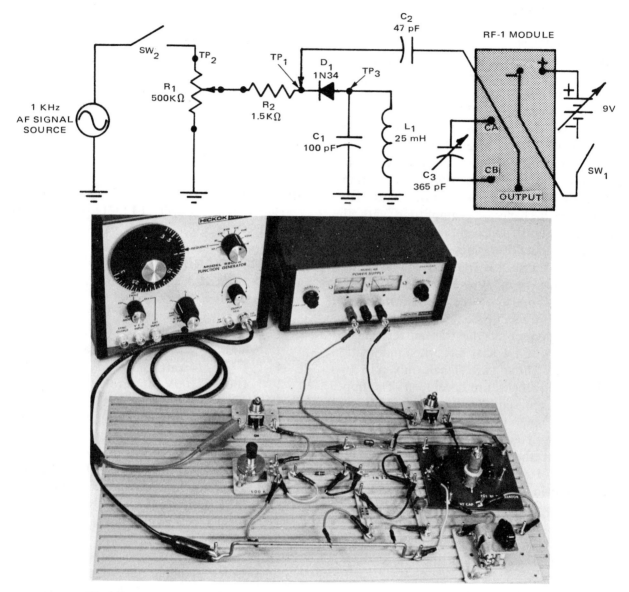

Fig. 15-2-1

set to 1 KHz, adjust its output control to a level that is equal to that of rf oscillator.

5. Move vertical probe of oscilloscope to $TP_3$. Horizontal sweep frequency should set to 500 Hz or to .5m sec horizontal/time.

6. Turn on $SW_1$ so that both rf and af signals are applied to diode ($D_1$).

7. Adjust $R_1$ while observing modulated signal. Modulation level is adjusted by $R_1$. At one extreme, no modulation occurs. At other extreme position, signal is over-modulated. This control also changes amplitude of modulated output signal to some extent.

8. Make a sketch of a 100 percent modulated, unmodulated and 50 percent modulated signals appearing at $TP_3$ in appropriate space provided in Fig. 15-2-2.

9. Turn off $SW_1$, $SW_2$, power supply, oscilloscope and signal generators. Disconnect circuit and return all components to storage cabinet.

100%
MODULATION _____
SIGNAL

UNMODULATED _____
SIGNAL

50%
MODULATED _____
SIGNAL

Fig. 15-2-2

## QUESTIONS

1. Which signal of the modulator circuit of this experiment represents the carrier wave? Which signal represents the modulating wave?

2. If a 50V peak-to-peak rf carrier changes in amplitude from 75V to 25V when modulated, what is the percent of modulation?

3. What causes an AM signal to be over-modulated?

## INTRODUCTION

An AM transmitter contains an rf oscillator and a low frequency modulation signal amplifier. The rf section of the transmitter produces a frequency of 30 KHz or higher. The specific rf frequency used by a transmitter is assigned by the Federal Communications Commission (FCC).

The modulating signal of a transmitter (af) represents frequencies that fall within the human range of hearing, which is 20 Hz to 20 KHz. Signals of this type are developed by a microphone, phono cartridges, magnetic tape heads or an audio frequency signal generator. The process of mixing rf and af signals produces modulation.

The volume level of the modulation signal determines the total amount of amplitude change of the rf signal. If the amplitude level of the modulating signal is greater than the rf signal, overmodulation takes place. Overmodulation, generally, is undesirable and should not occur for more than a few cycles at any one time. Otherwise, distortion and adjacent station interference will result.

In this experiment, you will build a simple AM transmitter system. The modulating signal is developed by a microphone and amplified by a single transistor. The rf signal is produced by an oscillator and mixed with the modulating signal.

### EXPERIMENT OBJECTIVES

As a result of this laboratory experience, you should be able to accomplish the following:
1. Construct a simple AM transmitter.
2. Observe both rf and af signals in the transmitter.
3. Observe modulation of the signal with an oscilloscope.

### REFERENCE

Gerrish and Dugger, ELECTRICITY AND ELECTRONICS, Chapter 15, pages 220 to 225.

### MATERIALS AND EQUIPMENT

1 — Variable dc power supply
1 — Oscilloscope
1 — Crystal microphone
1 — SPST toggle switch
1 — AM transmitter module (Hickok Teaching Systems) or the following components:
    2 — 2N3397 transistors
    1 — Hartley oscillator coil
    1 — Two-gang variable capacitor 365 pF/125 pF
    1 — 25 $\mu$ F, 50V capacitor
    1 — 0.1 $\mu$ F, 100V capacitor
    1 — 0.01 $\mu$ F, 100V capacitor
    1 — 0.001 $\mu$ F, 100V capacitor
    1 — 100 ohm, 1/4 watt resistor
    1 — 10K, 1/4 watt resistor
    1 — 100K, 1/4 watt resistor
    1 — 270K, 1/4 watt resistor
    1 — 500K, 2 watt potentiometer

## PROCEDURE

1. Connect AM transmitter module as shown in Fig. 15-3-1. If AM module is not available, connect equivalent transmitter circuit of Fig. 15-3-2 from separately mounted components.
2. Before turning on $SW_1$, turn on power supply and adjust it to 9V dc.
3. Connect a 24 in. length of wire to antenna terminal of transmitter.
4. Prepare oscilloscope for operation and connect ground lead to common negative terminal. Connect vertical probe to antenna of AM module. Make a sketch of observed waveform in provided space of Fig. 15-3-3 for unmodulated output.
5. Carefully adjust trimmer capacitor of module with a small screwdriver. What influence does this adjustment have upon unmodulated output signal? _____
   _____
6. Connect vertical probe of oscilloscope to positive signal input connection. Adjust sensitivity of microphone to a position that will produce a signal when speaking into microphone. This represents modulation input signal.

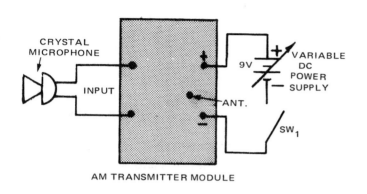

CRYSTAL
MICROPHONE

INPUT

AM TRANSMITTER MODULE

9V

VARIABLE
DC
POWER
SUPPLY

ANT.

SW$_1$

Fig. 15-3-1

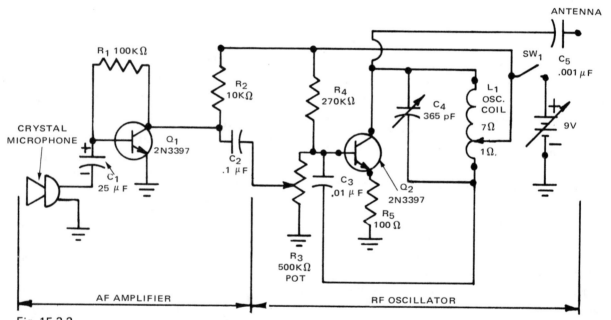

ANTENNA

R$_1$ 100KΩ

R$_2$
10KΩ

R$_4$
270KΩ

C$_4$
365 pF

L$_1$
OSC.
COIL

7Ω

1Ω.

SW$_1$

C$_5$
.001 μF

9V

CRYSTAL
MICROPHONE

Q$_1$
2N3397

C$_2$
.1 μF

C$_3$
.01 μF

Q$_2$
2N3397

R$_5$
100 Ω

C$_1$
25 μF

R$_3$
500KΩ
POT

AF AMPLIFIER

RF OSCILLATOR

Fig. 15-3-2

7. Make a sketch of very irregular modulation input signal in Fig. 15-3-3.
8. Move vertical probe of oscilloscope to AM module output terminal and speak into microphone while observing output. How does modulation influence output of transmitter? _____

_____

9. In Fig. 15-3-3, make a sketch of very irregular waveform appearing at output when modulation occurs.
10. If an AM radio receiver is available, place it near antenna wire of module. Speak into

microphone and adjust receiver to pick up transmitted signal. If a local station interferes with signal, adjust trimmer capacitor of module to a different frequency.
11. Receiver frequency is _____ KHz.
12. Move receiver to a location 10 ft. or so from transmitter module and test its operation. Try orienting antenna wire vertically, then horizontally. Reception of signal is best with which antenna polarity? _____

_____

13. Turn off power supply, receiver and oscilloscope. Return all parts to storage cabinet.

UNMODULATED
OUTPUT _____
SIGNAL

MODULATION
INPUT _____
SIGNAL

MODULATED
OUTPUT _____
SIGNAL

Fig. 15-3-3

## QUESTIONS

1. If the modulation signal is stronger than the rf signal of the transmitter of this experiment, what occurs?

2. How does a crystal microphone produce electrical energy from sound waves?

3. Make a sketch in the space below showing an unmodulated rf wave, 50 percent modulation, 100 percent modulation and an overmodulated wave.

UNMODULATED
RF WAVE _____

50 PERCENT
MODULATION _____

100 PERCENT
MODULATION _____

OVERMODULATED
RF WAVE _____

# Experiment 15-4   FREQUENCY MODULATION

## INTRODUCTION

In frequency modulation (FM), a modulating signal causes the radio frequency carrier to shift in frequency. Therefore, the amplitude of the rf signal of this type of transmitter remains at a constant level. When modulation is applied, its amplitude causes the rf carrier to shift above or below its center resting frequency. The frequency of the modulating signal determines the rate that rf signal shift occurs. Since FM is not influenced by amplitude changes, it is practically immune to noise caused by weather and electrical interference.

In this experiment, you will build a circuit that will permit you to see FM signals on an oscilloscope. An audio frequency signal applied to a special device known as a "varicap diode" causes the frequency of an rf oscillator to change. This diode functions as a variable capacitor that changes value with voltage. When connected across the capacitor of an LC tank circuit of an oscillator, it causes FM action to occur. If a low frequency af signal is applied to the diode, it produces a noticeable change or FM effect on the rf oscillator signal. As a general rule, FM signals are rather high in frequency and difficult to observe on a typical oscilloscope.

## EXPERIMENT OBJECTIVES

As a result of this laboratory experience, you should be able to accomplish the following:
1. Construct a circuit that will allow you to observe FM signals on an oscilloscope.
2. Become familiar with the frequency modulation (FM) principle.

## REFERENCE

Gerrish and Dugger, ELECTRICITY AND ELECTRONICS, Chapter 15, pages 226 to 228.

## MATERIALS AND EQUIPMENT

- 1 — Variable dc power supply
- 1 — AF signal source
- 1 — Oscilloscope
- 1 — Varicap diode, Motorola MV-1638 or equivalent
- 1 — .1 $\mu$F, 100V capacitor
- 1 — .01 $\mu$F, 100V capacitor
- 1 — .001 $\mu$F, 100V capacitor
- 1 — 100 pF, 100V capacitor
- 1 — 470K, 1/4 watt resistor
- 1 — 500K, 2 watt potentiometer
- 1 — SPST toggle switch
- 1 — RF-1 oscillator module (Hickok Teaching Systems) or equivalent components

## PROCEDURE

1. Connect FM transmitter test circuit as in Fig. 15-4-1. If rf oscillator module is not available, connect equivalent Hartley oscillator circuit as in Fig. 15-4-2.
2. Before turning on $SW_1$, turn on variable dc power supply and adjust it to 9V dc.
3. Prepare oscilloscope for operation with ground lead to negative or common circuit lead. Connect vertical probe to oscillator output. An rf signal should be displayed on oscilloscope if test circuit is functioning properly.
4. Adjust oscilloscope for 1.0 $\mu$ sec horizontal sweep time or to a sweep frequency of 1 MHz. Trace of scope must display a few distinct sine waves in order to observe FM effect of this circuit.
5. Turn on af signal source and adjust it to produce a frequency of 10 to 30 Hz.
6. Adjust potentiometer until FM occurs. Describe appearance of rf waveform with FM compared with the rf wave of step 3.

   _____

   _____

7. If possible, reduce frequency to 10 Hz while making next observation on oscilloscope. Adjust af amplitude control $R_1$ while observing output. Explain effect that amplitude has on waveform. _____

   _____

8. With amplitude control at its maximum output, change frequency from 10 to 60 Hz while observing oscilloscope display. What influence does frequency of af source

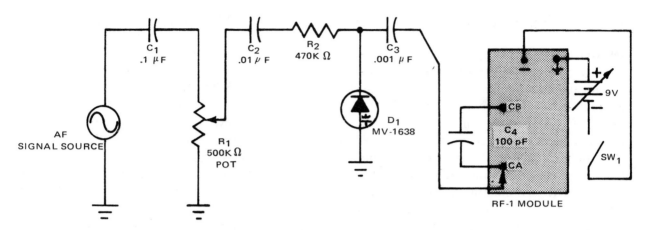

Fig. 15-4-1

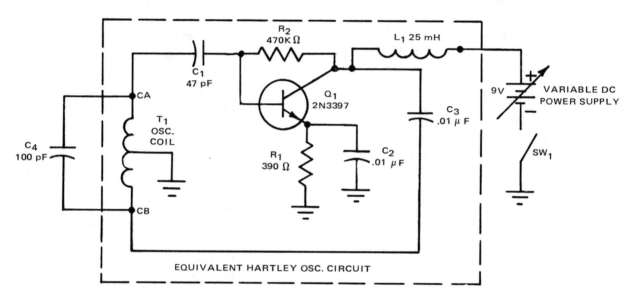

Fig. 15-4-2

have on display? _____

_____

9. Turn off SW$_1$, power supply, oscilloscope and af signal source. Disconnect circuit and return all parts to storage cabinet.

## QUESTIONS

1. If the amplitude of the modulating signal increases, what influence does this have on the output signal?

2. What influence does the frequency of the modulating signal have on the output of an FM signal?

3. Briefly, compare AM and FM transmitters with respect to the influence that the modulating signal amplitude and frequency has on the output signal.

### INTRODUCTION

Frequency modulation (FM) can be achieved when a modulating signal is connected to the tank circuit of an oscillator. When FM occurs, the modulating signal causes the frequency of the transmitter to deviate above and below its center resting frequency. The relationship between maximum carrier deviation and maximum modulation frequency is called the "modulation index." With the modulation index, the number of sidebands and total bandwidth can be calculated.

In this experiment, you will build an FM transmitter with completed module or from an equivalent circuit of discrete mounted components. Output of this transmitter is adjustable within the FM band of 88 to 108 MHz. Signals from the transmitter are picked up on an FM receiver and tested for frequency, distance and antenna orientation. Circuits of this type are commonly used in wireless microphone applications.

### EXPERIMENT OBJECTIVES

As a result of this laboratory experience, you should be able to accomplish the following:
1. Construct a simple FM transmitter.
2. Transmit FM signals through space.
3. Receive the transmitted FM signal on an FM receiver (if available).

### REFERENCE

Gerrish and Dugger, ELECTRICITY AND ELECTRONICS, Chapter 15, pages 228 to 232.

### MATERIALS AND EQUIPMENT

1 — Variable dc power supply
1 — Crystal microphone
1 — SPST toggle switch
1 — FM transmitter module (Hickok Teaching Systems) or an equivalent circuit containing the following parts:
   2 — 2N3644 transistors
   2 — 1 $\mu$F, 100V dc capacitors
   2 — .001 $\mu$F, 100V capacitors
   1 — 6.8 pF, 100V capacitor
   1 — Trimmer capacitor

1 — 1M, 1/4 watt resistor
2 — 10K, 1/4 watt resistors
1 — 4.7K, 1/4 watt resistor
1 — 470 ohm, 1/4 watt resistor
1 — 68 ohm, 1/4 watt resistor
1 — Miniduct 1/2 in. D, 7 turns tapped at 2 turns

### PROCEDURE

1. Connect FM transmitter module as shown in Fig. 15-5-1. If FM module is not available, connect equivalent transmitter circuit of Fig. 15-5-2, using separately mounted components.
2. Before turning on $SW_1$, turn on power supply and adjust it to 9V dc.
3. Connect a 24 in. length of wire to antenna

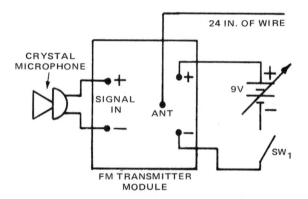

Fig. 15-5-1

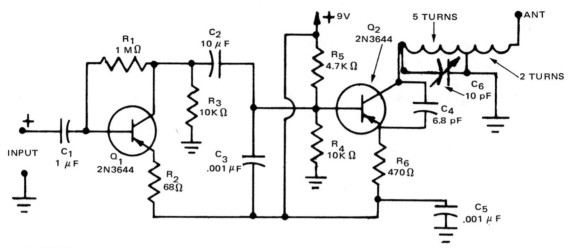

Fig. 15-5-2

terminal of transmitter.

4. If an FM radio receiver is available, place it near antenna wire of module. Speak into microphone and adjust receiver to pick up transmitted signal.

5. After station has been received, if interference from a local station occurs, adjust trimmer capacitor of module to a different frequency. Dial frequency is _____ MHz.

6. Frequency of transmitter can be adjusted by trimmer capacitor. When trimmer is adjusted to its minimum capacitance (when plates are extended), the tuning frequency becomes _____ (higher or lower).

7. When trimmer capacitor plates are compressed by adjusting screw (maximum capacitance), the tuning frequency changes to a _____ (higher or lower) value.

8. Test transmitting range of FM module by moving receiver to different locations. Maximum transmission distance tested is

_____

9. Try orienting transmitting antenna vertically, then horizontally. Reception of signal is best with antenna oriented

_____

_____

10. Turn off power supply. Disconnect circuit and return all parts to storage cabinet.

## QUESTIONS

1. In an FM transmitter, how does the modulating signal alter the output signal?

2. What is meant by the term "center resting frequency" of an FM transmitter?

3. What is meant by the term "modulating index?"

# Chapter 16

# RADIO RECEIVERS

## Experiment 16-1    AM COMMUNICATION SYSTEM

### INTRODUCTION

In an AM communication system, information is applied to the input of the transmitter and radiated into space. The rf waves carry the information to the receiver through the air. The receiver, in turn, picks up the wave, selects the correct frequency, rectifies the rf signal and reproduces the af signal through the earphones.

In this experiment, you will build a simple AM communication system. The transmitter section is the same as the one studied in Chapter 15. The receiver is a simple, solid state diode receiver or crystal diode. Functionally, the receiver must first pick up the original rf signal through the receiving antenna. Next, the $L_1 - C_1$ part of the receiver selects the desired station frequency and rejects all others. The diode rectifies the rf signal so that the af signal may be recovered. The af component then energizes the earphones which are designed to change electrical energy into sound energy. These basic principles of AM communication play a very important role in commercial AM radio, citizens band and television reception.

### EXPERIMENT OBJECTIVES

As a result of this laboratory experience, you should be able to accomplish the following:
1. Construct a simple AM communications system (transmitter and receiver).
2. Become familiar with the basic functions of an AM communications system.

### REFERENCE

Gerrish and Dugger, ELECTRICITY AND ELECTRONICS, Chapter 16, pages 235 to 238.

### MATERIALS AND EQUIPMENT

1 — Variable dc power supply
1 — AF signal generator
1 — Crystal microphone
1 — 1N34 diode
1 — 365 pF variable capacitor
1 — Ferrite strip transistor antenna rod
1 — 2K earphone
1 — AM transmitter module (Hickok Teaching Systems) or the equivalent separately mounted components

### PROCEDURE

1. Construct transmitter part of AM communication system as in Fig. 16-1-1. If AM transmitter module is not available, build equivalent circuit shown in Fig. 16-1-2 with mounted components.
2. Before turning on $SW_1$, turn on variable dc power supply and adjust it to 9V dc.
3. Connect a 24 in. length of wire to antenna and position it horizontally on top of workbench.
4. Adjust af signal source to produce a 400 Hz signal. If an AM receiver is available, place it near transmitter circuit and tune in signal. If a signal is not received, check wiring of transmitter circuit. An oscilloscope can be used to determine if rf and af part of circuit is not working properly.
5. Construct AM receiver part of system as in Fig. 16-1-1.
6. Place receiver antenna wire near transmitting antenna wire. Adjust variable capacitor of receiver through its range while listening for af signal.

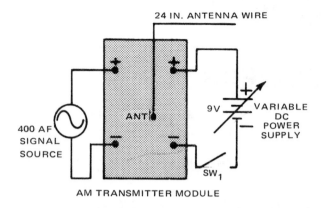

AM TRANSMITTER MODULE

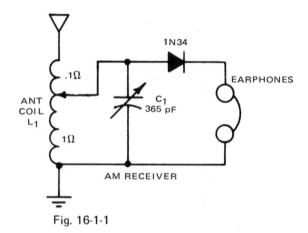

Fig. 16-1-1

7. When signal has been received, alter frequency of af signal source above and below

original 400 Hz setting. What is highest audio frequency that can be detected by receiver? _____

8. Change amplitude of af signal source while listening to received signal. What influence does af signal amplitude have on received signal? _____

9. Turn off $SW_1$ and disconnect af signal source. In its place, connect a crystal microphone.

10. Turn on $SW_1$ and ask someone to speak into microphone. If necessary, orient receiving antenna to produce strongest signal. What kind of reception range does system have? _____

11. Turn off $SW_1$ and power supply. Disconnect circuit and return all components to storage cabinet.

## QUESTIONS

1. What are the primary functions of an AM radio receiver?
2. What is the function of the diode in the AM receiver of this experiment?
3. What is the function of the antenna coil and $C_1$ capacitor?

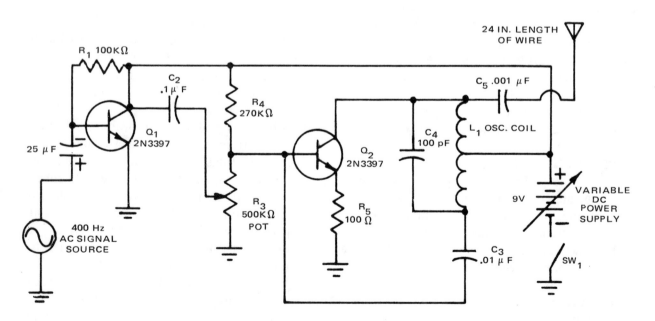

Fig. 16-1-2

## INTRODUCTION

One of the major functions of a radio receiver is to select a desired station frequency and to reject all unwanted stations. An rf tuning circuit is primarily used to carry out this "selectivity" function. This type of circuit typically employs an inductor and a variable capacitor. When adjusted, the capacitor changes the resonant frequency of the circuit. At resonance, a relatively high circulating current develops in the tank circuit. This frequency then passes to the rest of the receiver for additional processing.

In this experiment, you will build an rf tuner circuit with typical radio receiver parts. An rf signal generator is applied to the circuit input and an oscilloscope is connected to the output. When the circuit resonates with the rf signal generator, a maximum signal indication is displayed on the oscilloscope. You also will determine the tuning limits and bandwidth of the circuit. Bandwidth of a tuned circuit determines its ability to select a single frequency and reject other stations. The tuning principles of this experiment apply to a wide variety of communications circuit applications today.

## EXPERIMENT OBJECTIVES

As a result of this laboratory experience, you should be able to accomplish the following:
1. Construct an rf tuner circuit.
2. Apply an rf signal generator to the tuning circuit and observe the tuning action.
3. Determine the tuning limits of the circuit.

## REFERENCE

Gerrish and Dugger, ELECTRICITY AND ELECTRONICS, Chapter 16, pages 236 and 237.

## MATERIALS AND EQUIPMENT

1 — Volt-ohm-milliampere (VOM) meter
1 — RF signal generator
1 — Oscilloscope
1 — Ferrite strip transistor antenna rod
1 — 365 pF variable capacitor

## PROCEDURE

1. Remove ferrite antenna coil from storage cabinet and position it on circuit construction board. With a VOM, measure resistance of coil to locate center or tapped connection. Position coil as indicated in Fig. 16-2-1 with low resistant winding at top.
2. Prepare oscilloscope for operation. Connect common probe to test point B and vertical probe to test point C.

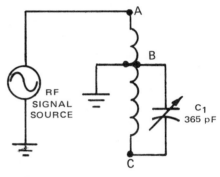

Fig. 16-2-1

3. Turn on rf signal source and adjust it to a frequency of approximately 800 KHz.
4. Adjust capacitor $C_1$ through its range while observing oscilloscope. At a specific capacitor position, tuned circuit will produce a maximum output signal indication. What does this demonstrate? _____

_____

5. Change capacitor to its maximum capacitance position. Adjust rf signal source to a position that produces greatest output signal indication for this tuned circuit setting. Low frequency tuning limit is _____ KHz.
6. Change capacitor to its minimum capacitance position. Adjust rf signal source to a position that produces greatest output signal indication for this tuned circuit setting. High frequency tuning limit is _____ KHz.
7. Adjust rf signal generator to an even

number indication such as 800 KHz on tuning dial. Then, tune circuit until it resonates at this frequency as indicated by maximum output of oscilloscope.

8. Adjust amplitude of signal source to produce 2 cm of vertical deflection. There should be five smaller divisions per centimetre or a total of 10 small divisions for 2 cm. This setting will serve as reference frequency for tuned circuit.

9. Carefully decrease frequency of signal generator until oscilloscope indicates a 30 percent reduction in amplitude. Three small divisions out of a total of 10 indicate this point. The frequency indication on rf signal generator that causes a 30 percent reduction in output amplitude is _____ KHz.

10. Return rf signal generator to original 800 KHz reference position.

11. Using same procedure outlined in step 9, carefully increase frequency of generator and locate point where a 30 percent reduction in amplitude occurs. High frequency amplitude reduction frequency is_____ KHz.

12. Tuning response bandwidth is high frequency amplitude reduction point minus low frequency point. Tuning response bandwidth of this circuit is _____ KHz.

13. Return rf signal generator to 800 KHz reference position. With an insulated screwdriver or an alignment screwdriver, adjust trimmer capacitor on one side of variable capacitor. Do not adjust screw too tight or it could possibly strip threads. How does this adjustment alter resonant tuning point indicated by oscilloscope?_____

_____

14. Turn off signal generator and disconnect circuit. Return all components to storage cabinet.

## QUESTIONS

1. What does the tuning response bandwidth of a radio receiver circuit represent?
2. What is meant by the term "tuning circuit selectivity?"
3. Why does a radio receiver need a tuning circuit on the input?

# Experiment 16-3  AM SIGNAL DEMODULATION

## INTRODUCTION

In the transmitter of an AM communication system, a modulating signal is mixed with an rf carrier so it can be radiated into space. After this signal has been transmitted, then picked up by the receiving antenna and applied to the tuning circuit, it must be "demodulated" before it can be effectively used. Today, the demodulation function of an AM receiver usually is achieved by a diode device.

The primary function of the demodulator (single solid state diode) of an AM receiver is rectification. The incoming rf wave is simply cut in half by the diode because it will only conduct when forward biased. Then, the rectified output of the diode is applied to a load resistor where it appears as a series of rf pulses changing in amplitude. These pulses are used to charge a capacitor connected across the load resistor. This charge voltage changes at the same rate as the original modulating signal. Through this process, the modulated part of the selected AM signal can be recovered by the receiver. The terms "detection" and "demodulation" are both used to describe this receiver function.

In this experiment, you will construct a diode detector circuit with discrete components. You will trace the signal path with an oscilloscope, observing the input signal, tuning, detection and rf filtering. The output of the detector circuit is also used to reproduce sound through an earphone.

## EXPERIMENT OBJECTIVES

As a result of this laboratory experience, you should be able to accomplish the following:
1. Construct a diode detector circuit.
2. Use an oscilloscope to trace the signal path.
3. Use an earphone to hear the output from the detector circuit.

## REFERENCE

Gerrish and Dugger, ELECTRICITY AND ELECTRONICS, Chapter 16, pages 237 to 239 and 246.

## MATERIALS AND EQUIPMENT

1 — RF signal generator with AM output
1 — Ferrite strip transistor antenna rod
1 — 365 pF variable capacitor
1 — 27K, 1/4 watt resistor
1 — 0.1 $\mu$ F, 100V capacitor
1 — 2K  earphone
1 — 1N34 diode

## PROCEDURE

1. Connect diode detector circuit of Fig. 16-3-1.
2. Turn on rf signal generator and adjust it to produce an AM signal of 1000 KHz. Connect generator output to $T_1$ as indicated.

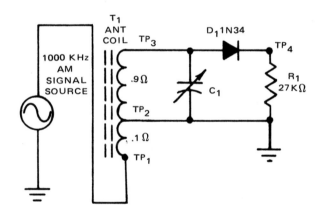

Fig. 16-3-1

3. Prepare oscilloscope for operation. Connect it to $TP_1$ and $TP_2$. The horizontal sweep frequency should be set to 100 Hz or to the 10m sec/cm range. Adjust modulation control of rf signal generator to produce approximately 100 percent modulation.
4. Make a sketch of observed input waveform in provided space in Fig. 16-3-2.
5. Move vertical probe of oscilloscope to $TP_3$ with ground probe remaining at $TP_2$. Adjust capacitor $C_1$ to produce a maximum signal indication on oscilloscope. What does this indicate about tuning circuit? _____

MODULATED
INPUT
WAVEFORM
(TP$_1$–TP$_2$) _____

DEMODULATED
WAVEFORM
(TP$_4$–TP$_2$
WITHOUT C$_2$) _____

DEMODULATED
WAVEFORM
(TP$_4$–TP$_2$
WITH C$_2$) _____

Fig. 16-3-2

6. Move vertical probe of oscilloscope to TP$_4$ with ground probe remaining at TP$_2$. Make a sketch of observed waveform in provided space in Fig. 16-3-2. How does this wave compare with observed wave in step 5?

_____

_____

7. Connect a 0.1 $\mu$F capacitor across TP$_2$

and TP$_4$ of the demodulator circuit. Make a sketch of waveform displayed on oscilloscope at TP$_4$ and TP$_2$ in provided space in Fig. 16-3-2. How does this display compare with step 6? _____

_____

8. Connect a set of earphones across TP$_2$ and TP$_4$ with capacitor remaining in circuit. What do you hear? _____

_____

9. Reduce modulation level of rf signal generator. What effect does this have on sound output? _____

_____

10. Turn off modulation so that only rf is supplied to demodulator circuit. What effect does this have on sound output?

_____

11. Disconnect rf signal generator from circuit. Connect TP$_1$ to an outside antenna and TP$_2$ to a good ground connection. Adjust tuner through its range to see if it will pick up a local AM station.

12. Disconnect circuit and return all parts to storage cabinet.

## QUESTIONS

1. Explain how the circuit in this experiment achieves demodulation of an applied AM signal.
2. What is the function of C$_2$ in the demodulator circuit of this experiment?
3. How does the earphone produce sound from electrical energy?

## INTRODUCTION

The heterodyning principle is a method of converting all signals applied to the input of a receiver to a single intermediate frequency (if). Through this process, the if signal can be amplified with a minimum of loss and distortion. To achieve this function, a local oscillator circuit mixes an unmodulated rf signal with the tuned incoming AM signal to produce an if signal. A tube or transistor usually is responsible for achieving the mixing or heterodyning function.

When two rf signals are applied to a common device with a nonlinear characteristic, the output produces four signals. This includes the two input signals, the addition of the two signals and the difference between the signals. The latter two signals are usually called "beats" or beat frequencies. The circuit is designed so that the local oscillator frequency is variable and tuned when selecting a given station frequency. A two-ganged variable capacitor achieves this function. The frequency of the local oscillator is designed to be the incoming station frequency plus the if signal frequency. An AM signal of 1000 KHz for example, would cause the local oscillator to produce a frequency of 1455 KHz in a typical AM receiver.

In an AM receiver, the difference frequency of the selected signal and local oscillator signal usually is 455 KHz. A single output frequency or intermediate frequency is therefore produced as a result of the heterodyning function.

In this experiment, you will build a single transistor heterodyne circuit and tune in a local station. You will be able to observe the resulting waveforms at key test points in this circuit and see how the circuit responds when the oscillator is turned off. The heterodyning principle is used in nearly all communication receiver circuits today.

### EXPERIMENT OBJECTIVES

As a result of this laboratory experience, you should be able to accomplish the following:

1. Construct a single transistor heterodyne circuit.

2. Tune this circuit to a local AM station.
3. Observe the resulting waveforms at key test points in the circuit.

## REFERENCE

Gerrish and Dugger, ELECTRICITY AND ELECTRONICS, Chapter 16, pages 240 to 243.

## MATERIALS AND EQUIPMENT

1 — Variable dc power supply
1 — Oscilloscope
1 — RF-1 oscillator module or a signal generator
1 — .455 KHz if transformer (J. W. Miller 10-C1 or equivalent)
1 — 2N3397 transistor
1 — Two-gang variable capacitor 365 pF/125 pF
1 — Ferrite strip transistor antenna rod

1 — 0.01 $\mu$F, 100V capacitor
1 — 47 pF, 100V capacitor
1 — 470K, 1/4 watt resistor
1 — 27K, 1/4 watt resistor
1 — 1.5K, 1/4 watt resistor
2 — SPST toggle switches
1 — Set of earphones

## PROCEDURE

1. Construct heterodyning circuit shown in Fig. 16-4-1. If an rf oscillator module is not available, use an unmodulated signal from an rf signal generator.
2. Before turning on $SW_1$, turn on power source and adjust it to 9V dc.
3. Turn on $SW_2$ which supplies source voltage to rf oscillator.
4. Adjust two-ganged tuning capacitor $C_{1A} - C_{1B}$ through its range. If area has a local AM station, you should be able to tune it in when an outside antenna is connected to top of $L_1$.
5. If an outside antenna or local station are not available, AM transmitter module or an rf signal generator may be employed as an AM source.
6. Tune receiver to one of selected AM signal

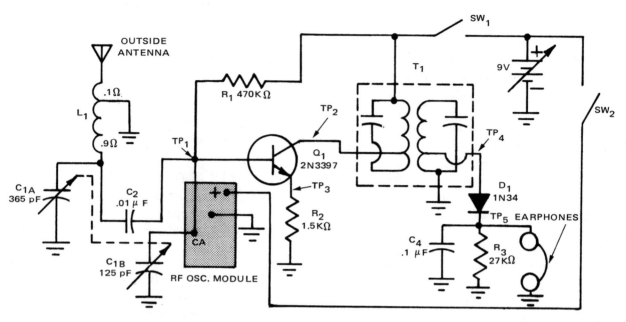

Fig. 16-4-1

sources. Earphone should reproduce modulating signal when proper tuning is achieved.

7. Turn off $SW_2$ momentarily while listening to earphone. What happens when local oscillator is removed from circuit? _____

_____

_____ Why? _____

_____

8. Prepare oscilloscope for operation. Connect negative probe to a common ground connection point. Observe waveforms at $TP_1$, $TP_2$, $TP_3$, and $TP_4$ with vertical probe. Signal at $TP_1$ is _____

$TP_2$ is _____

$TP_3$ is _____

$TP_4$ _____

9. Turn off local oscillator with $SW_2$ and observe waveforms at $TP_1$, $TP_2$, $TP_3$, $TP_4$ and $TP_5$. What signals appear at these test points with the oscillator off? _____

_____

10. Turn off power supply and oscilloscope. Disconnect circuit and return all components to storage cabinet.

### QUESTIONS
1. Why does turning off the oscillator kill the if signal?
2. What is meant by the term "heterodying?"
3. If the incoming AM signal is 1340 KHz, and the local oscillator produces a 1790 KHz signal, what signals would appear at collector of the heterodyning circuit of this experiment?
4. How is frequency of the local oscillator determined?

## INTRODUCTION

In a superheterodyne receiver, when the incoming station frequency is selected by the tuner, it mixes with an rf signal produced by the local oscillator. The resulting output of this heterodyning process is an intermediate frequency (if) signal. This signal is of a fixed value because the frequency of the local oscillator changes an equal amount each time the tuner is adjusted to receive a different station. In the mixer stage of a superheterodyne receiver, all incoming station frequencies are changed to a single if signal.

In this experiment, you will build a transistor if amplifier and apply an input signal to test its operation. You will adjust the transformer to resonance or align it to pass only the if signal. The basic principle of if amplification is extremely important in modern radio and television receiver circuits.

### EXPERIMENT OBJECTIVES

As a result of this laboratory experience, you should be able to accomplish the following:
1. Construct a transistor if amplifier.
2. Apply a signal to the if amplifier to test its operation.
3. Using an oscilloscope, trace the signal path through the if amplifier.

## REFERENCE

Gerrish and Dugger, ELECTRICITY AND ELECTRONICS, Chapter 16, pages 239 to 243.

## MATERIALS AND EQUIPMENT

1 — Variable dc power supply
1 — RF signal generator
1 — Oscilloscope
1 — 2N3397 transistor
1 — .455 KHz if transformer (J.W. Miller 10-C1 or equivalent)
1 — 0.01 $\mu$F, 100V capacitor
1 — 470K, 1/4 watt resistor
1 — 27K, 1/4 watt resistor
1 — 1.5K, 1/4 watt resistor
1 — SPST toggle switch

## PROCEDURE

1. Connect if amplifier circuit as shown in Fig. 16-5-1.
2. Before turning on $SW_1$, turn on variable dc power supply and adjust it to 9V dc.
3. Connect positive lead of rf signal source to $TP_1$. Connect negative lead to common circuit ground. Adjust frequency control of generator to produce a 455 KHz unmodulated signal.
4. Prepare oscilloscope for operation. Connect vertical probe to $TP_1$ and negative probe to

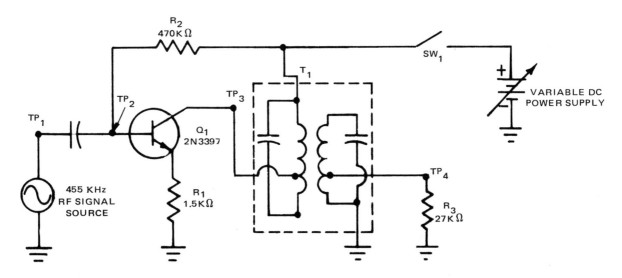

Fig. 16-5-1

ground. Use a slow horizontal sweep rate of 100 Hz or 1m sec/cm to observe input wave. Adjust amplitude control of signal generator to produce an rf peak-to-peak output of approximately 1V.

5. With oscilloscope vertical probe, follow rf signal path from $TP_1$ to $TP_2$ to $TP_3$.

6. Between $TP_1$ and $TP_3$ there should be substantial gain in signal level because of transistor amplification. Gain is _____

7. Connect vertical oscilloscope probe to $TP_4$. If there is a drop in signal amplitude between $TP_3$ and $TP_4$, this indicates that $T_1$ is detuned or that the input is not 455 KHz.

8. Adjust frequency of signal generator above and below its original setting to find resonant tuning point of transformer. Resonant frequency is _____ KHz.

9. If resonant point is something other than 455 KHz, adjust each tuning slug with alignment tool. Output after alignment should peak at 455 KHz when adjusting rf signal generator through its range. Be care-

ful not to force slugs together or to adjust them at same time.

10. If resonant point is at 455 KHz, carefully adjust top tuning slug while observing change in output. Then, return it to maximum output level. Adjust lower slug, using same procedure. Test alignment again by adjusting signal generator and observing oscilloscope for a 455 KHz peak output.

11. Turn off circuit switch, power supply, signal generator and oscilloscope. Disconnect circuit and return all parts to storage cabinet.

## QUESTIONS

1. What is physically being changed in the transformer when it is being aligned?

2. When the if transformer is tuned to 455 KHz, what happens to other frequencies that are applied?

3. What is meant by the term "intermediate frequency" or if in a superheterodyne receiver?

## INTRODUCTION

Sound transducers are devices designed to change electrical energy into sound energy or sound into electrical energy. Speakers and headphones (earphones) are two important sound transducers used in communication equipment today. Headphones provide private listening. Speakers provide sound for many people to hear over a large area.

A headphone is made of a coil of fine wire mounted in a housing at a fixed center position. A thin, soft iron diaphragm is suspended above the coil and supported only at its outer edge. Mechanically, the diaphragm is either attracted or repelled by the magnetic field of the wound coil. When a varying current is applied to the coil, it causes the diaphragm to move in and out. Through this action, electrical energy is effectively changed into sound energy. Headphones are designed with a large number of turns on an electromagnetic coil, making them very sensitive to minute changes in current.

A PM speaker has a permanent magnet attached to a frame. A small coil of wire is placed over the magnet and attached to a flexible cone. When electrical energy is applied to the voice coil, an interaction between the permanent magnet and the electromagnetic field causes movement. Voice coil movement causes the cone of the speaker to move which, in turn, sets volumes of air into motion. In this way, speaker action changes electrical energy into sound energy.

A speaker used in reverse serves as a transducer that changes sound into electrical energy. In this operation, sound waves strike the flexible cone and cause it to move. This, in turn, moves the voice coil through a magnetic field, which generates a small amount of electrical energy. The speaker in this case is a form of microphone, but it is not very sensitive to small changes in sound.

In this experiment, you will perform test procedures frequently used to determine the condition of headphones or a speaker. All communication systems that respond to sound must employ headphones or speakers.

## EXPERIMENT OBJECTIVES

As a result of this laboratory experience, you should be able to accomplish the following:
1. Test headphones and a speaker to see how they operate.
2. Use a signal generator and listen to the signal with earphones and a speaker.

## REFERENCE

Gerrish and Dugger, ELECTRICITY AND ELECTRONICS, Chapter 16, pages 243 to 246.

## MATERIALS AND EQUIPMENT

1 — Variable dc power supply
1 — 6.3V, 60 Hz ac source
1 — AF signal generator
1 — Headphones
1 — Speaker
1 — Volt-ohm-milliampere (VOM) meter

## PROCEDURE

1. Remove headphones from storage cabinet. Install headset on your head and position it over your ear.
2. Prepare VOM to measure resistance. Connect ohmmeter test probes to headset leads. What do you hear?_____

    _____

    What do you account for this?_____

    _____

3. The dc resistance of headset coil measures _____ ohms.
4. Remove headset and unscrew top cover cap from one earphone. Slide metal diaphragm to one side and remove it.
5. Make a sketch of inside structure of earphone in space provided in Fig. 16-6-1. Label parts of drawing.
6. Return diaphragm to top of earphone. What holds it in place? _____

    _____

7. Turn on variable dc power supply and adjust it to produce 10V dc.
8. Connect one lead of earphone to negative terminal and momentarily touch positive to

Fig. 16-6-1

other lead several times. Do you see diaphragm physically move? Describe action.

_____

_____

9. Disconnect dc power supply and plug filament transformer into power line.
10. Connect 6.3V ac to earphone. Gently place your finger on the diaphragm. Describe action of diaphragm. _____

_____

11. How do you account for this action? _____

_____

_____

12. Disconnect earphone from ac source. Return cover cap to earphone.
13. Again, place headset over your ears and connect leads to af signal generator. Increase signal amplitude to a level that can be heard. Run a frequency response test to find reproduction range of earphone. Sound range of earphone is _____ to _____ Hz.
14. Disconnect headset from signal generator and set it aside.
15. Remove speaker from storage cabinet and position it at location on top of workbench.
16. With VOM, measure resistance of speaker voice coil. Voice coil resistance is _____ ohms. Gently place your finger on cone of speaker, then touch ohmmeter to it. Do

you feel cone move? _____ What do you hear? _____

17. Adjust power supply to 3V dc. Connect negative lead to one speaker terminal. Gently place your finger on cone of speaker. Then, touch positive lead of power supply to other speaker terminal. Describe action._____

_____

18. Reverse polarity of dc power source and repeat step 17. Describe action. _____

_____

_____

19. Disconnect dc source from speaker. Connect speaker to 6.3V ac with your finger touching cone. Describe action._____

_____

_____

20. Disconnect ac source from speaker and prepare oscilloscope for operation. Set horizontal sweep selector to 20m sec range or 10 to 100 Hz sweep frequency. Adjust vertical input to its most sensitive range.
21. Connect oscilloscope probes to speaker terminals. Gently press cone of speaker down with your finger, then release it. Repeat this test several times. Gently rub your finger over speaker cone a few times. There should be a noticeable oscilloscope action. What causes generation of a signal voltage?_____

_____

_____

22. Try blowing, speaking or whistling toward cone of speaker. A speaker used in this manner serves as a _____
23. Turn off all equipment and return all components to storage cabinet.

## QUESTIONS
1. What is meant by the term "transducer?"
2. Explain how sound is produced by a speaker.
3. Why is an earphone more sensitive than a speaker?

## INTRODUCTION

An FM receiver employs the heterodyne principle of operation that is commonly used in typical AM receivers. FM receivers include an rf amplifier, local oscillator, mixer, if amplifiers, detector, af amplification, a speaker and a common power supply. The tuned station frequency, intermediate frequency and method of detection are the three primary differences between AM and FM receiver types.

In this experiment, you will look at a block diagram of an FM receiver, explain basic functions and calculate typical frequencies. Through this experience, you will become more familiar with basic operating principles of an FM receiver.

Part A of this experiment is a pencil and paper activity. Optional Part B can be pursued according to the availability of FM receivers and test equipment. In option Part C, an FM receiver kit can be built. In this case, the cost of the receiver kit and its availability will determine its selection.

## EXPERIMENT OBJECTIVES

As a result of this laboratory experience, you should be able to accomplish the following:
1. Study the FM receiver block diagram.
2. Explain the function of each part of the FM receiver block diagram.
3. Calculate certain frequencies that appear at certain points in an FM receiver.

## REFERENCE

Gerrish and Dugger, ELECTRICITY AND ELECTRONICS, Chapter 16, pages 248 to 251.

## PROCEDURE
### PART A—FM RECEIVER DIAGRAM

1. Refer to block diagram of an FM receiver in Fig. 16-7-1. Note that each block is labeled to designate function performed.
2. Function of each specific block of an FM receiver is similar to those of an AM receiver with exception of ratio detector. In provided space, briefly explain what each block of FM receiver does.

RF amplifiers_____

_____

Mixer_____

_____

Local oscillator _____

_____

1st and 2nd if amplifiers_____

_____

Ratio detector_____

_____

AVC_____

_____

1st af amplifier _____

_____

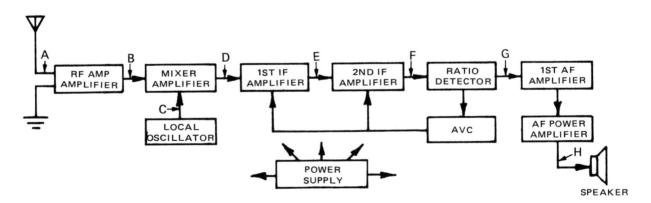

Fig. 16-7-1

AF output amplifier _____

_____

Speaker_____

_____

Power supply _____

_____

3. Again refer to Fig. 16-7-1. Assume that a 1 KHz audio tone is used to modulate an FM station operating at 100 MHz. If you pick up the 1 KHz tone at test point A, what frequencies will appear at points B, D, E, F, G and H? Assume, too, that the local oscillator is producing a frequency of 89.3 MHz and operates at received station frequency minus intermediate frequency.

4. If an FM station were tuned in at a frequency of 94 MHz, what frequency would local oscillator produce? What four frequencies would appear at point D?

5. If a schematic diagram of an FM receiver is available, study it and indicate receiver functions included in circuit.

## PROCEDURE
### PART B—FM SIGNAL TESTS

1. If your laboratory is equipped with an FM receiver, a schematic diagram of receiver and an FM signal generator, you may want to inject a representative test signal at key test points of Fig. 16-7-1. Your instructor will assist you in preparing for this procedure.

## PROCEDURE
### PART C—FM RECEIVER KITS

1. A number of FM receiver kits are available to construct. Build an FM receiver, align tuned circuits and test receiver operation. Your instructor will describe availability and price range of kits that are suitable for this option.

## QUESTIONS

1. What are the three primary differences in AM and FM superheterodyne receivers?
2. If an FM receiver tunes in a signal of 100 MHz, and a similar AM receiver tunes in a 1000 KHz signal, what is the primary difference in the physical components of the tuned circuits?

# Chapter 17
# TELEVISION

# Experiment 17-1 MONOCHROME TELEVISION RECEIVERS

## INTRODUCTION

A monochrome (black and white) television receiver employs many basic electronic communication principles in a single unit. The rf signal input (front end) of a TV receiver, for example, is a basic superheterodyne circuit. Both AM picture information and FM sound signals are processed through this part of the receiver at the same time. An rf amplifier, local oscillator and mixer circuit are all placed in the channel selecting chassis unit (tuner). The output of the tuner is applied to the if amplifier section. Both FM and AM detectors are connected to the output of the last if amplifier.

The sound (audio signal) is ultimately recovered by the FM detector, amplified and applied to the speaker. The picture signal (video information) also is recovered by the AM detector, amplified and applied to the picture tube where it is reproduced. The heterodyning principle is basically the same in this case as in AM and FM receivers in Chapters 15 and 16.

Television receivers also use oscillators to develop vertical and horizontal sweep signals that deflect the electron beam of the picture tube. These signals are synchronized by the incoming video signal. These circuits employ the same oscillator basics discussed in Chapter 14. Two distinct power supplies develop energy for circuit operation. Both full-wave and half-wave supplies usually are needed in a TV receiver. These circuits are very similar to those discussed in Chapter 12.

Many basic circuits of a TV receiver have been investigated in different places in this manual. Television receiver circuit applications, however, seem to be somewhat more complex when viewed in a composite diagram. A general understanding of the basic circuit principles, however, helps to reduce this mystery when familiar items can be picked out of a complex diagram.

In this experiment, you will work with the controls of a monochrome television receiver. Your instructor, however, may elect to demonstrate this experiment to the class as a group. In either case, you must be able to explain the function of each item and record the indicated data.

## EXPERIMENT OBJECTIVES

As a result of this laboratory experience, you should be able to accomplish the following:
1. Become familiar with the basic controls on a monochrome television receiver.
2. Become familiar with the basic operation of a monochrome receiver.

## REFERENCE

Gerrish and Dugger, ELECTRICITY AND ELECTRONICS, Chapter 17, pages 257 to 263.

## MATERIALS AND EQUIPMENT

1 — Operating black and white TV receiver

## PROCEDURE

1. Remove back cover so that chassis of TV receiver is exposed. If possible, remove receiver from its cabinet so that internal circuits can be observed. Place knobs on each control to improve receiver tuning.
2. DO NOT apply electrical power to receiver. DO NOT touch any part of set!

229

3. Locate picture tube (CRT) of receiver. Note front viewing area, backside of tube, neck and connection socket. Where are electron gun and tube elements located in the tube? _____

   _____

4. Locate deflection yoke on CRT. How would you describe this part? _____

   _____

5. Tuner of a TV receiver is mounted on a separate chassis unit. There should be one VHF tuner and one UHF tuner. Locate these units. What function does tuner actually perform? _____

   _____

6. How is tuner manipulated to achieve its function? _____

   _____

7. List receiver controls other than tuner that are accessible from front of cabinet. As a rule, these are called operator controls. Briefly explain function of each control.

a. _____
   _____

b. _____
   _____

c. _____
   _____

d. _____
   _____

e. _____
   _____

8. Refer to rear panel on backside of receiver. List all of controls found at this location. These controls are commonly called service controls.

a. _____
   _____

b. _____
   _____

c. _____
   _____

Fig. 17-1-1

d. _____

_____

e. _____

_____

f. _____

_____

g. _____

_____

h. _____

_____

9. Locate position of speaker. What is approximate size of cone area of speaker?

_____

10. How is ac supplied to TV receiver?

_____

_____

11. Why is an interlock plug used on ac power line cord? _____

12. How would this receiver be classified: solid state or vacuum tube?

13. Make a sketch of chassis of TV receiver used in this experiment, pointing out location or position of operator controls, service controls, tuners, transformers and ac line cord interlock. Use space provided in Fig. 17-1-1.

14. Briefly describe general construction of receiver circuit, pointing out such things as printed circuit boards, transformer locations, etc.

## QUESTIONS

1. Explain how a TV picture is produced by the scanning process. Point out such things as fields, frames, number of lines, retrace or flyback and trace time.

2. How is the horizontal frequency of a TV receiver derived?

3. What is the function of the deflection yoke?

# MONOCHROME TELEVISION RECEIVER CONTROLS

## INTRODUCTION

Monochrome TV receiver controls have three major classifications: operator controls, service controls and alignment controls. Operator controls are readily accessible from the front of the receiver. As a rule, these controls provide the operator some personal preference as to sound level, brightness, channel selection, contrast and power on or off. Service controls generally are less accessible to the operator. Adjustment of these controls usually requires some degree of technical understanding of receiver functions. Alignment controls are more complex and require specialized circuit information and test equipment. Avoid adjustment of these controls unless components are being replaced.

The three classifications of TV receiver controls varies between manufacturers. Some controls are interchanged while others are replaced by automatic adjustment circuits. New circuit developments tend to minimize the number of service and alignment controls.

In this experiment, you will have an opportunity to see how various controls influence TV receiver circuit operation. In some cases, your instructor may elect to demonstrate these adjustments because of the limited number of TV receivers. In either case, record the necessary data and respond to the procedures as indicated.

## EXPERIMENT OBJECTIVES

As a result of this laboratory experience, you should be able to accomplish the following:
1. Work with a TV monochrome receiver and see how various controls affect its operation.
2. Compare the schematic of the TV with the actual layout of the set.

## REFERENCE

Gerrish and Dugger, ELECTRICITY AND ELECTRONICS, Chapter 17, pages 261 to 263.

## MATERIALS AND EQUIPMENT

1 — Operating monochrome TV receiver
1 — Signal source from an antenna, a TV analyst or closed circuit cable system
1 — Set of receiver service literature

## PROCEDURE

1. Turn on TV receiver and tune in a station. If a signal source other than a local station is being supplied, adjust receiver to pick up applied signal. Keep sound level (receiver volume) very low.

2. Adjust each listed operator control and briefly explain influence this control has on receiver.
   a. Channel selector (VHF or UHF)
   _____
   _____
   b. Fine tuning _____
   _____
   c. Brightness _____
   _____
   d. Sound or volume _____
   _____
   e. Vertical hold _____
   _____
   f. Contrast _____
   _____
   g. ON/OFF switch _____
   _____
   h. Additional controls _____
   _____

3. Adjust following service controls over a range that will permit you to notice specific effect it produces. Note original control position with a mark or sketch and return it to this position on completion of adjustment.
   a. Horizontal hold _____
   _____
   b. AGC _____
   _____

c. Vertical height _____

_____

d. Vertical linearity _____

_____

e. Horizontal size or width _____

_____

f. Focus _____

_____

4. List other service controls that may be located on rear panel of receiver but not indicated in step 3. Do not attempt to adjust these controls without your instructor's assistance or permission.

a. _____

b. _____

c. _____

d. _____

5. Refer to schematic diagram of receiver and locate operator controls of step 2. Indicate which circuit of receiver is effected by adjustment of control.

a. Channel selector _____

b. Fine tuning _____

c. Brightness _____

d. Sound or volume _____

e. Vertical hold _____

f. Constrast _____

g. ON/OFF switch _____

h. Additional controls _____

6. Locate service controls of step 3 and indicate which circuit of receiver is effected by adjustment of control.

a. Horizontal hold _____

b. AGC _____

c. Vertical height _____

d. Vertical linearity _____

e. Horizontal size or width _____

f. Focus _____

7. Refer to schematic diagram of receiver and locate some alignment controls. Where are these controls located in receiver? _____

_____

8. Turn off TV receiver and disconnect it from antenna. Return receiver to storage cabinet.

## QUESTIONS

1. What is the primary difference between operator, service and alignment controls?

2. What receiver controls are used to change sweep frequencies?

3. What is the difference between brightness and contrast?

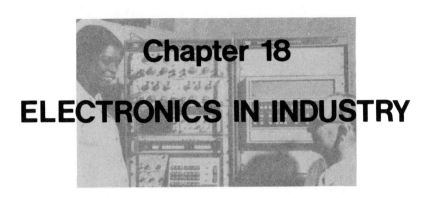

# Chapter 18
# ELECTRONICS IN INDUSTRY

## Experiment 18-1  LIGHT DETECTORS

### INTRODUCTION

Light detection electronic devices play an important role in industrial control circuits. These devices respond to light by changing their resistance, electron emission or developed voltage. The terms "light dependent resistor" (LDR), "photoemissive cell" and "photovoltaic cell" are commonly used to describe devices of this type.

A photoresistive device (LDR) is a very important light detection device. LDRs usually possess a rather high resistance between two terminals. When light energy is applied to a small window area, it causes a large reduction in resistance. A resistance ratio of dark to light ranges from 100 to 1 up to 10K to 1 in typical LDR units. This type of detector controls electrical energy from a source by changes in resistance. LDRs do not have a definite polarity and respond to current flow in either direction.

A photoemissive cell consists of an evacuated or gas-filled envelope housing a light sensitive cathode and an electron collecting anode. Light energy striking the cathode material causes it to emit (release) electrons. When the anode of the cell is made positive with respect to the cathode, it attracts emitted electrons. As a result, electron flow or current flow takes place when light is applied to the cell. Photoemissive cells have a definite polarity and will only produce current flow in one direction. Photodiodes are often classified as photoemissive cells or detectors.

Photovoltaic cells are a unique type of light sensitive device. These cells change light energy into voltage. When light energy strikes a thin layer of "N" type silicon, it causes electron movement in the material. These electrons move into a "P" material, forming a photocurrent. As a result of this action, light energy causes a charge difference across the cell. This is represented by a voltage or difference in potential across the PN junction. Voltages of less than one volt and current values up to 40 mA can be produced by a single cell. Cells of this type are frequently called "solar cells" because they are commonly used to convert sunlight into electrical energy.

In this experiment, you will test the operation of a photovoltaic cell and a light dependent resistor (LDR). Through this experience, you will observe light-to-electrical energy conversion and light energy circuit control techniques.

### EXPERIMENT OBJECTIVES

As a result of this laboratory experience, you should be able to accomplish the following:
1. Test the operation of two different light detection devices.
2. Observe the conversion of light to electrical energy.
3. Observe how light energy can control circuits in electronics.

### REFERENCE

Gerrish and Dugger, ELECTRICITY AND ELECTRONICS, Chapter 18, pages 271 to 273.

### MATERIALS AND EQUIPMENT

1 — Variable dc power supply
1 — Volt-ohm-milliampere (VOM) meter
1 — No. 47 lamp with socket

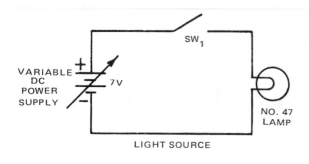

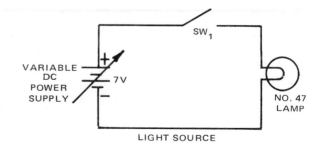

LIGHT SOURCE

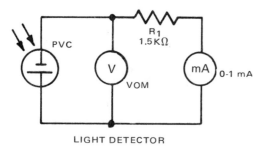

Fig. 18-1-1

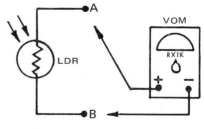

Fig. 18-1-2

1 — SPST toggle switch
1 — Solar cell
1 — Light dependent resistor
1 — 1.5K, 1/4 watt resistor
1 — 0-1 mA meter

## PROCEDURE

1. Connect photovoltaic cell test circuit as in Fig. 18-1-1.
2. Before turning on $SW_1$, turn on variable power supply and adjust it to 7V dc.
3. Move lamp as close as possible to cell window without touching cell.
4. Maximum current and voltage values indicated by VOM and mA meter are _____ volts and _____ mA.
5. Turn off $SW_1$. Indicate output of cell under conditions of normal room light. _____ volts and _____ mA.
6. Turn $SW_1$ on and off several times while observing voltage and current response time. How would you describe response time? _____ (instantaneous or slow)
7. Place cell part of test circuit near a window or in direct sunlight. How does output change? _____
8. Disconnect photovoltaic test circuit. Turn on LDR circuit shown in Fig. 18-1-2.

9. Prepare ohmmeter to measure resistance. Connect ohmmeter leads across test points A and B.
10. Cover cell with an opaque material that will block out ali light. Dark resistance of cell is _____ ohms.
11. Position lamp near window of LDR. Turn on $SW_1$ and record light resistance of cell. Light resistance is _____ ohms.
12. Reverse ohmmeter probes and measure light and dark resistance of LDR. Explain your findings. _____

_____

13. Prepare VOM to measure voltage across cell at test points A and B. Explain your findings. _____

_____

14. Turn off circuit switch and power supply. Disconnect circuit and return all parts to storage cabinet.

## QUESTIONS

1. Describe the measured differences in photovoltaic and photoresistive (LDR) devices.
2. Why does an LDR need an electrical energy source to achieve control?
3. What are some applications of photovoltaic cells?

# Experiment 18-2  LDR CONTROL CIRCUITS

## INTRODUCTION

A light dependent resistor (LDR) is frequently used as a light detector in photoelectric control circuits. An LDR is a form of variable resistance. Light energy applied to its window can be used to control electrical energy from a dc source.

An LDR achieves control when it is connected in series with the energy source and a sensitive relay. When a low level of light is applied to the window of an LDR, its internal resistance is quite high and circuit current is held to a minimum. When the applied light level is increased, it causes a decided reduction in the internal resistance of the LDR. This action, in turn, causes a corresponding increase in current flow, which is used to energize the relay. Circuits of this type are primarily used to achieve on and off control of an electrical device by changes in light level.

In this experiment, an LDR circuit uses light energy to control an incandescent lamp and to energize a relay. A latching circuit and a feedback light switch are also constructed. Through this experience, you will see some of the control possibilities of an LDR.

## EXPERIMENT OBJECTIVES

As a result of this laboratory experience, you should be able to accomplish the following:

1. Use a light dependent resistor (LDR) to control an incandescent lamp.

2. Use a light source to change the internal resistance of an LDR.

3. Construct a latching circuit and a feedback light switch circuit.

## REFERENCE

Gerrish and Dugger, ELECTRICITY AND ELECTRONICS, Chapter 18, pages 272 and 273.

## MATERIALS AND EQUIPMENT

1 — Volt-ohm-milliampere (VOM) meter
1 — Variable dc power supply
1 — 6.3V, 60 Hz ac source
1 — LDR cell
1 — 10V dc relay (Sigma 11F 100g 1A) or equivalent
1 — No. 47 lamp with sockets
1 — SPST toggle switch

## PROCEDURE

1. Connect LDR detector circuit as in Fig. 18-2-1. The ac source connected to a No. 47 lamp is controlled by switching action of relay.

2. Before applying electrical power to circuit, test relay switching contacts with an ohmmeter to determine proper contacts. This relay provides SPDT switching action. Normally open (N.O.) and normally closed (N.C.) conditions are present at three relay switching terminals. When relay is ener-

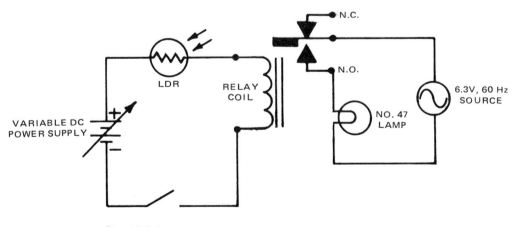

Fig. 18-2-1

gized, these conditions change to N.C. and N.O. respectively. N.O. switch is used in this part of experiment.

3. Apply 6.3V ac to lamp control circuit. If switch contacts are properly connected, lamp should be off. Lamp should turn on when relay armature is depressed to energized position with a pencil. If relay contacts do not function in this manner, turn off ac source and test contact points again with ohmmeter to find N.O. terminals.

4. Before turning on $SW_1$, turn on variable power supply and adjust it to 10V dc.

5. There should be enough existing light in room to energize circuit. If room has reduced light, sensitivity of circuit can be improved by increasing variable power supply voltage up to 15V dc.

6. Try triggering circuit with light from an external source, such as a flashlight or an additional 6V lamp. Reduce light sensitivity so that relay will not be energized by normal room light. Relay should only be energized when a light source is placed next to cell. Removing light should de-energize relay.

7. Another interesting effect is achieved when No. 47 lamp of control circuit is placed near LDR window. Energize relay circuit with flashlight or an external light source. How does circuit respond when external light source is removed? _____
_____

8. Turn off $SW_1$, then turn it on again. How does circuit respond? _____
_____

9. Again energize relay with a flashlight or external light source and test latching (locking) function.

10. Turn off 6.3V, 60 Hz source and switch relay switch contacts to N.C. terminals. Shield relay controlled lamp from LDR. Energize relay with a flashlight or external light source. How does it respond? _____
_____

11. With relay de-energized and lamp on, position lamp near LDR window. How does circuit respond? _____
_____

12. Turn off circuit switch and two power supplies. Disconnect circuit and return all parts to storage cabinet.

## QUESTIONS
1. What causes the lamp to flash on and off in step 11?
2. How does the light latch circuit of step 7 operate?
3. Why does an increase in source voltage cause increase sensitivity to light?

## INTRODUCTION

An RC timer is a precise circuit that can be used to achieve different timing operations. The term "RC" refers to a resistor capacitor network used to perform the timing operation. Production line control, motor running time and light flashing circuits are typical applications of this circuit.

When dc voltage is applied to a capacitor, it quickly charges to the value of the source. The capacitor has the ability to hold this charge voltage for a certain length of time. If a resistor is connected across a charged capacitor, it will discharge through the resistor according to the value of RC. Large value capacitors and resistors will cause a rather long discharge rate.

In this experiment, an RC circuit is used to control the conduction time of a transistor relay circuit. To ready this circuit for the operating cycle, a capacitor is charged to the dc source voltage. When switched to the START position, the capacitor begins to discharge through a resistor network. In this position, the charge voltage of the capacitor is used to forward bias a transistor into conduction. Then, when the charge voltage drops below a certain value, the transistor becomes nonconductive. Through this type of circuit, a starting operation can be delayed or turned on for a precise length of time. RC timers play a very important role in industrial control circuitry.

### EXPERIMENT OBJECTIVES

As a result of this laboratory experience, you should be able to accomplish the following:
1. Construct an RC timer.
2. Adjust the RC timer circuit to vary the time delay.

### REFERENCE

Gerrish and Dugger, ELECTRICITY AND ELECTRONICS, Chapter 18, page 273.

### MATERIALS AND EQUIPMENT

1 — Variable dc power supply
1 — Volt-ohm-milliampere (VOM) meter
1 — 6.3V, 60 Hz ac source
1 — 0-1 mA meter
1 — 10V dc relay (Sigma 11F 100g 1A) or equivalent
1 — 2N3397 transistor
1 — No. 47 lamp with socket
1 — 25 $\mu$F, 50V capacitor
1 — 680 $\mu$F, 50V dc capacitor from power supply module or an equivalent value
1 — 500K, 2 watt potentiometer
1 — 100K, 1/4 watt resistor
1 — 27K, 1/4 watt resistor
1 — 100 ohm, 1/4 watt resistor
1 — SPST toggle switch
1 — SPDT toggle switch

### PROCEDURE

1. Construct delay timer circuit, Fig. 18-3-1.
2. Before turning on $SW_1$, turn on variable power supply and adjust it to 9V dc.
3. To operate this circuit, place $SW_2$ in READY position. $C_1$, in this case, charges to dc value of power supply. In this first operating condition, transistor is inoperative because base is reversed biased through $R_1$ and $R_2$. Relay is not energized. Lamp is _____ (on or off) in this state.
4. When $SW_2$ is changed to START position, $C_1$ forward biases base circuit which, in turn, causes transistor to be conductive and energize relay. How does lamp respond with $SW_2$ in START position? _____
_____
5. Adjust potentiometer $R_2$ to its maximum clockwise position. Turn switch $SW_2$ to READY position momentarily, then back to START position. Note delay time. Delay time is _____ seconds.
6. Change potentiometer $R_2$ to its maximum counterclockwise position. Repeat READY and START switching action. Delay time is _____ seconds.
7. Why does value of $R_2$ alter delay time of relay circuit? _____
_____
8. Turn off $SW_1$ and connect a 0-1 mA meter into circuit at $TP_1$.

Electricity and Electronics Laboratory Manual

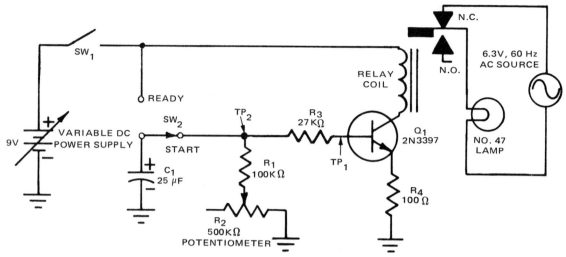

Fig. 18-3-1

9. Turn on $SW_1$ and adjust $R_2$ to longest delay position. Cycle timer by changing $SW_2$ to READY, then START positions. How does mA meter respond? _____

_____

10. Turn off $SW_1$ and remove $C_1$ from circuit. Connect 680 $\mu F$ capacitor from power supply module or an equivalent mounted capacitor in place of $C_1$. Be certain to connect capacitor polarity as indicated.

11. Turn on $SW_1$ and cycle timer to READY, then START positions. Delay time is _____ _____ seconds.

12. If a high impedance voltmeter such as a VTVM or FET VOM is available, connect it across $TP_2$ and ground.

13. Cycle timer and observe voltage indication at $TP_2$. Describe how voltage responds.

_____

_____

14. Turn off $SW_1$ and power supply. Disconnect circuit and return all parts to storage cabinet.

## QUESTIONS
1. What is meant by the term "delay timer?"
2. What determines the delay time of the circuit used in this experiment?
3. Why must the circuit be switched to the READY position first before the cycle is started?

240

## INTRODUCTION

Radio control applications are commonly used to energize circuits from distant locations. Garage door openers are typical examples. An rf signal sent out from an automobile some distance from the garage will activate a relay circuit which, in turn, starts a door opening mechanism. Typical radio control frequencies are 27 MHz, 53 MHz and 72 MHz.

The radio control circuit in this experiment utilizes an rf signal that is approximately 1 MHz and less than the 100 mW. This type of circuit does not require a license to operate as long as the transmitter unit is not applied to an outside antenna.

When an rf signal is sent out by the transmitter, it is picked up by the receiver circuit. The tuned circuit of the receiver is adjusted to select the rf signal. A diode in the receiver rectifies the rf signal and applies its output to a capacitor. The average value of the rectified rf pulses is used to develop a dc voltage across the capacitor. This voltage is amplified by two transistors, and it is used to drive a relay. Relay control, then, can be used to actuate a wide variety of electrical devices. In this experiment, the lamp serves as a load control device.

The rf circuit used in this experiment is similar in general theory to that of a radio control system. More rf power, at a higher frequency, with a narrow frequency assignment or channel are typically found in commercial radio control units. The circuit of this experiment is used only to demonstrate the basic principles of rf control. The transmitter part of the circuit should not be changed effectively without a license or knowledge of the legal limits of rf transmission at this frequency.

## EXPERIMENT OBJECTIVES

As a result of this laboratory experience, you should be able to accomplish the following:

1. Construct a low frequency, low power radio control circuit.
2. Perform some basic tasks with the radio control circuit.

## REFERENCE

Gerrish and Dugger, ELECTRICITY AND ELECTRONICS, Chapter 18, pages 273 to 276.

## MATERIALS AND EQUIPMENT

1 — Variable dc power supply
1 — 6.3V, 60 Hz ac source
1 — Volt-ohm-milliampere (VOM) meter
1 — AM transmitter module rf oscillator, or equivalent rf signal source
1 — Antenna coil
2 — SPST toggle switches
1 — 365 pF variable capacitor
1 — 25 $\mu$F, 50V dc capacitor
1 — 100K, 1/4 watt resistor
1 — 27K, 1/4 watt resistor
1 — 2N3397 transistor
1 — 2N3702 transistor
1 — 10V dc relay (Sigma 11F 100g 1A) or equivalent
1 — No. 47 lamp with socket

## PROCEDURE

1. Construct radio control circuit shown in Fig. 18-4-1.
2. The rf signal source of system uses an AM transmitter module without a microphone. $SW_2$ is used as a key to control rf signal. An rf signal generator that produces a signal of 100 KHz may be used in place of AM module if it is not available. The rf oscillator module or an equivalent circuit may also be used as an rf source.
3. Before turning on $SW_1$ and $SW_2$, turn on variable dc power supply and adjust it to 10V dc. Same dc source is used to supply both rf source and circuit.
4. Prepare oscilloscope for operation. Connect vertical probe to $TP_1$ and connect ground to common circuit ground or negative power supply terminal.
5. Touch antenna of rf source against receiving antenna. Tune capacitor $C_1$ of circuit for maximum rf signal indication on oscilloscope. If circuit is working properly, relay should be energized and turn on lamp. If it does not work, turn off $SW_2$ and

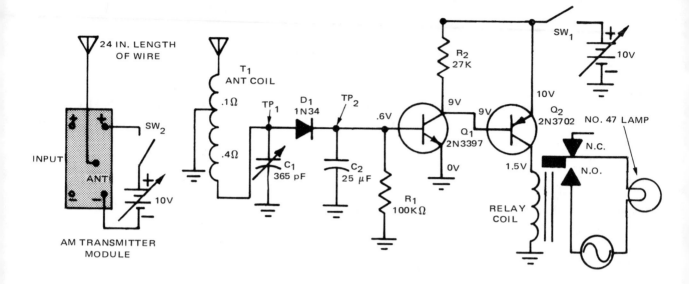

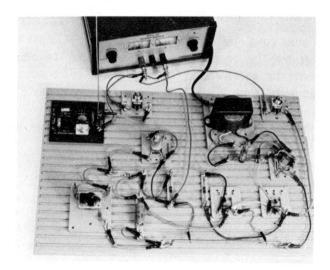

Fig. 18-4-1

measure dc voltages at transistor elements. Measured values should approximate those indicated on diagram.

6. Turn on $SW_2$ again with the two antennas touching. Measure dc voltage at $TP_2$. Tune $C_1$ for maximum voltage. The dc voltage at $TP_2$ is _____ volts. If a dc voltage cannot be obtained at this test point, check tuner circuit wiring and rf signal source for output. If voltage is present at $TP_2$, re-check wiring of two transistors and relay circuit. Relay should be energized at this time.

7. Measure energized voltage values at transistor elements.

8. Key circuit on OFF position by turning $SW_2$ on and off.

9. Separate two antenna wires and test circuit for control. Maximum distance that control can be achieved is _____ ft.

10. Turn off power supply and equipment. Disconnect circuit and return all parts to storage cabinet.

## QUESTIONS

1. Give one application of a radio control circuit.

2. What is the function of the diode in the circuit used in this experiment?

3. What kind of signal is developed across capacitor $C_2$ of this experiment?

# Chapter 19
# TEST INSTRUMENTS

## Experiment 19-1 BRIDGE MEASURING CIRCUITS

### INTRODUCTION

A Wheatstone bridge circuit is used in many electronic test instruments. Basically, a Wheatstone bridge employs two series resistor branch circuits connected across a common voltage source. When the resistance of the right hand branch equals the resistance of the left hand branch, a zero or balanced bridge condition will occur between the center connected resistor points. When any change in resistance occurs, the bridge becomes imbalanced and produces a voltage across its center connection points.

Vacuum tube voltmeters and transistorized voltmeters use the Wheatstone bridge principle in their operation. With no voltage applied to the bridge circuit, it is adjusted to produce a balanced condition. When voltage to be measured is applied to a transistor or vacuum tube, it will cause a resistance change in the device and in the total bridge circuit. This circuit change then produces a corresponding deflection of a meter connected across the midpoints of the bridge. As a result, very accurate voltage, current and resistance measurements can be achieved.

In this experiment, you will build and test a Wheatstone bridge circuit. When the bridge is balanced, the corresponding voltage values across resistors are of an equal value. An imbalanced condition is used to show what occurs when the circuit values change.

### EXPERIMENT OBJECTIVES

As a result of this laboratory experience, you should be able to accomplish the following:
1. Construct a Wheatstone bridge circuit.
2. Test bridge circuit operation.
3. Observe how this circuit can be applied to a test instrument.

### REFERENCE

Gerrish and Dugger, ELECTRICITY AND ELECTRONICS, Chapter 19, pages 282 to 284.

### MATERIALS AND EQUIPMENT

1 — Volt-ohm-milliampere (VOM) meter
1 — 0-1 mA meter
1 — Variable dc power supply
1 — SPST toggle switch
1 — Resistor decade module or following 1/4 watt resistors:
    2 — 2K, 1/4 watt resistors
    2 — 220 ohm, 1/4 watt resistors
1 — 5K, 2 watt potentiometer

### PROCEDURE

1. Construct Wheatstone bridge circuit as in Fig. 19-1-1. If resistor decade module is not available, separately mounted resistors may be used.
2. Before turning on $SW_1$, adjust variable dc power supply to 5V.
3. Prepare a VOM to measure dc voltage across $R_1$, $R_2$, $R_3$ and $R_4$. $V_{R_1}$ is _____, $V_{R_2}$ is _____, $V_{R_1}$ is _____ and $V_{R_4}$ is _____
4. If bridge is perfectly balanced, $V_{R_1}$ should be equal to $V_{R_2}$. $V_{R_3}$ should equal $V_{R_4}$. In this condition, no voltage will appear across points C-D.
5. Connect VOM across $TP_3$ and $TP_4$ to determine if there is voltage present. If

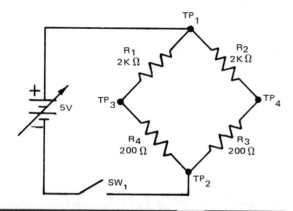

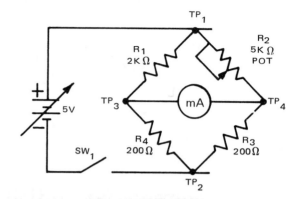

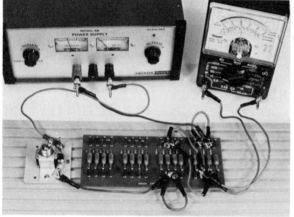

Fig. 19-1-1

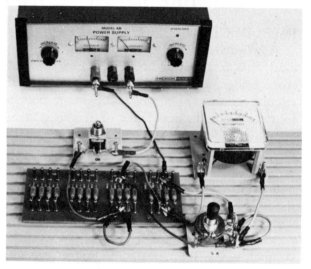

Fig. 19-1-2

meter deflection is "on scale," polarity of meter matches polarity of bridge. An "off scale" deflection indicates meter polarity reversal with respect to bridge voltage. $TP_1$ is _____ (positive or negative), while $TP_2$ is _____ (positive or negative).

6. Turn off $SW_1$ and remove $R_2$ from circuit. In its place, connect a 5K potentiometer as indicated in Fig. 19-1-2. Connect a 0-1 mA meter across $TP_3$ and $TP_4$ to indicate balanced condition of circuit.

7. Adjust $R_2$ to approximate center of its resistance range. Then, turn on $SW_1$.

8. Adjust $R_2$ again to produce a balanced condition indicated by a zero meter indication.

9. Prepare VOM to measure voltage across $R_1$,

$R_2$, $R_3$ and $R_4$ with bridge balanced. $V_{R_1}$ is _____. $V_{R_2}$ is _____. $V_{R_3}$ is _____. $V_{R_4}$ is _____.

10. Turn off power supply and $SW_1$. Disconnect circuit and return all parts to storage cabinet.

## QUESTIONS

1. Why does a zero reading at $TP_3$ and $TP_4$ indicate a balanced condition?

2. In measuring voltages of a bridge circuit: $V_{R_1}$ is 3V. $V_{R_2}$ is 2.8V. $V_{R_3}$ is 2.2V. $V_{R_4}$ is 2V. Give polarity of $TP_3$ and $TP_4$.

3. What is the function of the potentiometer in Fig. 19-1-2?

## INTRODUCTION

A number of testers are available that will determine the operating condition of solid state devices. With these units, you can test bipolar transistors, field effect transistors, unijunction transistors, diodes, silicon controlled rectifiers, triacs, diacs and integrated circuits. Meter deflecting instruments, oscilloscope display units and sound producing testers are three different classes of testers. These devices may be used to test the device either in or out of an operating circuit.

In this experiment, you will build a transistor tester that will reveal leakage current, gain, transistor type and material type. This particular circuit is used only to make out-of-circuit tests of transistors. Through this experiment, you will become familiar with transistor measurement techniques and test procedures.

Leakage current is an important transistor test condition. This measurement is made by applying voltage between the emitter-collector elements with the base open. The term "$I_{CBO}$" is commonly used to describe this condition. Leakage current should be below 10 microamperes in either NPN and PNP transistors.

The gain or beta ($\beta$) test indicates the ability of a transistor to amplify. This measurement is made by forward biasing the emitter-base junctions and reverse biasing the collector. A small base current should produce a rather sizable collector current. In this test, gain is found by multiplying the collector current reading by the range switch setting of X10 or X100. Typical beta values may range around 200.

Polarity testing shows whether a transistor is an NPN or PNP type. You can make this test by forward biasing the base collector junction. If deflection occurs when the NPN-PNP select switch is in the NPN position, the transistor is of the PNP type. Deflection in the PNP select position indicates an NPN type of transistor. No deflection in either position means the transistor is "open."

The material testing function of the transistor tester is achieved after transistor type has been determined. Germanium transistors will produce a current indication of less than 1 mA. Silicon transistors will not show current flow at this small value of base voltage.

The transistor tester of this experiment may be built from a circuit board module or from individually mounted components. This tester also can be built as a take-home project.

## EXPERIMENT OBJECTIVES

As a result of this laboratory experience, you should be able to accomplish the following:
1. Construct a simple transistor tester.
2. Use this tester to check some transistors for leakage current, gain, type and material.

## REFERENCE

Gerrish and Dugger, ELECTRICITY AND ELECTRONICS, Chapter 19, pages 288 and 289.

## MATERIALS AND EQUIPMENT

1 — Volt-ohm-milliampere meter, a 10 mA dc meter or a 1 mA dc meter with a shunt resistor to extend its range
1 — SPST toggle switch
1 — Variable dc power supply
1 — Transistor tester module or following components:
    1 — DPDT toggle switch
    3 — SPST push button switches, N.O.
    1 — 47 ohm, 1/4 watt resistor
    1 — 56K, 1/4 watt resistor
    1 — 510K, 1/4 watt resistor
    4 — 1N4004 diodes
    3 — Alligator clip leads
1 — 2N3397 transistor
1 — 2N3702 transistor

## PROCEDURE

1. Turn on variable dc power supply of Fig. 19-2-1 and adjust it to 6V. Then, connect it to transistor test module. If a test module is not available, construct circuit from separately mounted components, using Fig. 19-2-2.
2. Connect a 2N3397 transistor to emitter-base-collector test leads of tester.

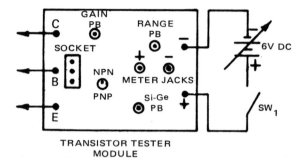

Fig. 19-2-1

surable $I_{CBO}$ in a good transistor. Acceptable values are generally below 10 microamperes. Measured $I_{CBO}$ is _____

4. Depress Si-Ge (silicon-germanium) push button. If meter deflects with select switch in NPN position, transistor is PNP type. If no deflection occurs, change select switch to PNP position. Deflection in this position indicates an NPN transistor type. No deflection with select switch in either NPN or PNP position indicates an "open" transistor. Transistor being tested is a _____ (PNP or NPN) type.

5. Release Si-Ge push button and set NPN-PNP select switch to transistor type determined in step 4.

6. Depress Si-Ge push button again. A zero reading indicates a silicon transistor. A reading less than 1 mA reveals a germanium type. Transistor being tested is a _____ (silicon or germanium) type.

7. Release Si-Ge push button.

8. Depress gain push button. To compute gain, multiply meter reading by range setting switch position of X100 or X10.

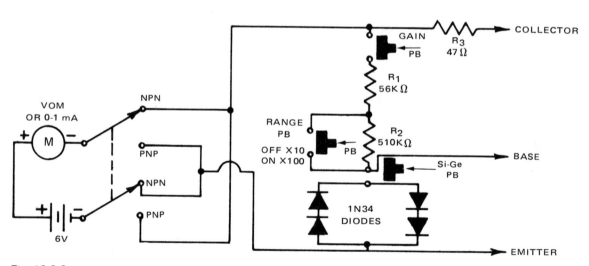

Fig. 19-2-2

3. Place select switch in NPN position: meter reads transistor leakage current between emitter-collector with base open. Term $I_{CBO}$ is commonly used to denote this value. There should be practically no mea-

Gain is _____

9. Remove 2N3397 transistor. Install a 2N3702 transistor in its place.

10. To test transistor:
   a. Set select switch to NPN.

b. Depress Si-Ge push button. Meter deflection signals type opposite of switch position. Type is _____ (NPN or PNP).

c. Set select switch to determined type, then depress Si-Ge push button. Transistor is _____ (silicon or germanium).

d. Depress gain push button. To compute gain, multiply meter reading by range setting. Gain is _____

11. Ask your instructor for another transistor for testing. Test it, using procedure outlined in step 10. Condition of transistor is _____ (good or bad). Type is _____ (NPN or PNP). Transistor is _____ (silicon or germanium). Gain is _____

12. Disconnect tester circuit or module. Turn off power supply and return all parts to storage cabinet.

## QUESTIONS

1. What is $I_{CBO}$?
2. How would an open transistor respond in the testing procedure?
3. How would a shorted transistor test in the $I_{CBO}$ position of procedure step 3?

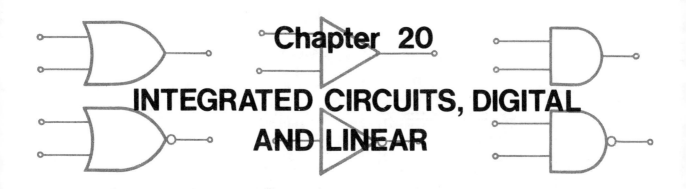

# Chapter 20

# INTEGRATED CIRCUITS, DIGITAL AND LINEAR

## Experiment 20-1 AND GATES

### INTRODUCTION

One important application of an integrated circuit (IC) is in the field of digital electronics. The IC field primarily deals with circuits that process information in only two operating states or conditions. The ON state or 1 condition denotes when a circuit has voltage applied to it. Rather low voltage values of 5V or less are typical of this state of operation. The OFF state or 0 condition denotes when a circuit has no voltage applied to it. Digital circuits that process 1 and 0 information are frequently called "two state" or "binary logic" circuits.

In this experiment, you will build and test a two input AND gate. You will apply different combinations of 0V and 5V to the input of this logic gate, then measure and record corresponding output. In addition, you will build a three input AND gate, using the two input gates in a combination circuit.

When the input and output relationship of an AND gate is plotted in a table, it shows the unique characteristics of the gate. The term "truth table" is commonly used to describe this setup. Knowing basic logic functions is essential in the study of digital electronic devices.

### EXPERIMENT OBJECTIVES

As a result of this laboratory experience, you should be able to accomplish the following:
1. Construct a two input AND gate.
2. Test the AND gate circuit.
3. Construct a three input AND gate and test it.

### REFERENCE

Gerrish and Dugger, ELECTRICITY AND ELECTRONICS, Chapter 20, pages 294 and 295.

### MATERIALS AND EQUIPMENT
1 — Volt-ohm-milliampere (VOM) meter
1 — Variable dc power supply
1 — IC circuit construction module or following equivalent parts:
    4 — 5V light emitting diodes
    4 — SPDT toggle switches
    4 — 390 ohm, 1/8 watt resistors
    1 — IC construction board or socket
1 — SN7408 integrated circuit
1 — SPST toggle switch

### PROCEDURE
1. Connect AND gate test circuit as in Fig. 20-1-1, using IC construction module. If IC module is not available, construct circuit with separately mounted components. See Fig. 20-1-2.
2. Before turning on $SW_1$, turn on power supply and adjust it to 5V dc.
3. Light emitting diodes or LEDs are lettered A, B and C. A and B serve as inputs to logic gate. LED C serves as output indicator.
4. Test logic switch wiring by moving $SW_A$ to 5V or 1 position. LED A should turn on if circuit is wired properly. Turn $SW_A$ off.
5. Using same procedure outlined in step 4, test LED B.
6. If both LED indicators A and B are working properly, you are ready to test operation of logic gate. If they are not working properly, test 5V power supply and polarity of each diode with a VOM.

LOGIC MODULE IC-1

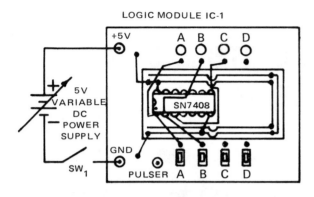

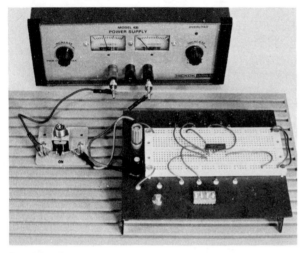

Fig. 20-1-1

Check circuit wiring again to determine if it is correct.

7. Test logic gate according to switch position alternatives shown in Fig. 20-1-3. Record status of output LED.

| SWITCH A LED A | | SWITCH B LED B | | OUTPUT LED C | |
|---|---|---|---|---|---|
| 0 | V | 0 | V | | V |
| 0 | V | 1 | V | | V |
| 1 | V | 0 | V | | V |
| 1 | V | 1 | V | | V |

Fig. 20-1-3

8. Prepare VOM to measure dc voltage. Determine corresponding voltage values related to 0 and 1 of switches A, B and output. Record voltage values in provided spaces of Fig. 20-1-3.
9. Turn off $SW_1$ and add $SW_C$ to IC. Also change LED connections to conform with Fig. 20-1-4.
10. Turn on $SW_1$ and test logic switch position alternatives shown in Fig. 20-1-5. Record status of gate output at LED D.
11. Turn off circuit switch and disconnect logic circuit. Return all parts to storage cabinet.

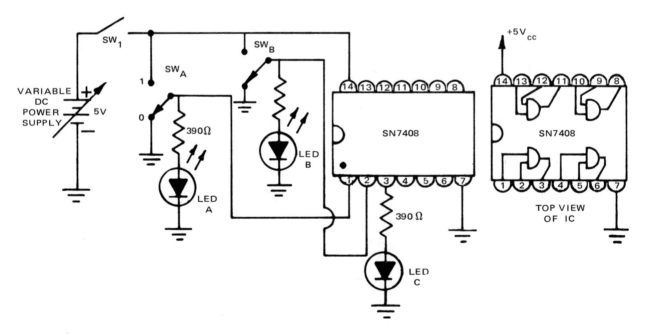

Fig. 20-1-2

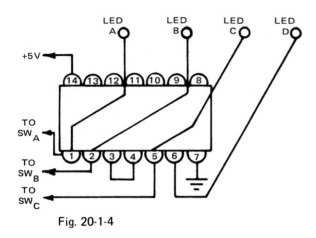

Fig. 20-1-4

| SWITCH A | SWITCH B | SWITCH C | LED D OUTPUT |
|----------|----------|----------|--------------|
| 0 | 0 | 0 | |
| 0 | 0 | 1 | |
| 0 | 1 | 0 | |
| 0 | 1 | 1 | |
| 1 | 0 | 0 | |
| 1 | 0 | 1 | |
| 1 | 1 | 0 | |
| 1 | 1 | 1 | |

Fig. 20-1-5

## QUESTIONS

1. Draw a logic symbol of two gates constructed in this experiment, showing input and leads with corresponding letter labels.

2. Prepare a statement that describes logic function of first gate of this experiment.

3. Using logic symbols, make a sketch of the two logic gates set up in procedure step 9 and in Fig. 20-1-4.

## INTRODUCTION

An OR gate performs an important primary logic function in computers. This type of logic gate produces a 1 output when either one or the other of its inputs is a 1. The other alternative shows that if all inputs are 0, the output will also be 0. Typically, an OR gate is used in applications that need to determine if any one of the inputs of a circuit is present. In this regard, an OR gate is often called an ANY or ALL gate. It will develop a 1 output when any or all of its inputs are a 1.

In this experiment, you will build an OR gate with an integrated circuit and observe its output as voltage or as LED indicators. A truth table will show measured voltages and 1s or 0s to indicate the input and output possibilities of the OR function. Positive logic, which considers a turned on LED or voltage as a 1 and an off LED or no voltage as 0, is used in this experiment.

## EXPERIMENT OBJECTIVES

As a result of this laboratory experience, you should be able to accomplish the following:
1. Construct an OR gate, using an IC.
2. Test the operation of the OR gate.
3. Complete a truth table for the OR gate.

## REFERENCE

Gerrish and Dugger, ELECTRICITY AND ELECTRONICS, Chapter 20, page 295.

## MATERIALS AND EQUIPMENT

   1 – Volt-ohm-milliampere (VOM) meter
   1 – Variable dc power supply
   1 – IC circuit construction module or following equivalent parts:
      4 – 5V light emitting diodes
      4 – SPDT toggle switches
      4 – 390 ohm, 1/8 watt resistors
      1 – IC construction board or socket
   1 – SN7432 integrated circuit
   1 – SPST toggle switch

## PROCEDURE

1. Connect OR gate test circuit as shown in Fig. 20-2-1, using IC construction module. If IC module is not available, circuit may be constructed with separately mounted components according to Fig. 20-2-2.

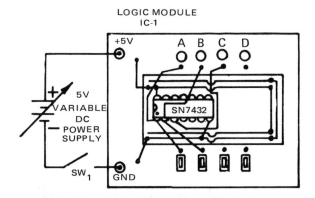

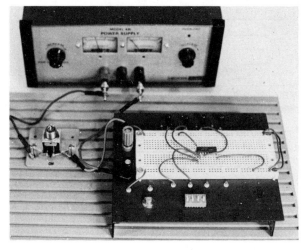

Fig. 20-2-1

2. Before turning on $SW_1$, turn on power supply and adjust it to 5V dc.
3. Light emitting diodes labeled A and B serve as input indicators. LED C is output.
4. Test logic switch wiring, placing $SW_A$ in 1 position. If properly wired, LED A should turn on. Using same procedure, test LED B.
5. If both $SW_A$ and $SW_B$ control their respective LEDs, you are ready to test logic gate. If they do not control, test power supply connections, polarity of diodes and circuit voltage with a VOM.
6. Test logic gate according to switch position

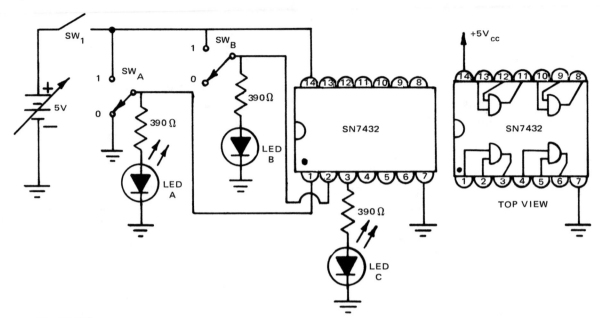

Fig. 20-2-2

| SWITCH A LED A | | SWITCH B LED B | | OUTPUT LED C | |
|---|---|---|---|---|---|
| 0 | ____ V | 0 | ____ V | ____ | ____ V |
| 0 | ____ V | 1 | ____ V | ____ | ____ V |
| 1 | ____ V | 0 | ____ V | ____ | ____ V |
| 1 | ____ V | 1 | ____ V | ____ | ____ V |

Fig. 20-2-3

alternatives shown in Fig. 20-2-3. Record 1 or 0 status of output LED indicator.

7. Prepare VOM to measure dc voltage and determine voltage values for each 0 or 1 condition of $SW_A$, $SW_B$ and resulting output of LED C. Record measured voltages and 1 or 0 alternatives in provided space in Fig. 20-2-3.

8. Turn off $SW_1$ and add switch C to IC. Change LED connections to conform with those in Fig. 20-2-4.

9. Turn on $SW_1$ and test logic switch position alternatives shown in Fig. 20-2-5. Record status of gate output appearing under LED D in chart in Fig. 20-2-5.

10. If time permits, test other two gates of SN7432 IC.

11. Turn off circuit switch and disconnect logic circuit. Return all parts to storage cabinet.

## QUESTIONS

1. Draw a logic symbol of the two gate circuits constructed in this experiment. Show the

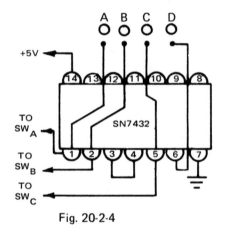

Fig. 20-2-4

| SWITCH A | SWITCH B | SWITCH C | LED D OUTPUT |
|---|---|---|---|
| 0 | 0 | 0 | |
| 0 | 0 | 1 | |
| 0 | 1 | 0 | |
| 0 | 1 | 1 | |
| 1 | 0 | 0 | |
| 1 | 0 | 1 | |
| 1 | 1 | 0 | |
| 1 | 1 | 1 | |

Fig. 20-2-5

input and output with corresponding letter labels.

2. Prepare a statement that describes the logic function of the gate constructed in step 1 of this experiment.

3. Using logic symbols, make a sketch of the two logic gate connections of step 9.

# Experiment 20-3  NOT GATES

## INTRODUCTION

A NOT gate is the third basic logic function of a digital electronic system. Bascially, this type of gate is designed to the inversion function. When a 1 is applied to its input, a 0 will appear at the output. This function is described by a statement, "A one applied to the input is NOT a one in the output." In two states (binary logic): if the output is not 1, it can only be 0.

In this experiment, you will test the input and output possibilities of a NOT gate built on an integrated circuit chip. The particular IC used in this experiment contains six separate gates and is described as a "hex inverter." All of the NOT gates are tested, then connected to achieve other logic functions. Due to the inverting capability of a NOT gate, a combination of them can be used to build AND and OR gates.

## EXPERIMENT OBJECTIVES

As a result of this laboratory experience, you should be able to accomplish the following:
1. Construct and test a NOT gate.
2. Observe the input and output of the NOT gate.

## REFERENCE

Gerrish and Dugger, ELECTRICITY AND ELECTRONICS, Chapter 20, pages 295 and 296.

## MATERIALS AND EQUIPMENT

   1 — Variable dc power supply
   1 — SN7404 IC
   1 — SPST toggle switch
   1 — IC circuit construction module or following equivalent parts:
      4 — 5V light emitting diodes
      4 — SPDT toggle switches
      4 — 390 ohm, 1/8 watt resistors
      1 — IC construction board or socket

## PROCEDURE

1. Connect logic gate of Fig. 20-3-1, using IC circuit construction module. If IC module is not available, circuit can be constructed with separately mounted components according to Fig. 20-3-2.

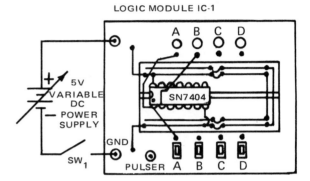

LOGIC MODULE IC-1

Fig. 20-3-1

2. Before turning on $SW_1$, turn on power supply and adjust it to 5V dc.
3. LED and switch labeled A serve as input. LED B serves are output.
4. Place $SW_A$ in GND position, then in +5V position while observing LEDs A and B. Describe action of LEDs. _____

_____

5. Test other logic gates of IC at locations 3-4, 5-6, 8-9, 10-11 and 12-13 by moving leads from 1 and 2 to other pin combinations.
6. Turn off $SW_1$. Connect a combination gate circuit with $SW_A$ and LED A attached to pin 1, and pins 2 and 3 connected together. Connect output pin 4 to LED B.
7. Turn on $SW_1$ and test combination circuit with $SW_A$. How does output or LED B respond? _____

_____

8. Turn off $SW_1$ and connect combination circuit of Fig. 20-3-3. NOTE: Only gate diagram of circuit is shown.
9. Using LEDs A and B as input, and C as output, complete truth table for test circuit. Assume that an ON LED is 1 and an OFF condition is 0. What logic function is achieved by this circuit? _____

_____

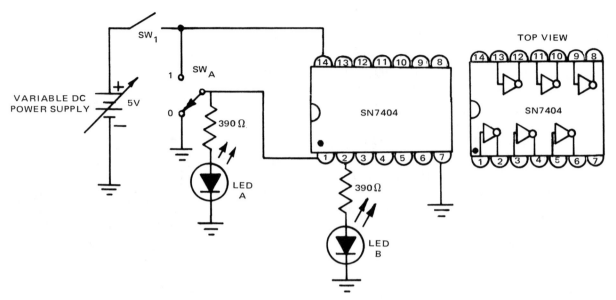

Fig. 20-3-2

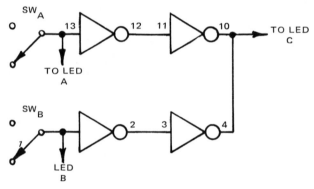

Fig. 20-3-3

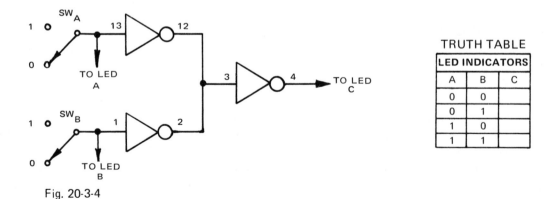

Fig. 20-3-4

**TRUTH TABLE**

| LED INDICATORS | | |
|---|---|---|
| A | B | C |
| 0 | 0 | |
| 0 | 1 | |
| 1 | 0 | |
| 1 | 1 | |

10. Turn off $SW_1$. Change circuit of Fig. 20-3-3 to conform with circuit of Fig. 20-3-4.

11. Turn on $SW_1$ and test circuit. Complete truth table, using positive logic indicators for 1 and 0. What logic function is

achieved by this circuit? _____

_____

12. Turn off circuit switch and disconnect circuit. Return all parts to storage cabinet.

## QUESTIONS

1. When the output of one NOT gate is connected to the input of a second NOT gate, how will the output of the second gate compare with the input?

2. What is meant by the term "positive logic?" Give an example.

3. What is the statement that describes the function of a NOT gate?

## INTRODUCTION

Today, a NAND gate usually is classified as a combination logic function. This gate function is achieved by combining an AND gate and a NOT gate. The word NAND is a contraction of the words NOT AND. A statement describing this function indicates that "The inputs applied to a NAND gate appear as a NOT AND at the output."

Several discrete NAND gates are commonly built on a single IC chip. Since this type of gate performs an inversion function, it can be used in combination circuits to build AND, OR, NOT, NAND and NOR logic functions. A NAND gate serves as a basic building block in one family of integrated circuits.

In this experiment, you will first build a NAND gate, using a combination of AND and NOT logic gates. Secondly, NOT gates in a combination logic circuit are used to produce the NAND function. In the last part of the experiment, one NAND gate of a quad NAND gate IC is used to achieve this logic function. In this way, you will become familiar with the NAND logic function and be able to construct it in a number of ways.

## EXPERIMENT OBJECTIVES

As a result of this laboratory experience, you should be able to accomplish the following:
1. Construct a NAND gate.
2. Test the operation of the NAND gate, using different methods.

## REFERENCE

Gerrish and Dugger, ELECTRICITY AND ELECTRONICS, Chapter 20, page 296.

## MATERIALS AND EQUIPMENT

1 — Variable dc power supply
1 — SN7400 IC
1 — SN7404 IC
1 — SN7408 IC
1 — SPST toggle switch
1 — IC circuit construction module or following equivalent parts:
    4 — 5V light emitting diodes
    2 — SPDT toggle switches
    4 — 390 ohm, 1/8 watt resistors
    1 — IC construction board or socket

## PROCEDURE

1. Connect combination logic gate circuit shown in Fig. 20-4-1, using IC circuit construction module. If IC module is not available, circuit can be constructed with separately mounted components according to Fig. 20-4-2.
2. Before turning on $SW_1$, turn on variable power supply and adjust it to 5V dc.
3. Complete truth table for output C, using alternatives in Fig. 20-4-1. What logic function is indicated by output C? _____

_____

4. Complete truth table for output D, using alternatives listed in truth table in Fig.

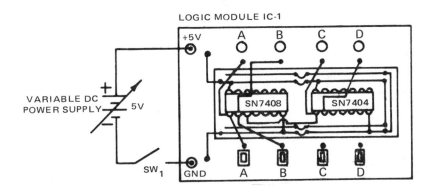

LOGIC MODULE IC-1

Fig. 20-4-1

| TRUTH TABLE | | | |
|---|---|---|---|
| LED INDICATORS | | | |
| A | B | C | D |
| 0 | 0 | | |
| 0 | 1 | | |
| 1 | 0 | | |
| 1 | 1 | | |

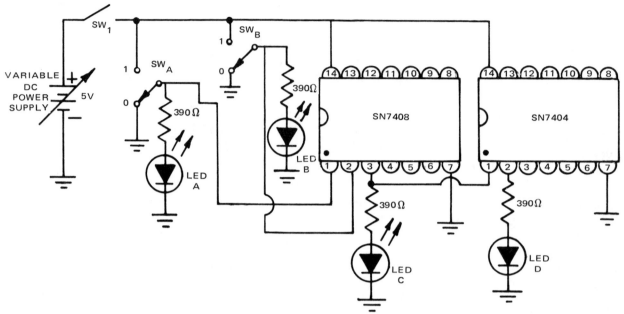

Fig. 20-4-2

20-4-1. What logic function is indicated by output D? _____

_____

5. Turn off SW$_1$ and disconnect IC logic circuit in Fig. 20-4-1. Connect combination logic circuit of Fig. 20-4-3, using an SN7404 IC. NOTE: Only gate part of circuit is shown to simplify diagram.

circuit? _____

7. Turn off SW$_1$ and disconnect SN7404 circuit.

8. Connect SN7400 gate test circuit shown in Fig. 20-4-4. NOTE: Only gate part of circuit is shown for simplicity.

9. Turn on SW$_1$ and test the logic gate, using alternatives in truth table in Fig. 20-4-4.

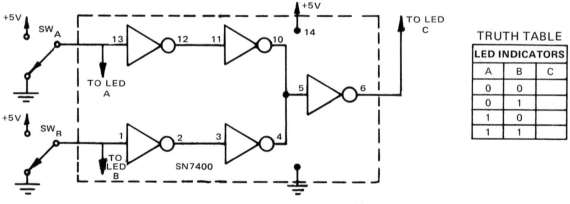

| TRUTH TABLE | | |
|---|---|---|
| LED INDICATORS | | |
| A | B | C |
| 0 | 0 | |
| 0 | 1 | |
| 1 | 0 | |
| 1 | 1 | |

Fig. 20-4-3

6. Turn on SW$_1$ and test circuit, using alternatives in truth table in Fig. 20-4-3. Record output of logic gate indicated by LED C. What logic function is achieved by this gate

Record output of logic gate indicated by LED C. What logic function is achieved by this gate circuit? _____

10. If time permits, test operation of remaining

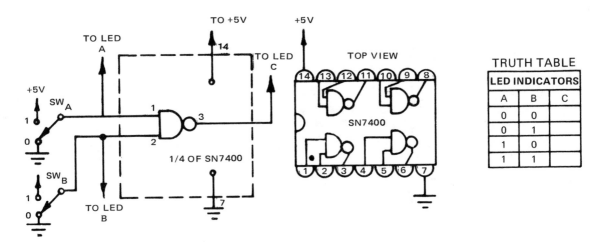

Fig. 20-4-4

three gates of SN7400 IC.

11. Turn off $SW_1$ and power supply. Disconnect circuit and return all parts to storage cabinet.

## QUESTIONS

1. Sketch a gate diagram of the combination logic circuit you have constructed, based on Fig. 20-4-1 or Fig. 20-4-2.

2. What statement describes the NAND function?

3. What logic function would be performed if the output of a NAND gate is applied to a NOT gate?

## INTRODUCTION

A NOR gate is an important combination logic gate. This gate function is achieved by combining an OR gate and a NOT gate. The word NOR is a contraction of the words NOT OR. A statement used to describe this function indicates that "The inputs applied to a NOR gate appear as a NOT OR function at the output."

Today, discrete NOR gates are commonly built on single IC chips. Since this type of gate accomplishes an inverting function, it can be used in combination circuits to build AND, OR, NOT, NAND and NOR logic functions. The NOR gate serves as a basic building block for one integrated circuit family.

In this experiment, you will build the NOR logic function using OR and NOT gates. NOT gates only and with a quad NOR gate IC. In this manner, you will become familiar with the NOR logic function by achieving it in several different ways.

## EXPERIMENT OBJECTIVES

As a result of this laboratory experience, you should be able to accomplish the following:
1. Construct a NOR gate.
2. Test the operation of the NOR gate, using different methods.

## REFERENCE

Gerrish and Dugger, ELECTRICITY AND ELECTRONICS, Chapter 20, page 296.

## MATERIALS AND EQUIPMENT

1 — Variable dc power supply
1 — SN7402 IC
1 — SN7404 IC
1 — SN7432 IC
1 — SPST toggle switch
1 — IC circuit construction module or following equivalent parts:
    4 — 5V light emitting diodes
    2 — SPDT toggle switches
    4 — 390 ohm, 1/8 watt resistors
    1 — IC construction board or socket

## PROCEDURE

1. Connect combination logic gate circuit shown in Fig. 20-5-1, using IC circuit construction module. If IC module is not available, circuit can be constructed with separately mounted components according to Fig. 20-5-2.

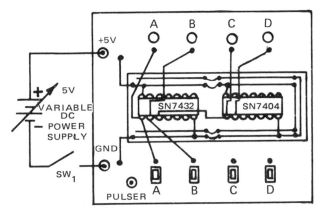

TRUTH TABLE

| LED INDICATORS | | | |
|---|---|---|---|
| A | B | C | D |
| 0 | 0 | | |
| 0 | 1 | | |
| 1 | 0 | | |
| 1 | 1 | | |

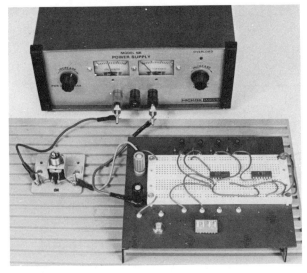

Fig. 20-5-1

263

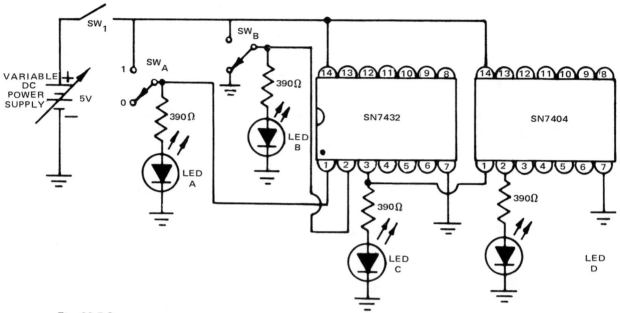

Fig. 20-5-2

2. Before turning on $SW_1$, turn on variable power supply and adjust it to 5V dc.
3. Complete truth table for output C, using alternatives in Fig. 20-5-1. What logic function is indicated by output C? _____

_____

4. Complete truth table for output D, using alternatives listed in Fig. 20-5-1. What logic function is achieved by output D?

_____

_____

5. Turn off $SW_1$ and disconnect IC logic circuit shown in Fig. 20-5-1. Connect

combination logic circuit as in Fig. 20-5-3, using an SN7404 IC.
6. Turn on $SW_1$ and test logic function of circuit, using truth table alternatives given in Fig. 20-5-3. Record output observed at C and D. What logic functions are indicated?

_____

_____

7. Turn off $SW_1$ and disconnect SN7404 circuit.
8. Connect SN7402 gate test circuit shown in Fig. 20-5-4.
9. Turn on $SW_1$ and test logic gate, using

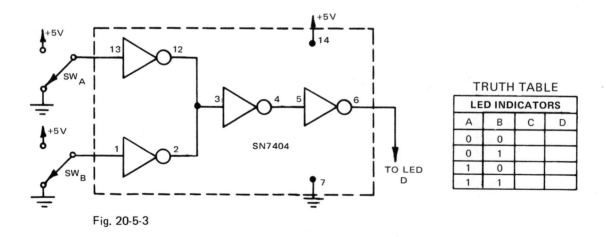

Fig. 20-5-3

TRUTH TABLE

| LED INDICATORS | | | |
|---|---|---|---|
| A | B | C | D |
| 0 | 0 | | |
| 0 | 1 | | |
| 1 | 0 | | |
| 1 | 1 | | |

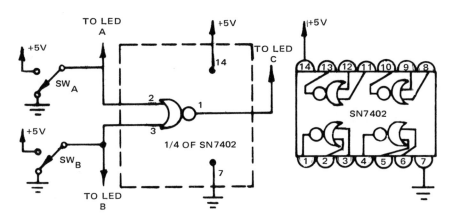

Fig. 20-5-4

| TRUTH TABLE | | |
|---|---|---|
| **LED INDICATORS** | | |
| A | B | C |
| 0 | 0 | |
| 0 | 1 | |
| 1 | 0 | |
| 1 | 1 | |

alternatives in truth table in Fig. 20-5-4. Record output of logic gate indicated by LED C. What logic function is performed by this gate circuit? _____

_____

10. Test remaining three gates of SN7402.
11. Turn off SW$_1$ and power supply. Disconnect circuit and return all parts to storage cabinet.

## QUESTIONS

1. Using logic gate symbols, sketch a diagram of the circuit shown in Fig. 20-5-1 and indicate input and output terminals.
2. What statement describes the NOR gate function?
3. What logic function is achieved when the output of a NOR gate is connected to a NOT gate?

## INTRODUCTION

The primary numbering system of a computer deals with operational states that are either 1 or 0. This numbering process is based on the powers of two, so it is commonly called a "binary system." Precise computer functions can be performed by this type of numbering system.

A binary counter is an important part of a computer system. It must accept two-state information and produce an accurate count that is based upon the applied data. The binary counter used in this experiment contains four devices known as "flip-flops" housed in a single integrated circuit. These flip-flops will produce a state change each time a clock pulse or voltage level change occurs.

When a pulse is applied to the input of the first flip-flop, it initiates a state change that causes a 1 to appear at its output. Arrival of the next pulse causes another state change and a 0 appears at its output. As a result, two input pulses will produce one output pulse or a "divide by two" function. Four flip-flops connected so the output of one drives the input of the next will achieve binary counting. LEDs attached to the output of each flip-flop will indicate a count in binary numbers.

In this experiment, you will build a binary counter that drives four LED indicators that denote the binary number count. Single pulses are applied to the counter initially, then they are processed one at a time for study. A clock circuit or pulse generator is used to produce automatic counting. Through this experiment, you will be able to observe a binary counter in operation and become familiar with the binary numbering system.

## EXPERIMENT OBJECTIVES

As a result of this laboratory experience, you should be able to accomplish the following:

1. Construct a binary counter.
2. Use it to count individual input pulses.
3. Use a clock circuit to generate input pulses so that the binary counter will count multiple pulses.

## REFERENCE

Gerrish and Dugger, ELECTRICITY AND ELECTRONICS, Chapter 20, pages 292 to 294.

## MATERIALS AND EQUIPMENT

1 — Variable dc power supply
1 — SN7493 IC
1 — SPST toggle switch
1 — IC circuit construction module or following equivalent parts:
    4 — 5V LEDs
    4 — 390 ohm, 1/8 watt resistors
    1 — SPDT push button, N.C.
    1 — SPST toggle switch
1 — Function generator, square wave generator or following equivalent parts:
    1 — SE/NE555 IC
    1 — 4 $\mu$F, 25V capacitor
    1 — .01 $\mu$F, 100V capacitor
    2 — 200K, 1/4 watt resistors
    1 — SPST toggle switch

## PROCEDURE

1. Construct binary counter as in Fig. 20-6-1, using IC circuit construction module. If IC module is not available, circuit can be constructed with separately mounted components according to Fig. 20-6-2.

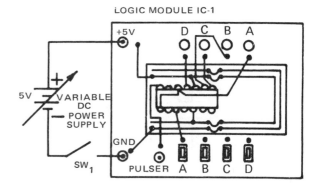

Fig. 20-6-1

2. Before turning on $SW_1$, turn on power supply and adjust it to 5V dc.
3. Place RESET/COUNT switch in RESET

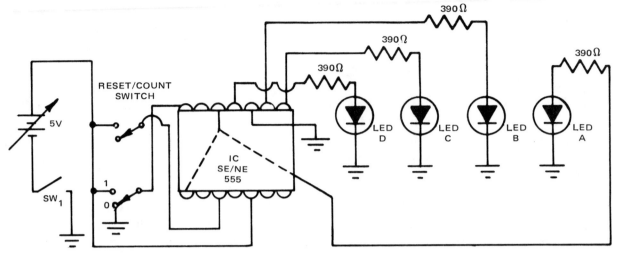

Fig. 20-6-2

position momentarily, then return it to COUNT position. All four LED readouts should be in OFF state.

4. Depress pulser button one time. This action will inject a binary 1 count into LED display.

5. Using binary number table in Fig. 20-6-3, cycle counter through its counting sequence. If counter skips a number in sequence, reset it and repeat procedure. NOTE: Switching action of manual push button or pulser control circuit may initiate "bouncing switch contact" problems at times.

6. Turn off $SW_1$ and disconnect pulser switch or push button.

| LED INDICATORS (BINARY COUNT) | D | C | B | A | DECIMAL COUNT |
|---|---|---|---|---|---|
| | 0 | 0 | 0 | 0 | 0 |
| | 0 | 0 | 0 | 1 | 1 |
| | 0 | 0 | 1 | 0 | 2 |
| 0 = OFF | 0 | 0 | 1 | 1 | 3 |
| 1 = ON | 0 | 1 | 0 | 0 | 4 |
| | 0 | 1 | 0 | 1 | 5 |
| | 0 | 1 | 1 | 0 | 6 |
| | 0 | 1 | 1 | 1 | 7 |
| | 1 | 0 | 0 | 0 | 8 |
| | 1 | 0 | 0 | 1 | 9 |
| | 1 | 0 | 1 | 0 | 10 |
| | 1 | 0 | 1 | 1 | 11 |
| | 1 | 1 | 0 | 0 | 12 |
| | 1 | 1 | 0 | 1 | 13 |
| | 1 | 1 | 1 | 0 | 14 |
| | 1 | 1 | 1 | 1 | 15 |

Fig. 20-6-3

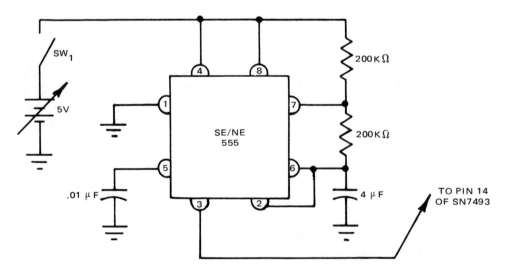

Fig. 20-6-4

7. Connect output of a square wave generator or function generator to pin 14 of SN7493. If a square wave generator is not available, square wave generator circuit of Fig. 20-6-4 may be constructed with discrete components.

8. Turn on $SW_1$ (counter circuit switch) and reset counter to a zero display. Turn on generator or square wave circuit and observe counting action. With a generator, counting rate can be adjusted to different values. If possible, make this adjustment while observing counter action.

9. If time permits (using a counter from another lab group), you may want to cascade two counters. To do this, connect D output from pin 11 to input of second counter at pin 14. Use only one generator and connect ground commonly together. The maximum binary count that can be had with this counter is _____

10. Turn off power supply, generator and circuit switch. Disconnect circuit and return all parts to storage cabinet.

## QUESTIONS

1. Explain the difference between counting in values and binary numbers.

2. The largest binary count that can be achieved with four LED readouts is

_____

3. What is the function of a flip-flop?

# MATERIALS AND EQUIPMENT LIST

The following items are required for use in conducting the experiments presented in this ELECTRICITY AND ELECTRONICS LABORATORY MANUAL.

## EQUIPMENT

1 — Variable dc power supply, 0-15V, 2A
1 — Volt-ohm-milliampere (VOM) meter, preferably FET type
1 — RF signal generator with AM modulation capabilities
1 — AF signal source or function generator, 50 Hz to 50 KHz
1 — 12.6V CT, 60 Hz filament transformer, 2A
1 — 0-1 mA meter
1 — 10 MHz oscilloscope (with calibrated horizontal sweep preferred)

## OPTIONAL EQUIPMENT

1 — 0-100V, 20 mA dc power supply

## COMPOSITE LABORATORY MATERIALS

(Available through Hickok Teaching Systems, # 2 Wheeler Ave., Woburn, MA 01801)
1 — Audio frequency module
1 — Power supply module
1 — Resistor decade module
1 — RF oscillator module
1 — AM transmitter module
1 — FM transmitter module
1 — Transistor tester module

## SPECIALIZED ITEMS

(Available through Hickok Teaching Systems)
1 — Set of permanent magnets
1 — Transformer (Hickok coil 1 - 3320-383; coil 2 - 3320-393; core - 12180-38)
1 — Gilley coil with 5/8 in. D x 2 1/2 in. L iron core
1 — Modified St. Louis motor/generator unit
1 — Voltaic cell kit
1 — Electroscope
1 — Hartley oscillator coil (J. W. Miller A-5496-C)

## DISCRETE MOUNTED COMPONENTS

3 — 2N3397 NPN silicon transistors
2 — 2N3644 PNP silicon transistors
1 — 2N3702 PNP silicon transistor
1 — Assortment of used transistors
1 — 1N34A signal diode
4 — 1N4004 diodes
1 — Varicap diode (Motorola MV-1638)
1 — 2.9V zener diode
2 — No. NE-2 neon lamps
1 — Light dependent resistor (LDR), 500 mW (Vactec Inc. VT 50L or Clairex CL 505L)
4 — Light emitting diodes (LED), (Chicago Miniature CM 4-20 or equivalent)
1 — Solar cell (International Rectifier Corp. S1020 E8 PL or equivalent)
2 — No. 47 incandescent lamps with sockets

## TRANSMITTING, RECEIVING ITEMS

1 — Rechargeable "C" cell
4 — "C" cells and holders
1 — "C" type Ni-Cad cell
2 — "D" cells
1 — Assortment of dry cells (No. 6, alkaline, mercury)
1 — Speaker, 3.2 ohm
1 — 10V dc relay (Sigma 11F 100 g 1A or equivalent)
1 — 100 KHz crystal
1 — Mounted phono cartridge (Astatic 62-1)
1 — Code key
1 — Crystal microphone
1 — Headphones, 2K

## RESISTORS, CAPACITORS

2 — 0.47 ohm, 1/4 watt resistors
1 — 2 ohm, 1/4 watt resistor
1 — 4 ohm, 1 watt resistor
2 — 20 ohm, 1/4 watt resistors
1 — 47 ohm, 1/4 watt resistor
1 — 68 ohm, 1/4 watt resistor
1 — 100 ohm, 1/4 watt resistor
2 — 200 ohm, 1/4 watt resistors
2 — 220 ohm, 1/4 watt resistors
1 — 270 ohm, 1 watt resistor

4 — 390 ohm, 1/8 watt resistors
1 — 390 ohm, 1/4 watt resistor
1 — 470 ohm, 1/4 watt resistor
1 — 1K, 1/4 watt resistor
1 — 1.5K, 1/4 watt resistor
2 — 2K, 1/4 watt resistors
1 — 2.2K, 1/4 watt resistor
1 — 2.7K, 1/4 watt resistor
1 — 4.7K, 1/4 watt resistor
1 — 5K, 1/4 watt resistor
1 — 6.8K, 1/4 watt resistor
1 — 10K, 1/4 watt resistor
1 — 15K, 1/4 watt resistor
1 — 27K, 1/4 watt resistor
1 — 47K, 1/4 watt resistor
1 — 56K, 1/4 watt resistor
1 — 100K, 1/4 watt resistor
2 — 200K, 1/4 watt resistors
1 — 270K, 1/4 watt resistor
1 — 470K, 1/4 watt resistor
1 — 1M, 1/4 watt resistor
1 — 5K, 2 watt potentiometer
1 — 10K, 2 watt potentiometer
1 — 500K, 2 watt potentiometer
2 — 680 $\mu$ F, 50V dc capacitors
1 — 100 $\mu$ F, 25V dc capacitor
1 — 25 $\mu$ F, 50V dc capacitor
1 — 10 $\mu$ F, 50V dc capacitor
1 — 4 $\mu$ F, 25V dc capacitor
1 — .22 $\mu$ F, 100V dc capacitor
1 — .1 $\mu$ F, 100V dc capacitor
1 — .01 $\mu$ F, 100V dc capacitor
1 — .001 $\mu$ F, 100V dc capacitor
1 — 6.8 pF, 100V dc capacitor
1 — 47 pF, 100V dc capacitor
1 — 100 pF, 100V dc capacitor
1 — 365 pF/125 pF, two-gang variable capacitor
1 — Trimmer capacitor, 0-10 pF (Erie 513-010-A 2-10)

## INDUCTORS, TRANSFORMERS, SWITCHES

1 — 25 mH inductor, 10 mA (J. W. Miller 70F252AF or equivalent)
1 — 4.5 H inductor, 50 mA (Essex-Stancor C-1706 or equivalent)
1 — Ferrite strip transistor antenna rod (J. W. Miller 2004 or equivalent)
1 — 455 KHz if transformer and alignment tool (J. W. Miller KHz 455)
1 — Audio input transformer (Argonne AR-109 or Essex-Stancor TA-35)
1 — Audio output transformer (Argonne AR-119 or Stancor TA-21)
2 — SPST toggle switches
4 — SPDT toggle switches
1 — DPDT toggle switch
1 — SPST push button switch, N.O.
1 — SPDT push button switch, N.C.

## LOGIC CIRCUIT ITEMS

1 — IC circuit construction module (Hickok)
1 — SN7400 IC
1 — SN7402 IC
1 — SN7404 IC
1 — SN7408 IC
1 — SN7432 IC
1 — SN7493 IC
1 — SE/NE555 IC
1 — IC construction board (E. L. Co.)

## OPTIONAL TV EQUIPMENT

1 — Operating black and white TV receiver
1 — Service literature for black and white TV receivers

## STATIC ELECTRICITY ITEMS

1 — Vulcanite rod, 3/4 in. x 8 in.
1 — 6 in. square of wool cloth
1 — 1/2 in. x 8 in. glass rod or equivalent lucite rod
1 — 6 in. square of silk cloth
1 — 30 in. No. 22 enamel wire
1 — Balloon
1 — Pith ball assembly
1 — Support stand

## MISCELLANEOUS ITEMS

1 — Assortment of connecting wires
1 — Assortment of solid and stranded wires
1 — Magnetic compass
1 — Circuit construction board
1 — Thermocouple or 6 in. lengths of copper wire and iron constantan wire
1 — American Standard wire gauge
1 — Assortment of straight pins
3 — Alligator clip leads